KT-370-603

PENGUIN BOOKS
ITALIAN PHRASE BOOK

OTHER PENGUIN PHRASE BOOKS

Dutch
French
German
Greek
Polish
Portuguese
Russian
Spanish
Turkish

ITALIAN
PHRASE BOOK

THIRD EDITION

JILL NORMAN

PIETRO GIORGETTI

DAPHNE TAGG

PENGUIN BOOKS

PENGUIN BOOKS

Published by the Penguin Group
Penguin Books Ltd, 27 Wrights Lane, London W8 5TZ, England
Penguin Putnam Inc., 375 Hudson Street, New York, New York 10014, USA
Penguin Books Australia Ltd, Ringwood, Victoria, Australia
Penguin Books Canada Ltd, 10 Alcorn Avenue, Toronto, Ontario, Canada M4V 3B2
Penguin Books (NZ) Ltd, Private Bag 102902, NSMC, Auckland, New Zealand

Penguin Books Ltd, Registered Offices: Harmondsworth, Middlesex, England

First published 1968
Second edition 1979
Third edition 1988
11 13 15 17 19 20 18 16 14 12

Printed in England by Clays Ltd, St Ives plc
Set in Linotron 202 Ehrhardt

CONTENTS

INTRODUCTION

To the Third Edition

In this series of phrase books only those words and phrases that might be called essential to a traveller have been included, but the definition of 'traveller' has been made very wide, to include not only the business traveller and the holiday-maker, whether travelling alone, with a group or the family, but also the owner of a house, an apartment or a time-share. Each type of traveller has his or her own requirements, and for easy use the phrases are arranged in sections which deal with specific situations.

Pronunciation is given for each phrase and for all words in the extensive vocabulary. An explanation of the system used for the pronunciation guide is to be found on pages xiii–xv. It is essential to read this section carefully before starting to use this book.

Some of the Italian phrases are marked with an asterisk* – these give an indication of the kind of reply you might get to your question, and of questions you may be asked in your turn.

For those who would like to know a little more about the Italian language, a brief survey of the main points of its grammar is provided at the end of the book (pages 210–19).

PRONUNCIATION

The pronunciation guide is intended for people with no knowledge of Italian. As far as possible the system is based on English pronunciation. This means that complete accuracy may sometimes be lost for the sake of simplicity, but readers should be able to understand Italian pronunciation, and make themselves understood, if they read this section carefully.

VOWELS

All vowels are sounded distinctly; unstressed vowels keep their pure sound and are never slurred as in English. Final 'e' is always sounded.

Pronounce:	a as a in father	symbol a	e.g. pane – bread (pa-neh)
and	a as in apple	symbol a	e.g. alto – high (al-to)
	e as e in wet	symbol e or eh	e.g. ponte – bridge (pon-teh)
and	e as e in eight	symbol ai	e.g. aperto – open (a-pair-to)
	i as i in machine	symbol ee	e.g. litro – litre (lee-tro)
	o as o in soft	symbol o	e.g. opera – opera (o-pair-a)
	u as oo in moon	symbol oo or u	e.g. punto – point (poon-to)

COMPOUND VOWELS

In the combinations ie, io, iu the i tends to be shortened and sounds rather like y in yet. This is shown as y in the pronunciation guide, e.g. pensione – boarding house (pen-syo-neh), piede – foot (pye-deh).

In the combinations ue, ui, uo the u sounds like w in wet and is represented by w in the pronunciation guide, e.g. guida – guide (gwee-da), buono – good (bwo-no).

Au is like ow in how,   e.g. autunno – autumn (ow-toon-no).
Ei is like ay in day,   e.g. Lei – you (lay).

CONSONANTS

In general consonants are pronounced much as in English, although r is always pronounced very distinctly. Note the following:

c followed by e or i is pronounced as ch in church   symbol ch
    e.g. cibo – food (chee-bo)
c followed by a, o, u is pronounced as k in king   symbol k
    e.g. casa – house (ka-za)
g followed by e or i is pronounced as j in joy   symbol j
    e.g. gente – people (jen-teh)
g followed by a, o, u is pronounced as g in good   symbol g
    e.g. gatto – cat (gat-to)

s has two sounds – as in taste and in nose. Symbols s and z are used respectively, e.g. sigaro – cigar (see-ga-ro) and rosa – rose (ro-za).
z also has two sounds – ts as in cuts and ds as in birds. Symbols ts and dz, e.g. zio – uncle (tsee-o) and mezzo – half (med-zo).

GROUPS OF CONSONANTS

Double consonants, like cc, gg, always represent a single but more heavily stressed sound.
The following groups also represent a single sound:

ch is pronounced k as in king	symbol **k**
e.g. chiesa – church (kye-za)	
gh is pronounced g as in good	symbol **g**
e.g. ghiaccio – ice (gya-cho)	
gl followed by i is like lli of million	symbol **ly**
e.g. figlio – son (feel-yo)	
gn is like ni of onion	symbol **ny**
e.g. bagno – bath (ban-yo)	
sc followed by e or i pronounced sh as in ship	symbol **sh**
e.g. sciarpa – scarf (shar-pa)	
sc followed by a, o, u is pronounced sk	symbol **sk**
e.g. scuola – school (skwo-la)	

STRESS

Most Italian words are stressed on the next to last syllable. If the last syllable is stressed it is written with an accent. Irregular stress is indicated in the pronunciation guide by printing the stressed syllable in **bold type**.

ESSENTIALS

FIRST THINGS

Yes	**Sì**	See
No	**No**	No
Please	**Per favore/per piacere**	Pair fa-vor-eh/pair pya-chair-eh
Thank you	**Grazie**	Gra-zyeh
No, thank you	**No, grazie**	No, gra-zyeh
Sorry	**Mi scusi/mi dispiace**	Mee skoo-zee/mee dees-pya-cheh

LANGUAGE PROBLEMS

I'm English/American	**Io sono inglese/americano**	Ee-o so-no een-gle-zeh/a-me-ree-ka-no

Do you speak English?	**Parla inglese?**	Par-la een-gle-zeh
Does anyone here speak English?	**C'è qualcuno qui che parla inglese?**	Cheh kwal-koo-no kwee keh par-la een-gle-zeh
I don't speak Italian	**Non parlo italiano**	Non par-lo ee-tal-ya-no
I understand	**Capisco**	Ka-pee-sko
I speak a little Italian	**Parlo un po' d'italiano**	Par-lo oon po dee-tal-ya-no
Do you understand (me)?	***(Mi) capisce?**	(Mee) ka-pee-sheh
I don't understand	**Non capisco**	Non ka-pee-sko
Would you say that again, please?	**Vuole ripetere, per favore?**	Vwo-leh ree-pe-tair-eh, pair fa-vor-eh
Please speak slowly	**Parli più lentamente, per favore**	Par-lee pyoo len-ta-men-teh, pair fa-vor-eh
What does that mean?	**Cosa vuol dire questo?**	Ko-za vwol dee-reh kwes-to
Can you translate this for me?	**Me lo può tradurre?**	Meh lo pwo tra-door-reh
Please write it down	**Per cortesia, lo vuole scrivere?**	Pair kor-te-zee-a, lo vwo-leh scree-vair-eh
What do you call this in Italian?	**Come si chiama questo in italiano?**	Ko-meh see kya-ma kwes-to een ee-tal-ya-no
I will look it up in my phrase book	**Guardo nel mio manuale di conversazione**	Gwar-do nel mee-o man-wa-leh dee kon-vair-sat-syo-neh
Please show me the word in the book	**Può mostrarmi la parola nel libro?**	Pwo mos-trar-mee la pa-ro-la nel lee-bro

QUESTIONS

Who?	**Chi?**	Kee
Where is/are...?	**Dov'è/dove sono...?**	Dov-eh/do-veh so-no
When	**Quando?**	Kwan-do
Why	**Perchè?**	Per-keh
Where?	**Dove?**	Do-veh
What?	**Cosa/che cosa?**	Ko-za/keh ko-za
How?	**Come?**	Ko-meh
How much/many?	**Quanto/quanti?**	Kwan-to/kwan-tee
How much is/are...?	**Quanto costa/ costano?**	Kwan-to kos-ta/**kos-ta-no**
How long?	**Quanto tempo?**	Kwan-to tem-po
How far?	**A che distanza è?**	A keh dees-tant-sa eh
What's this?	**Cos'è questo?**	Koz-eh kwes-to
What do you want?	**Cosa desidera/cosa vuole?**	Ko-za de-zee-dair-a/ko-za vwo-leh
What must I do?	**Cosa devo fare?**	Ko-za de-vo far-eh
What is the matter?	**Cosa c'è/cosa succede?**	Ko-za cheh/ko-za soo-che-deh
Have you .../do you sell ...?	**Ha .../vende ...?**	A .../ven-deh ...
Is there ...?	**C'è ...?**	Cheh ...
Have you seen ...?	**Ha visto ...?**	A vees-to ...
Where can I find ...?	**Dove posso trovare ...?**	Do-veh pos-so tro-var-eh ...
May I have ...?	**Posso avere ...?**	Pos-so a-vair-eh ...

I want/should like ...	Vorrei/ho bisogno di ...	Vor-ray/o bee-zon-yo dee ...
I don't want ...	Non voglio ...	Non vol-yo ...
Can you help me?	Potrebbe aiutarmi?	Pot-reb-beh a-yoo-tar-mee
Can I help you?	*Posso aiutarla?	Pos-so a-yoo-tar-la
Can you tell/give/show me ...?	Può dirmi/darmi/mostrarmi ...?	Pwo deer-mee/dar-mee/mos-trar-mee ...

USEFUL STATEMENTS

It is ...	E ...	Eh ...
It isn't ...	Non è ...	Non eh ...
I have ...	Ho ...	O ...
I don't have ...	No ho ...	Non o ...
I want ...	Voglio ...	Vol-yo ...
I would like ...	Vorrei ...	Vor-ray ...
I need ...	Ho bisogno di ...	O bee-zon-yo dee ...
I like it	Mi piace	Mee pya-cheh
OK/that's fine	OK/va bene	O-kay/va be-neh
I'm lost	Sono perduto	So-no pair-doo-to
We're looking for ...	Cerchiamo ...	Chair-kya-mo ...
Here is/are ...	Ecco ...	Ek-ko ...
Here it is	Eccolo	Ek-ko-lo
There they are	Eccoli	Ek-ko-lee
There is/are ...	C'è/ci sono ...	Cheh/chee so-no ...

It's important	**E importante**	Eh eem-por-tan-teh
It's urgent	**E urgente**	Eh oor-jen-teh
You are mistaken	**Lei si sbaglia**	Lay see zbal-ya
I like it/them	**Mi piace/mi piacciono**	Mee pya-cheh/mee pya-cho-no
I don't like it/them	**Non mi piace/ piacciono**	Non mee pya-cheh/pya-cho-no
I know	**Lo so**	Lo so
I don't know	**Non lo so**	Non lo so
I didn't know	**Non lo sapevo**	Non lo sa-pe-vo
I think so	**Credo di sì**	Kre-do dee see
I'm hungry/thirsty	**Ho fame/sete**	O fa-meh/se-teh
I'm tired	**Sono stanco**	So-no stan-ko
I'm in a hurry	**Ho fretta**	O fret-ta
I'm ready	**Sono pronto**	So-no pron-to
Leave me alone	**Mi lasci in pace/mi lasci stare**	Mee la-shee een pa-cheh/mee la-shee star-eh
Just a moment	***Mi scusi un momento**	Mee skoo-zee oon mo-men-to
This way, please	***Da questa parte, per favore**	Da kwes-ta par-teh, pair fa-vor-eh
Take a seat	***Si accomodi/si metta a sedere**	See ak-ko-mo-dee/see met-ta a se-dair-eh
Come in!	***Entri, prego/avanti, prego!**	Ent-ree, pre-go/a-van-tee, pre-go
It's cheap	**Costa poco/non è molto caro**	Kos-ta po-ko/non eh mol-to kar-o

It's too expensive	E molto caro/costa troppo	E mol-to kar-o/kos-ta trop-po
That's all	Nient'altro/questo è tutto	Nyent-alt-ro/kwes-to eh toot-to
You're right	Lei ha ragione	Lay a ra-jo-neh
You're wrong	Lei si sbaglia	Lay see zbal-ya

GREETINGS

Good morning/good day	Buon giorno	Bwon jor-no
Good afternoon	Buon giorno/buona sera	Bwon jor-no/bwo-na se-ra
Good evening	Buona sera	Bwo-na se-ra
Good night	Buona notte	Bwo-na not-teh
Hallo	Ciao	Chow
How are you?	Come sta?	Ko-me sta
Very well, thank you	Molto bene, grazie	Mol-to be-neh, gra-zyeh
Good-bye	Arrivederla/arrivederci/ciao	Ar-ree-ve-dair-la/ar-ree-ve-dair-chee/chow
See you soon	A presto	A pres-to
See you tomorrow	A domani	A do-ma-nee
Have a good journey	Buon viaggio	Bwon vyad-jo
Good luck/all the best	Buona fortuna/i migliori auguri	Bwo-na for-too-na/ee meel-yor-ee ow-goo-ree
Have a good time	Buon divertimento	Bwon dee-vair-tee-men-to

POLITE PHRASES

Sorry	**Mi scusi/mi dispiace**	Mee skoo-zee/mee dees-pya-cheh
Excuse me	**Mi scusi**	Mee skoo-zee
Excuse me (*to pass*)	**Permesso**	Pair-mes-so
That's all right	**Va benissimo**	Va be-**nees**-see-mo
Not at all	**Nient'affatto**	Nyent-af-fat-to
With pleasure	**Prego**	Pre-go
Don't mention it (*after thanks*)	**Prego**	Pre-go
Don't worry	**Non si preoccupi**	Non see pre-ok-koo-pee
It doesn't matter	**Non importa/non fa niente**	Non eem-por-ta/non fa nyen-teh
Is everything all right?	**Tutto bene?**	Toot-to be-neh
I beg your pardon?	**Prego?**	Pre-go
Am I disturbing you?	**La disturbo?**	La dees-toor-bo
I'm sorry to have troubled you	**Mi scusi per il disturbo**	Mee skoo-zee pair eel dees-toor-bo
Good/that's fine	**Bene/va bene così**	Be-neh/va be-neh ko-zee

OPPOSITES

before/after	**prima/dopo**	pree-ma/do-po
early/late	**presto/tardi**	pres-to/tar-dee
first/last	**primo/ultimo**	pree-mo/ool-tee-mo

now/later, then	**ora/dopo, poi**	or-a/do-po, poy
far/near	**lontano/vicino**	lon-ta-no/vee-chee-no
here/there	**qui/lì**	kwee/lee
in/out	**dentro/fuori**	den-tro/fwo-ree
inside/outside	**dentro/fuori**	den-tro/fwo-ree
under/over	**sotto/sopra**	sot-to/sop-ra
big, large/small	**grande/piccolo**	gran-de/peek-ko-lo
deep/shallow	**profondo/basso**	pro-fon-do/bas-so
empty/full	**vuoto/pieno**	vwo-to/pye-no
fat/lean	**grasso/magro**	gras-so/mag-ro
heavy/light	**pesante/leggero**	pe-zan-teh/led-je-ro
high/low	**alto/basso**	al-to/bas-so
long, tall/short	**lungo, alto/breve, basso**	lun-go, al-to/bre-veh, bas-so
narrow/wide	**stretto/largo**	stret-to/lar-go
thick/thin	**spesso, grosso/ sottile, fine**	spes-so, gros-so/sot-tee-leh, fee-neh
least/most	**minimo/massimo**	mee-nee-mo/mas-see-mo
many/few	**molti/pochi**	mol-tee/po-kee
more/less	**più/meno**	pyoo/me-no
much/little	**molto/poco**	mol-to/po-ko
beautiful/ugly	**bello/brutto**	bel-lo/broot-to
better/worse	**meglio/peggio**	mel-yo/ped-jo
cheap/expensive	**a buon mercato/ costoso, caro**	a bwon mair-ka-to/kos-to-zo, kar-o
clean/dirty	**pulito/sporco**	poo-lee-to/spor-ko

cold/hot, warm	freddo, fresco/caldo, tiepido	fred-do, fres-ko/kal-do, tye-pee-do
easy/difficult	facile/difficile	fa-chee-leh/deef-fee-chee-leh
fresh/stale	fresco/stantio, andato a male	fres-ko/stan-tee-o, an-da-to a ma-leh
good/bad	buono/cattivo	bwo-no/kat-tee-vo
new, young/old	nuovo, giovane/vecchio	nwo-vo, jo-va-neh/vek-kyo
nice/nasty	buono/cattivo, disgustoso	bwon-o/kat-tee-vo, deez-goos-to-zo
right/wrong	giusto/sbagliato	joos-to/zbal-ya-to
vacant/occupied	libero/occupato	lee-bair-o/ok-koo-pa-to
open/closed, shut	aperto/chiuso	a-pair-to/kyoo-zo
quick/slow	rapido/lento	ra-pee-do/len-to
quiet/noisy	quieto, silenzioso/rumoroso	kye-to, see-lent-syo-zo/roo-mo-ro-zo
sharp/blunt	affilato/non taglia	af-fee-la-to/non tal-ya

SIGNS & PUBLIC NOTICES[1]

Acqua potabile	Drinking water
Acqua non potabile	Not for drinking
Affittasi	To let
Aperto	Open
Aperto dalle ore ... alle ore ...	Open from ... to ...
Ascensore	Lift/elevator
Attenzione	Caution
Banca	Bank
Bussare	Knock
Carabinieri	Police station
Chiuso	Closed
Divieto di entrata	No entry
Entrata	Entrance

1. See also SIGNS TO LOOK FOR AT AIRPORTS AND STATIONS (p. 19) and ROAD SIGNS (p. 40).

Gabinetto	Lavatory/toilet
Gabinetto per signore/donne	Ladies
Gabinetto per signori/uomini	Gentlemen
Guida	Guide
Ingresso	Entrance
Ingresso libero	Admission free
Interprete	Interpreter
In vendita	For sale
I signori sono pregati di non ...	You are requested not to ...
I trasgressori verranno puniti a termini di legge	Trespassers will be prosecuted
Libero	Vacant/free/unoccupied
Occupato	Engaged/occupied
Pedoni	Pedestrians
Pericolo	Danger
Posto di polizia	Police station
Posti in piedi	Standing room only
Privato	Private
Riservato	Reserved
Si prega di non ...	Do not ...
Spingere	Push
Stanza da affittare	Room to let
Suonare	Ring
Svendita	Sale
Tenere la destra	Keep right
Tirare	Pull

Tutto esaurito	House full (*cinema, etc.*)
Tutto occupato	No vacancies
Ufficio informazioni	Information
Ufficio postale	Post office
Uscita	Exit
Uscita di emergenza	Emergency exit
Vietato fumare	No smoking
Vietato l'ingresso	No admission

MONEY[1]

Is there a bank that changes money near here?	C'è una banca/un'ufficio cambi qui vicino?	Cheh oon-a ban-ka/oon oof-fee-cho kam-bee kwee vee-chee-no
Do you change travellers' cheques?	Può cambiare dei travellers' cheques?	Pwo kam-byar-eh day travellers' cheques
Where can I change travellers' cheques?	Dove posso cambiare dei travellers' cheques?	Do-veh pos-so kam-byar-eh day travellers' cheques
Please cash this Eurocheque	Vuol incassare questo euroassegno	Vwol een-kas-sar-eh kwes-to e-oo-ro-as-sen-yo
Will you take a personal cheque?	Accetta assegni di conto corrente?	A-chet-ta as-sen-yee dee kon-to kor-ren-teh
Will you take a credit card?	Accetta una carta di credito?	A-chet-ta oon-a kar-ta dee kre-dee-to

1. In Italy, banks are open from 0800 to 1300, closed Saturday.

Do you have any identification?	*Ha un documento d'identità?	A oon do-koo-men-to dee-den-tee-ta
I want to change some pounds/dollars	Vorrei cambiare delle sterline/dei dollari	Vor-ray kam-byar-eh del-le ster-lee-neh/day dol-la-ree
What is the exchange rate?	Quanto è il cambio oggi?	Kwan-to eh eel kam-byo od-jee
Can you give me some small change?	Può darmi degli spiccioli?	Pwo dar-mee del-yee spee-cho-lee
Where do I sign?	Dove devo firmare?	Do-veh de-vo feer-mar-eh
Sign here, please	*Vuol firmare qui, per favore	Vwol feer-mar-eh kwee, pair fa-vor-eh
Go to the cashier	*Si accomodi alla cassa	See ak-ko-mo-dee al-la kas-sa
I arranged for money to be transferred from England. Has it arrived yet?	Ho dato istruzioni di trasferire del denaro dall'Inghilterra. E arrivato?	O da-to is-troot-syo-nee dee tras-fe-reer-eh del de-na-ro dal-leen-geel-ter-ra. Eh ar-ree-va-to
I want to open a bank account	Vorrei aprire un conto in banca	Vor-ray ap-reer-eh oon kon-to een ban-ka
Please credit this to my account	Vuol versare questo sul mio conto	Vwol vair-sar-eh kwes-to sool mee-o kon-to
I'd like to get some cash with my credit card	Vorrei avere dei contanti con la mia carta di credito	Vor-ray a-vair-eh day kon-tan-tee kon la mee-a kar-ta dee kre-dee-to
current account	il conto corrente	kon-to kor-ren-teh
deposit account	il conto deposito	kon-to de-po-zee-to

statement	**l'estratto conto** *m*	es-trat-to kon-to
balance	**il saldo**	sal-do
cheque book	**il libretto degli assegni**	leeb-ret-to del-yee as-sen-yee

CURRENCY

Italian currency is the **lira** (plural **lire**).

TRAVEL

ON ARRIVAL

PASSPORTS

Passport control	***Controllo passaporti**	Kon-trol-lo pas-sa-por-tee
Your passport, please	***Passaporto, prego**	Pas-sa-por-to, pre-go
Are you together?	***I signori sono insieme?**	Ee seen-yor-ee so-no een-sye-meh
I'm travelling alone	**Viaggio da solo**	Vyad-jo da so-lo
I'm travelling with my wife/a friend	**Viaggio con mia moglie/un amico (un'amica)**	Vyad-jo kon mee-a mol-yeh/oon a-mee-ko (un-a-mee-ka)
I'm here on business/ on holiday	**Sono qui per affari/ vengo in vacanza**	So-no kwee pair af-far-ee/ven-go een va-kant-sa

| What is your address in Italy/Milan? | *Qual'è il suo indirizzo in Italia/a Milano? | Kwal-eh eel soo-o een-dee-reet-so een ee-tal-ya/a mee-la-no |
| How long are you staying here? | *Quanto tempo rimane? | Kwanto tem-po ree-ma-neh |

CUSTOMS

Customs	*Dogana	Do-ga-na
Goods/nothing to declare	Merci/niente da dichiarare	Mair-chee/nyen-teh da dee-kya-rar-eh
Which is your luggage?	*Quali sono i suoi bagagli?	Kwal-ee so-no ee swoy ba-gal-yee
Have you anything to declare?	*Ha niente da dichiarare?	A nyen-teh da dee-kya-rar-eh
I have a carton of cigarettes and a bottle of gin/wine	Ho una stecca di sigarette e una bottiglia di gin/vino	O oon-a stek-ka dee see-ga-ret-teh eh oon-a bot-teel-ya dee gin/vee-no
You will have to pay duty on this	*Deve pagare il dazio per questo	De-veh pa-gar-eh eel dat-syo pair kwes-to
This is my luggage	Ecco i miei bagagli	Ek-ko ee myay ba-gal-yee
Do you have any more luggage?	*Ha altri bagagli?	A alt-ree ba-gal-yee
I have only my personal things in it	Ci sono solo effetti personali	Chee so-no so-lo ef-fet-tee pair-so-nal-ee
Open this bag, please	*Apra questa valigia, per favore	Ap-ra kwes-ta va-lee-ja, pair fa-vor-eh
Can I shut my case now?	Posso chiudere la valigia?	Pos-so kyoo-dair-eh la va-lee-ja

| May I go? | **Posso andare?** | Pos-so an-dar-eh |

LUGGAGE

Porter	**Facchino/ portabagagli**	Fak-kee-no/por-ta-ba-gal-yee
My luggage has not arrived	**I miei bagagli non sono arrivati**	Ee myay ba-gal-yee non so-no ar-ree-va-tee
My luggage is damaged	**I miei bagagli sono sciupati**	Ee myay ba-gal-yee so-no shoo-pa-tee
One suitcase is missing	**Manca una valigia**	Man-ka oon-a va-lee-ja
Are there any luggage trolleys?	**Ci sono dei carelli?**	Chee so-no day ka-rel-lee
Where is the left luggage office?	**Dov'è il deposito bagagli?**	Dov-eh eel de-po-zee-to ba-gal-yee
Luggage lockers	**La custodia automatica dei bagagli**	Koos-to-dya ow-to-ma-tee-ka day ba-gal-yee
Would you take these bags to a taxi/the bus?	**Vuol portare questi bagagli al taxi/ all'autobus?**	Vwol por-tar-eh kwes-tee ba-gal-yee al taxi/al-low-to-bus
What's the price for each piece of luggage?	**Quanto costa a collo?**	Kwan-to kos-ta a kol-lo
I shall take this myself	**Questa la porto io**	Kwes-ta la por-to ee-o
That's not mine	**Questa non è mia**	Kwes-ta non eh mee-a
Would you call a taxi?	**Mi può chiamare un taxi, per favore?**	Mee pwo kya-mar-eh un taxi, pair fa-vor-eh
How much do I owe you?	**Quanto le devo?**	Kwan-to leh de-vo

MOVING ON

Where is the information bureau, please?	Dov'è l'ufficio informazioni, per favore?	Dov-eh loof-fee-cho een-for-mat-syo-nee, pair fa-vor-eh
Is there a bus/train into the town?	C'è un autobus/un treno che va al centro?	Cheh oon ow-to-bus/oon tre-no keh va al chen-tro
How can I get to ...?	Come si arriva a ...?	Ko-meh see ar-ree-va a ...

SIGNS TO LOOK FOR AT AIRPORTS AND STATIONS

Arrivals	**Arrivi**
Booking office	**Prenotazioni**
Buses	**Autobus/pullman**
Car rental	**Noleggio macchina**
Connections	**Coincidenze**
Departures	**Partenze**
Exchange	**Cambio/cambiavalute**
Gentlemen	**Signori/gabinetti/toilette**
Hotel reservations	**Prenotazioni alberghi**
Information	**Informazioni**
Ladies' room	**Signore/gabinetti per signora**
Left luggage	**Deposito bagagli**
Lost property	**Oggetti smarriti**

Main lines	**Linee principali**
News-stand	**Edicola**
No smoking	**Vietato fumare**
Refreshments	**Rinfreschi/ristoratore**
Reservations	**Prenotazioni**
Smoker	**Fumatori**
Suburban lines	**Linee locali**
Taxis	**Taxi**
Tourist office	**Ufficio turistico**
Transit desk	**Passaggeri in transito**
Tickets	**Biglietti**
Underground	**Metropolitana**
Waiting room	**Sala d'aspetto**

BUYING A TICKET

Where's the nearest travel agency?	**Dov'è l'agenzia di viaggi la più vicina?**	Dov-eh la-jent-see-a dee vyad-jee la pyoo vee-chee-na
Have you a timetable, please?	**Ha un orario, per favore?**	A oon or-ar-yo, pair fa-vor-eh
What's the tourist return fare to …?	**Quanto costa un biglietto turistico di andata e ritorno per …?**	Kwan-to kos-ta oon beel-yet-to too-rees-tee-ko dee an-da-ta e ree-tor-no pair …
How much is it first class to …?	**Quanto costa un biglietto di prima classe per …?**	Kwan-to kos-ta oon beel-yet-to dee preem-a klas-seh pair …

A second class single to ...	Un biglietto di seconda classe, solo andata, per ...	Oon beel-yet-to dee se-kon-da klas-seh, so-lo an-da-ta, pair ...
A single ticket to ...	Un biglietto di solo andata per ...	Oon beel-yet-to dee so-lo an-da-ta pair ...
A return ticket to ...	Un biglietto di andata e ritorno per ...	Oon beel-yet-to dee an-da-ta eh ree-tor-no pair ...
A day return to ...	Un biglietto a ridiuzione per ...	Oon beel-yet-to a ree-doot-syo-neh pair ...
Is there a cheaper midweek/weekend fare?	C'è un biglietto feriale/festivo?	Cheh oon beel-yet-to fer-ya-leh/fes-tee-vo
When are you coming back?	*Quando ritorna?	Kwan-do ree-tor-na
Is there a cheaper day ticket?	C'è un biglietto a riduzione?	Cheh oon beel-yet-to a ree-doot-syo-neh
Is there a special rate for children?	C'è uno sconto per i ragazzi?	Che oon-o skon-to pair ee ra-gat-see
How old is he (she)/are they?	*Quanti anni ha/hanno?	Kwan-tee an-nee a/an-no
How long is this ticket valid?	Per quanti giorni è valido questo biglietto?	Pair kwan-tee jor-nee eh va-lee-do kwes-to beel-yet-to
A book of tickets, please	Un mazzetto di biglietti, per favore	Oon mad-zet-to dee beel-yet-tee, pair fa-vor-eh
Can I use it on the bus/underground too?	E pure valido per l'autobus/la metropolitana?	Eh poo-reh va-lee-do pair low-to-bus/la met-ro-po-lee-ta-na

| Is there a supplementary charge? | C'è da pagare un supplemento? | Cheh da pa-gar-eh oon soop-le-men-to |

BY TRAIN[1]

RESERVATIONS AND INQUIRIES

Where's the railway station?	Dov'è la stazione?	Dov-eh la stat-syo-neh
Where is the ticket office?	Dov'è la biglietteria?	Dov-eh la beel-yet-tair-ee-a
Two seats on the 11.15 tomorrow to ...	Due posti sul treno delle undici e quindici di domani per ...	Doo-eh pos-tee sool tre-no del-leh oon-dee-chee eh kween-dee-chee dee do-ma-nee pair ...
I want	Vorrei	Vor-ray
a window seat	un posto vicino al finestrino	oon pos-to vee-chee-no al fee-nes-tree-no
a corner seat	un posto nell'angolo	oon pos-to nel-lan-go-lo
a seat in a non-smoking compartment	un posto in uno scompartimento per non fumatori	oon pos-to een oon-o skom-par-tee-men-to pair non foo-ma-tor-ee

1. For help in understanding the answers to these and similar questions see TIME (p. 195), NUMBERS (p. 201), DIRECTIONS (p. 34).

I want to reserve a sleeper	Vorrei riservare un posto in vagone letto	Vor-ray ree-zair-var-eh un pos-to een va-go-neh let-to
How much does a couchette cost?	Quanto costa una cuccetta?	Kwan-to kos-ta oon-a koo-chet-ta
When is the next train to ...?	Quando parte il prossimo treno per ...?	Kwan-do par-teh eel pros-see-mo tre-no pair ...
I want to register this luggage through to ...	Vorrei spedire questi bagagli raccomandati a ...	Vor-ray spe-deer-eh kwes-tee ba-gal-yee rak-ko-man-da-tee a ...
Is it an express or a local train?[2]	E un treno diretto o locale?	Eh oon tre-no dee-ret-to o lo-ka-leh
Is there an earlier/later train?	Ci sono altri treni prima di questo/ dopo questo?	Chee so-no alt-ree tre-nee pree-ma dee kwes-to/do-po kwes-to
Is there a restaurant car on the train?	C'è un vagone ristorante su questo treno?	Cheh oon va-go-neh rees-tor-an-teh soo kwes-to tre-no
I'd like to make a motorail reservation	Vorrei fare una riservazione per i servizi treni con auto accompagnate	Vor-ray far-eh oon-a ree-zair-vat-syo-neh pair ee sair-veet-see tre-nee kon ow-to ak-kom-pan-ya-teh

2. Trains are classified as follows: **Rapido** – fast trains running between main towns, sometimes only first class. A supplement is charged (about 25 per cent of normal single fare). **Espresso** – long distance express trains, first and second class. **Diretto** – express trains, first and second class. **Locale** – local trains. Luggage can often be transported for the whole journey in the luggage car, and this service is called **bagaglio a seguito passaggero**. Certain Trans-European Express trains go through Italy. They are only first class and a supplement must be paid.

| Where is the motorail loading platform? | Dov'è il binario motorail? | Dov-eh eel bee-nar-yo motorail |

CHANGING

Is there a through train to ...?	C'è un treno diretto per ...?	Cheh oon tre-no dee-ret-to pair ...
Do I have to change?	Devo cambiare?	De-vo kam-byar-eh
Where do I change?	Dove devo cambiare?	Do-veh de-vo kam-byar-eh
What time is there a connection to ...?	A che ora c'è la coincidenza per ...?	A keh or-a cheh la ko-een-chee-dent-sa pair ...
Change at ... and take the local train	*Cambiare a ... e prendere il treno locale	Kam-byar-eh a ... eh pren-dair-eh eel tre-no lo-ka-leh

DEPARTURE

When does the train leave?	A che ora parte questo treno?	A keh or-a par-teh kwes-to tre-no
Which platform does the train to ... leave from?	Da quale binario parte il treno per ...?	Da kwal-eh bee-nar-yo par-teh eel tre-no pair ...
Is this the train for ...?	E questo il treno per ...?	Eh kwes-to eel tre-no pair ...
There will be a delay of ...	*Ci sarà un ritardo di ...	Chee sa-ra oon ree-tar-do dee ...

ARRIVAL

When does it get to ...?	A che ora arriva a ...?	A keh or-a ar-ree-va a ...
Does the train stop at ...?	Ferma a ... questo treno?	Fer-ma a ... kwes-to tre-no
How long do we stop here?	Quanto ci fermiamo qui?	Kwan-to chee fer-mya-mo kwee
Is the train late?	E in ritardo questo treno?	Eh een ree-tar-do kwes-to tre-no
When does the train from ... get in?	A che ora arriva il treno da ...?	A keh or-a ar-ree-va eel tre-no da ...
At which platform?	Su quale binario?	Soo kwa-leh bee-nar-yo

ON THE TRAIN

We have reserved seats	Abbiamo posti riservati	Ab-bya-mo pos-tee ree-zair-va-tee
Is this seat free?	E libero questo posto?	Eh lee-bair-o kwes-to pos-to
This seat is taken	Questo posto è occupato	Kwes-to pos-to eh ok-koo-pa-to
Is this a smoking/ non-smoking compartment?	E per fumatori/non fumatori questo scompartimento?	Eh pair foo-ma-tor-ee/ non foo-ma-tor-ee kwes-to skom-par-tee-men-to
Dining car	La carrozza ristorante	Kar-rot-sa rees-tor-an-teh
Two tickets for lunch please	Due biglietti per il pranzo, per favore	Doo-eh beel-yet-tee pair eel prand-zo, pair fa-vor-eh

When is the buffet car open?	Quando è aperta la carrozza ristorante?	Kwan-do eh a-pair-ta la kar-rot-sa rees-tor-an-teh
Where is the sleeping car?	Dov'è il vagone letto?	Dov-eh eel va-go-neh let-to
Which is my sleeper?	Qual'è la mia cuccetta?	Kwal-eh la mee-a koo-chet-ta
The heating is too high/too low	Bisogna abbassare/alzare il riscaldamento	Bee-zon-ya ab-bas-sar-eh/alt-sar-eh eel rees-kal-da-men-to
I can't open/close the window	Non riesco ad aprire/a chiudere il finestrino	Non ree-es-ko ad ap-reer-eh/a kyoo-dair-eh eel fee-nes-tree-no
What station is this?	Che stazione è?	Keh stat-syo-neh eh
How long do we stop here?	Quanto tempo si ferma qui?	Kwan-to tem-po see fair-ma kwee

BY AIR

Where's the Alitalia office?	Dov'è l'ufficio dell'Alitalia?	Dov-eh loof-fee-cho del-lal-ee-tal-ya
I'd like to book two seats on Monday's plane to ...	Vorrei prenotare due posti sull'aereo di lunedì per ...	Vor-ray pre-no-tar-eh doo-eh pos-tee sool-la-air-yo dee loo-ne-dee pair ...
Is there a flight to Milan next Thursday?	Ci sono servizi aerei per Milano giovedì prossimo?	Chee so-no sair-veet-see a-air-yee pair mee-la-no jo-ve-dee pros-see-mo

What is the flight number?	Qual'è il numero di volo?	Kwal-eh eel noo-mair-o dee vo-lo
When does it leave/arrive?	A che ora parte/arriva?	A keh or-a par-teh/ar-ree-va
When does the next plane leave?	A che ora parte il prossimo aereo?	A keh or-a par-teh eel pros-see-mo a-air-yo
Is there a bus to the airport/to the town?	C'è un autobus per l'aeroporto/per andare in città?	Cheh oon ow-to-bus pair la-air-o-por-to/pair an-dar-eh een cheet-ta
When must I check in?	A che ora c'è il controllo?	A keh or-a cheh eel kon-trol-lo
Please cancel my reservation to ...	Vorrei disdire la mia prenotazione per ...	Vor-ray dees-deer-eh la mee-a pre-no-tat-syo-neh pair ...
I'd like to change my reservation to ...	Vorrei cambiare la mia prenotazione per ...	Vor-ray kam-byar-eh la mee-a pre-no-tat-syo-neh pair ...
I have an open ticket	Ho un biglietto aperto	O oon beel-yet-to a-pair-to
Can I change my ticket?	Posso cambiare il mio biglietto?	Pos-so kam-byar-eh eel mee-o beel-yet-to
Will it cost more?	Costerà in più?	Kos-te-ra een pyoo

BY BOAT

Is there a boat from here to ...?	C'è un servizio marittimo per ...?	Cheh oon sair-veet-syo mar-eet-tee-mo pair ...
How long does it take to get to ...?	Quanto tempo mette per arrivare a ...?	Kwan-to tem-po met-teh pair ar-ree-var-eh a ...

How often do the boats leave?	Ogni quanto partono i battelli?	On-yee kwan-to par-to-no ee bat-tel-lee
Where does the boat put in?	Dove fa scalo questo battello?	Do-veh fa ska-lo kwes-to bat-tel-lo
Does it call at …?	Si ferma a …?	See fer-ma a …
When does the next boat leave?	Quando parte il prossimo battello?	Kwan-do par-teh eel pros-see-mo bat-tel-lo
Can I book a single berth cabin?	Posso riservare una cabina ad un letto?	Pos-so ree-zair-var-eh oon-a ka-bee-na ad oon let-to
How many berths are there in this cabin?	Quante cuccette ci sono in questa cabina?	Kwan-teh koo-chet-teh chee so-no een kwes-ta ka-been-na
When must we go on board?	A che ora dobbiamo essere a bordo?	A keh or-a dob-bya-mo es-sair-eh a bor-do
How do we get on to the deck?	Come si arriva al ponte?	Ko-meh see ar-ree-va al pon-teh
When do we dock?	A che ora arriviamo in porto?	A keh or-a ar-ree-vya-mo een por-to
How long do we stay in port?	Quanto rimaniamo in porto?	Kwan-to ree-ma-nya-mo een por-to
(car) ferry	il traghetto	tra-get-to
hovercraft	l'hovercraft m	hovercraft
hydrofoil	l'aliscafo m	a-lee-ska-fo
lifebelt	la cintura di salvataggio	cheen-too-ra dee sal-va-tad-jo
lifeboat	il batello di salvataggio	ba-tel-lo dee sal-va-tad-jo

BY UNDERGROUND

Where is the nearest underground station?	Dov'è la stazione della metropolitana la più vicina?	Dov-eh la stat-syo-neh del-la met-tro-po-lee-ta-na la pyoo vee-chee-na
Which line goes to ...?	Quale linea va a ...?	Kwa-leh lee-ne-a va a ...
Does this train go to ...?	Questo treno va a ...?	Kwes-to tre-no va a ...
Where do I change for ...	Dove si cambia per ...?	Do-veh see kam-bya pair ...
Is the next station ...?	La prossima stazione è ...?	La pros-see-ma stat-syo-neh eh ...
What station is this?	Qual'è questa stazione?	Kwal-eh kwes-ta stat-syo-neh
Do you have an underground map?	Ha una carta della metropolitana?	A oon-a kar-ta del-la met-ro-po-lee-ta-na

BY BUS OR COACH

Where's the bus station?	Dov'è la stazione degli autobus?	Dov-eh la stat-syo-neh del-yee ow-to-bus
Where's the coach station?	Dov'è la stazione dei pullman?	Dov-eh la stat-syo-neh day pullman
Bus stop	*Fermata dell'autobus	Fair-ma-ta del-low-to-bus
Request stop	*Fermata a richiesta	Fair-ma-ta a ree-kyes-ta

When does the coach leave?	Quando parte il pullman?	Kwan-do par-teh eel pullman
What time do we get to ...?	A che ora arriviamo a ...?	A keh or-a ar-ree-vya-mo a ...
What stops does it make?	In quali posti si ferma?	Een kwa-lee pos-tee see fair-ma
Is it a long journey?	E un viaggio molto lungo?	E oon vyad-jo mol-to loon-go
We want to take a sightseeing tour round the city	Vogliamo fare un giro turistico della città	Vol-ya-mo far-eh oon jeer-o toor-ees-tee-ko del-la cheet-ta
Is there an organized tour of the town?	Ci sono giri organizzati della città?	Chee so-no jeer-ee or-ga-neet-sa-tee del-la cheet-ta
What is the fare?	Quanto costa?	Kwan-to kos-ta
Does the bus/coach call at our hotel?	Questo autobus/ pullman passa dal nostro albergo?	Kwes-to ow-to-bus/pull-man pas-sa dal nos-tro al-bair-go
Is there an excursion to ... tomorrow?	C'è una gita a ... domani?	Cheh oon-a jee-ta a ... do-ma-nee
What time is the next bus?	A che ora c'è il prossimo autobus?	A keh or-a cheh eel pros-see-mo ow-to-bus
How often does the ... run?	Ogni quanto passa l'autobus ...?	On-yee kwan-to pas-sa low-to-bus ...
Has the last bus gone?	E già partito l'ultimo autobus?	Eh ja par-tee-to lool-tee-mo ow-to-bus
Does this bus go to the centre?	Passa dal centro questo autobus?	Pas-sa dal chen-tro kwes-to ow-to-bus
Does it go to the beach?	Passa vicino alla spiaggia?	Pas-sa vee-chee-no al-la spyad-ja

Does this bus go to the station?	Va alla stazione questo autobus?	Va al-la stat-syo-neh kwes-to ow-to-bus
Does it go near ...?	Passa vicino a ...?	Pas-sa vee-chee-no a ...
Where can I get a bus to ...?	Dove posso prendere un autobus per ...?	Do-veh pos-so pren-dair-eh oon ow-to-bus pair ...
Is this the right stop for ...?	E questa la fermata giusta per ...?	Eh kwes-ta la fair-ma-ta joos-ta pair ...
Which bus goes to ...?	Quale autobus va a ...?	Kwal-eh ow-to-bus va a ...
I want to go to ...	Voglio andare a ...	Vol-yo an-dar-eh a ...
Where do I get off?	Dove devo scendere?	Do-veh de-vo shen-dair-eh
I want to get off at ...	Voglio scendere a ...	Vol-yo shen-dair-eh a ...
The bus to ... stops over there	*L'autobus per ... ferma là	Low-to-bus pair ... fair-ma la
A number ... goes to ...	*Il numero ... va a ...	Eel noo-mair-o ... va a ...
You must take a number ...	*Lei deve prendere il numero ...	Lay de-ve pren-dair-eh eel noo-mair-o ...
You get off at the next stop	*Scenda alla prossima fermata	Shen-da al-la pros-see-ma fair-ma-ta
The buses run every ten minutes/every hour	*C'è un autobus ogni dieci minuti/ogni ora	Cheh oon ow-to-bus on-yee dye-chee mi-noo-tee/on-yee or-a

BY TAXI

Please get me a taxi	Vuol chiamarmi un taxi, per favore?	Vwol kya-mar-mee oon taxi, pair fa-vor-eh
Where can I get a taxi?	Dove posso prendere un taxi?	Do-veh pos-so pren-dair-eh oon taxi
Are you free?	E libero?	Eh lee-bair-o
Please take me	Mi vuol portare	Mee vwol por-tar-eh
to Hotel Central	all'Hotel Centrale	al-lo-tel chen-tra-leh
to the station	alla stazione	al-la stat-syo-neh
to this address	a questo indirizzo	a kwes-to een-dee-reet-so
Can you hurry, I'm late?	Può andare più in fretta, sono in ritardo?	Pwo an-dar-eh pyoo een fret-ta, so-no een ree-tar-do
I want to go through the centre	Vorrei passare dal centro	Vor-ray pas-sar-eh dal chen-tro
Please wait a minute	Aspetti un momento, per favore	As-pet-tee oon mo-men-to, pair fa-vor-eh
Stop here	Fermi qui	Fair-mee kwee
Is it far?	E molto lontano?	Eh mol-to lon-ta-no
How far is it to …?	Quanto c'è di qui a …?	Kwan-to cheh dee kwee a …
Turn right/left at the next corner	Si gira a destra/ sinistra al prossimo angolo	See jeer-a a des-tra/see-nees-tra al pros-see-mo an-go-lo
Straight on	Va diritto	Va dee-reet-to

How much do you charge by the hour/ for the day?	Quanto prende all'ora/a giornata?	Kwan-to pren-deh al-lor-a/a jor-na-ta
I'd like to go to ... How much would you charge?	Vorrei andare a ... Quanto costa?	Vor-ray an-dar-eh a ... kwan-to kos-ta
How much is it?	Quanto è?	Kwan-to eh
That's too much	E troppo	Eh trop-po
I am not prepared to spend that much	No, grazie, è più di quanto posso spendere	No, gra-zyeh, eh pyoo dee kwan-to pos-so spen-dair-eh
It's a lot, but all right	E un po' caro, ma va bene	Eh oon po kar-o, ma va be-neh

DIRECTIONS

Excuse me, could you tell me the way to …?	Mi scusi, può indicarmi la strada per …?	Mee skoo-zee, pwo een-dee-kar-mee la stra-da pair …
Where is …?	Dov'è	Dov-eh …
Is this the way to …?	E questa la strada per …?	Eh kwes-ta la stra-da pair …
Which is the road for …?	Qual'è la strada per …?	Kwal-eh la stra-da pair …
How far is it to …?	Quanto c'è di qui a …?	Kwan-to cheh dee kwee a …
How many kilometres?	Quanti chilometri?	Kwan-tee kee-lo-met-ree
We want to get on to the motorway to …	Vorremmo prendere l'autostrada per …	Vor-rem-mo pren-dair-eh low-to-stra-da pair …
Which is the best road to …?	Qual'è la migliore strada per …?	Kwal-eh la meel-yor-eh stra-da pair …
Is this the right road for …?	E questa la strada giusta per …?	Eh kwes-ta la stra-da joos-ta pair …

Where does this road lead to?	Dove porta questa strada?	Do-veh por-ta kwes-ta stra-da
Is it a good road?	E una strada in buone condizioni?	Eh oon-a stra-da een bwo-neh kon-deet-syo-nee
Is it a motorway?	E un'autostrada?	Eh oon ow-to-stra-da
Is there a toll?	C'è un pedaggio?	Cheh oon pe-dad-jo
Is the tunnel/pass open?	E aperta la galleria/aperto il passo?	Eh a-pair-ta la gal-lair-ee-a/a-pair-to eel pas-so
Is the road to ... clear?	E aperta la strada per ...?	Eh a-pair-ta la stra-da pair ...
How far is the next village/petrol station?	A che distanza è il prossimo paese/la prossima stazione di rifornimento?	A keh dees-tand-za eh eel pros-see-mo pa-e-zeh/la pros-see-ma stat-syo-neh dee ree-for-nee-men-to
Is there any danger of avalanches?	C'è pericolo di valanghe?	Cheh pair-ee-ko-lo dee va-lan-geh
Will we get to ... by evening?	Arriveremo a ... prima di sera?	Ar-ree-vair-em-o a ... pree-ma dee se-ra
How long will it take	Quanto tempo ci si mette	Kwan-to tem-po chee see met-teh
by car?	in macchina?	een mak-kee-na
by bicycle?	in bicicletta?	een bee-chee-klet-ta
on foot?	a piedi?	a pye-dee
Where are we now?	Dove siamo adesso?	Do-veh sya-mo a-des-so
What is the name of this place?	Come si chiama questo posto?	Ko-meh see kya-ma kwes-to pos-to

Please show me on the map	Può farmi vedere sulla mappa, per favore	Pwo far-mee ve-dair-eh sool-la map-pa, pair fa-vor-eh
It's that way	*E in questa direzione/di qui	Eh een kwes-ta dee-ret-syo-neh/dee kwee
It isn't far	*Non è lontano di qui	Non eh lon-ta-no dee kwee
Follow signs for ...	*Segua direzioni per ...	Seg-wa dee-ret-syo-nee pair ...
Follow this road for ... kilometres	*Segua questa strada per ... chilometri	Seg-wa qwes-ta stra-da pair ... kee-lo-met-ree
Keep straight on	*Continui diritto	Kon-teen-wee dee-reet-to
Turn right at the crossroads	*Al crocevia volti a destra	Al kro-che-vee-a vol-tee a des-tra
Take the second road on the left	*Prenda la seconda strada a sinistra	Pren-da la se-kon-da stra-da a see-nees-tra
Turn right at the traffic-lights	*Al semaforo, volti a destra	Al se-ma-fo-ro, vol-tee a des-tra
Turn left after the bridge	*Dopo il ponte giri a sinistra	Do-po eel pon-teh jee-ree a see-nees-tra
The best road is ...	*La migliore strada è ...	La meel-yor-eh stra-da eh ...
Take this road as far as ... and ask again	*Segua questa strada fino a ... e chieda di nuovo	Seg-wa kwes-ta stra-da fee-no a ... eh kye-da dee nwo-vo
You are going the wrong way	*Ha sbagliato strada	A zbal-ya-to stra-da
one-way system	la circolazione a senso unico	cheer-ko-lat-syo-neh a sen-so oo-nee-ko

north	norte	nor-teh
south	sud	sood
east	est	est
west	ovest	o-vest

DRIVING

Have you a road map, please?	Ha una carta stradale, per favore?	A oon-a kar-ta stra-da-leh, pair fa-vor-eh
Where is a car park?	Dov'è un parcheggio?	Dov-eh oon par-ked-jo
(How long) can I park here?	(Per quanto tempo) si può parcare qui?	(Pair kwan-to tem-po) see pwo par-kar-eh kwee
Can I park here?	Si può tenere la macchina qui?	See pwo te-nair-eh la mak-kee-na kwee
Have you any change for the meter, please?	Ha mica degli spiccioli per il parchimetro?	A mee-ka del-yee spee-cho-lee pair eel par-kee-met-ro
No parking	*Divieto di parcheggio/ parcheggio vietato	Dee-vye-to dee par-ked-jo/par-ked-jo vye-ta-to
Is this your car?	E sua questa macchina?	Eh soo-a kwes-ta mak-kee-na
May I see your licence, please?	*Posso vedere la sua patente, per favore?	Pos-so ve-dair-eh la soo-a pa-ten-teh, pair fa-vor-eh

How far is the next petrol station?	A che distanza è il più vicino distributore (di benzina)?	A keh dees-tand-za eh eel pyoo vee-chee-no dees-tree-boo-tor-eh (dee bend-zee-na)
Speed limit	Limite di velocità	Lee-mee-teh dee ve-lo-chee-ta
Pedestrian precinct	Zona pedonale	Dzo-na pe-do-na-leh

CAR HIRE

Where can I hire a car?	Dove posso noleggiare una macchina?	Do-veh pos-so no-led-jar-eh oon-a mak-kee-na
I want to hire a car and a driver/a self-drive car	Vorrei noleggiare una macchina con autista/vorrei prendere a nolo una macchina	Vor-ray no-led-jar-eh oon-a mak-kee-na kon ow-tees-ta/vor-ray pren-dair-eh a no-lo oon-a mak-kee-na
I want to hire an automatic	Vorrei noleggiare una macchina automatica	Vor-ray no-led-jar-eh oon-a mak-kee-na ow-to-ma-tee-ka
Is there a weekend rate/a midweek rate?	C'è una tariffa festiva/feriale?	Cheh oon-a ta-reef-fa fes-tee-va/fer-ya-leh
How much is it	Quanto costa	Kwan-to kos-ta
by the hour?	all'ora?	al-lor-a
by the day?	a giornata?	a jor-na-ta
by the week?	per settimana?	pair set-tee-ma-na

I need a car for two days/a week	Ho bisogno di una macchina per due giorni/una settimana	O bee-zon-yo dee oon-a mak-kee-na pair doo-eh jor-nee/oon-a set-tee-ma-na
Does that include mileage?	Il chilometraggio è compreso?	Eel kee-lo-met-rad-jo eh kom-pre-zo
The charge per kilometre is …	*La tariffa è di lire … a chilometro	La ta-reef-fa eh dee leer-eh … a kee-lo-met-ro
What kind of insurance do you want?	*Che tipo di assicurazione vuole?	Keh tee-po dee as-see-koo-rat-syo-neh vwol-eh
Do you want a deposit?	Vuole una cauzione?	Vwo-leh oon-a kowt-syo-neh
I will pay by credit card	Pagherò con la carta di credito	Pa-ge-ro kon la kar-ta dee kre-dee-to

ROAD SIGNS

Caduta massi	Falling stones
Cautela	Caution
Curve	Winding road
Diluvio	Flooding
Diversione	Diversion
Disco blu	Parking disc required
Dogana	Customs
Fermata	Stop
Lavori in corso	Road works ahead

Limite di velocità	Speed limit
Parcheggio vietato	No parking
Passaggio a livello	Level crossing
Pericolo	Danger
Prudenza	Attention/caution
Rallentare	Slow
Salita ripida	Steep hill
Semaforo	Traffic lights
Senso unico	One way (street)
Senso vietato	No entry
Sosta autorizzata	Parking allowed
Strada interrotta	Road blocked
Superficie irregolare/ sdrucciolevole	Uneven/slippery surface
Superficie ghiacciata	Icy surface
Svolte/curve	Bends/curves
Tenere la destra	Keep right
Tenersi in corsia	Keep in lane
Usare i fanali	Lights on/use headlights
Uscita autoveicoli	Exit for lorries
Zona pedonale	Pedestrians only

AT THE GARAGE OR PETROL STATION

Where is the nearest petrol station?	Dov'è il distributore più vicino?	Dov-eh eel dees-tree-boo-tor-eh pyoo vee-chee-no
How far is the next petrol station?	A che distanza è il distributore più vicino?	A keh dees-tand-za eh eel dees-tree-boo-tor-eh pyoo vee-chee-no
... litres of petrol, and please check the oil and water	... litri di benzina, e per favore controlli l'olio e l'acqua	... leet-ree dee bend-zee-na, eh pair fa-vor-eh kon-trol-lee lol-yo eh lak-wa
... litres of diesel	... litri di nafta	... leet-ree dee naf-ta
Fill it up	Faccia il pieno	Fa-cha eel pye-no
How much is petrol a litre?	Quanto costa un litro di benzina?	Kwan-to kos-ta oon leet-ro dee bend-zee-na
... lire worth of petrol, please	... lire di benzina, per favore	... leer-eh dee bend-zee-na, pair fa-vor-eh
The oil needs changing	Bisognerebbe cambiare l'olio	Bee-zon-yair-eb-beh kam-byar-eh lol-yo
Please change the tyre	Vuol cambiare la gomma, per favore	Vwol kam-byar-eh la gom-ma, pair fa-vor-eh
Please check	Per favore, controlli	Pair fa-vor-eh, kon-trol-lee
the battery	la batteria	la bat-tair-ee-a
the brakes	i freni	ee fre-nee
the oil	l'olio	lol-yo

the transmission fluid	il giunto idraulico	eel joon-to ee-**drow**-lee-ko
the tyre pressure, including the spare	le gomme, inclusa la ruota di scorta	leh gom-meh, een-kloo-za la rwo-ta dee skor-ta
Would you clean the windscreen, please?	Può pulirmi il parabrezza, per favore?	Pwo poo-leer-mee eel pa-ra-bred-za, pair fa-vor-eh
Please wash the car	Vuol lavare la macchina, per favore	Vwol la-var-eh la **mak**-kee-na, pair fa-vor-eh
Can I garage the car here?	Posso lasciare la macchina in questo garage?	Pos-so la-shar-eh la mak-kee-na een kwes-to ga-raj
What time does the garage close?	A che ora chiude il garage?	A keh or-a kyoo-deh eel ga-**raj**
Where are the toilets?	Dove sono le toilette?	Do-veh so-no leh twa-let-teh

REPAIRS

My car's broken down	Ho un guasto alla macchina	O oon gwas-to al-la mak-kee-na
Can you give me a lift to a telephone?	Può darmi un passaggio al telefono più vicino?	Pwo dar-mee oon pas-sad-jo al te-le-fo-no pyoo vee-chee-no
Please tell the next garage to send help	Dica al garage più vicino di mandare soccorso	Dee-ka al ga-**raj** pyoo vee-chee-no dee man-dar-eh sok-kor-so

Can I use your phone?	Posso usare il telefono?	Pos-so oo-zar-eh eel te-le-fo-no
Where is there a ... agency?	Dov'è l'agenzia della ...?	Dov-eh la-jent-see-a del-la ...
Have you a breakdown service?	Ha un servizio riparazioni?	A oon sair-veet-syo ree-pa-rat-syo-nee
Is there a mechanic?	C'è un meccanico?	Cheh oon mek-ka-nee-ko
Can you send someone to repair it/tow it away?	Può mandare qualcuno a ripararla/rimorchiarla?	Pwo man-dar-eh kwal-koo-no a ree-pa-rar-la/ree-mor-kyar-la
It is an automatic and cannot be towed	E automatica, e non si può rimorchiare	Eh ow-to-ma-tee-ka, eh non see pwo ree-mor-kyar-eh
Where is your car?	*Dov'è la macchina?	Dov-eh la mak-kee-na
Where are you now?	*Dove si trova lei adesso?	Do-veh see tro-va lay a-des-so
I am on the road from ... to ... near kilometre post ...	Sono sulla strada da ... a ... vicino al chilometro ...	So-no sool-la stra-da da ... a ... vee-chee-no al kee-lo-met-ro ...
How long will you be?	Fra quanto tempo sarà qui?	Fra kwan-to tem-po sa-ra kwee
I want the car serviced	Vorrei far revisionare l'automobile	Vor-ray far re-vee-zyo-nar-eh low-to-mo-bee-leh
The battery is flat, it needs charging	La batteria è scarica, ha bisogno di essere caricata	La bat-tair-ee-a eh ska-ree-ka, a bee-zon-yo dee es-sair-eh ka-ree-ka-ta

This tyre is flat/punctured	**Questa gomma è sgonfia/forata**	Kwes-ta gom-ma eh zgon-fya/fo-ra-ta
The exhaust is broken	**Lo scappamento è guasto**	Lo skap-pa-men-to eh gwas-to
The windscreen wipers do not work	**Non funzionano i tergicristalli**	Non foont-syo-na-no ee tair-jee-krees-tal-lee
The valve is leaking	**Questa valvola perde**	Kwes-ta val-vo-la pair-deh
The radiator is leaking	**Il radiatore perde acqua**	Eel ra-dya-tor-eh pair-deh ak-wa
My car won't start	**La mia macchina non parte**	La mee-a mak-kee-na non par-teh
It's not running properly	**Procede a scosse**	Pro-che-deh a skos-seh
The engine is overheating	**Il motore riscalda troppo**	Eel mo-tor-eh rees-kal-da trop-po
I've got electrical trouble	**Dev'esserci un guasto nel sistema elettrico**	Dev-es-sair-chee oon gwas-to nel sees-te-ma el-et-tree-ko
The lock is broken/jammed	**La serratura è rotta/bloccata**	La ser-ra-too-ra eh rot-ta/blok-ka-ta
The engine is firing badly	**L'accensione è difettosa**	La-chen-syo-neh eh dee-fet-to-za
Can you change this plug?	**Può cambiare questa candela?**	Pwo kam-byar-eh kwes-ta kan-de-la
There's a petrol/oil leak	**C'è una perdita di benzina/d'olio**	Cheh oon-a pair-dee-ta dee bend-zee-na/dol-yo
There's a smell of petrol/rubber	**Si sente odore di benzina/di gomma**	See sen-teh o-dor-eh dee bend-zee-na/dee gom-ma

The carburettor needs adjusting	Il carburatore dev'essere regolato	Eel kar-boo-ra-tor-eh dev-es-sair-eh re-go-la-to
Something is wrong with	Ho un guasto	O oon gwas-to
my car	alla macchina	al-la mak-kee-na
the engine	nel motore	nel mo-tor-eh
the lights	ai fanali	a-ee fa-na-lee
the clutch	nella frizione	nel-la freet-syo-neh
the gearbox	nella scatola del cambio	nel-la ska-to-la del kam-byo
the brakes	ai freni	a-ee fre-nee
the steering	allo sterzo	al-lo stairt-so
Can you repair it?	Può ripararla?	Pwo ree-pa-rar-la
How long will it take to repair?	Quanto tempo ci vuole per ripararla?	Kwan-to tem-po chee vwo-leh pair ree-pa-rar-la
What will it cost?	Quanto costerà?	Kwan-to kos-tair-a
When can I pick the car up?	Quando posso venire a prendere la macchina?	Kwan-do pos-so ve-neer-eh a pren-dair-eh la mak-kee-na
I need it	Ne ho bisogno	Neh o bee-zon-yo
as soon as possible	il più presto possible	eel pyoo pres-to pos-see-bee-leh
in three hours	fra tre ore	fra treh or-eh
tomorrow morning	domani mattina	do-ma-nee mat-tee-na
It will take two days	*Ci vorranno due giorni	Chee vor-ran-no doo-eh jor-nee

We can repair it temporarily	*La possiamo riparare provvisoriamente	La pos-sya-mo ree-pa-rar-eh prov-vee-zor-ya-men-teh
We haven't the right spares	*Non abbiamo i pezzi di ricambio	No ab-bya-mo ee pet-see dee ree-kam-byo
We have to send for the spares	*Dobbiamo far venire i pezzi di ricambio	Dob-bya-mo far ve-neer-eh ee pet-see dee ree-kam-byo
You will need a new ...	*Ci vuole un nuovo ...	Chee vwo-leh oon nwo-vo ...
Could I have an itemized bill, please?	Può farmi il conto articolo per articolo, per favore?	Pwo far-mee eel kon-to ar-tee-ko-lo pair ar-tee-ko-lo, pair fa-vor-eh

PARTS OF A CAR AND OTHER USEFUL WORDS

accelerate (to)	accelerare	a-che-le-rar-eh
accelerator	l'acceleratore m	a-che-le-ra-tor-eh
air pump	la pompa d'aria	pom-pa dar-ya
alternator	l'alternatore m	al-ter-na-tor-eh
anti-freeze	l'anticongelante m	an-tee-kon-je-lan-teh
automatic transmission	la trasmissione automatica	traz-mees-syo-neh ow-to-ma-tee-ka
axle	l'asse m	as-seh
battery	la batteria	bat-tair-ee-a
bonnet	il cofano	ko-fa-no

boot/trunk	**il portabagagli**	por-ta-ba-gal-yee
brake	**il freno**	fre-no
brake lights	**le luci dei freni**	loo-chee day fre-nee
brake lining	**la guarnizione del freno**	gwar-neet-syo-neh del fre-no
brake pads	**la ganascia del freno**	ga-na-sha del fre-no
breakdown	**il guasto**	gwas-to
bulb	**la lampadina**	lam-pa-dee-na
bumper	**il paraurti**	pa-ra-oor-tee
carburettor	**il carburatore**	kar-boo-ra-tor-eh
choke	**la presa d'aria**	pre-za dar-ya
cooling system	**il sistema di raffreddamento**	sees-te-ma dee raf-fred-da-men-to
crankshaft	**la manovella**	ma-no-vel-la
cylinder	**il cilindro**	chee-leen-dro
differential gear	**il differenziale**	deef-fer-ent-sya-leh
dip stick	**la coppa dell'olio**	kop-pa del-lol-yo
distilled water	**l'acqua distillata** *f*	ak-wa dees-teel-la-ta
distributor	**il distributore**	dees-tree-boo-tor-eh
door	**lo sportello/la portiera**	spor-tel-lo/por-tyair-a
doorhandle	**la maniglia dello sportello**	ma-neel-ya del-lo spor-tel-lo
drive (to)	**guidare**	gwee-dar-eh
drive shaft	**l'albero di trasmissione** *m*	al-be-ro dee tras-mees-syo-neh
driver	**l'autista** *m*	ow-tees-ta

dynamo	la dinamo	dee-na-mo
engine	il motore	mo-tor-eh
exhaust	lo scappamento	skap-pa-men-to
fan	il ventilatore	ven-tee-la-tor-eh
fanbelt	la cinghia del ventilatore	cheen-gya del ven-tee-la-tor-eh
(oil) filter	il filtro (dell'olio)	feel-tro (del-lol-yo)
flat tyre	la gomma sgonfia	gom-ma zgon-fya
foglamp	il fanale antinebbia	fan-al-eh an-tee-neb-bya
fusebox	la valvola	val-vo-la
gasket	la guarnizione	gwar-neet-syo-neh
gear	la marcia/la velocità	mar-cha/ve-lo-chee-ta
gear box	la scatola del cambio	ska-to-la del kam-byo
gear lever	la leva del cambio	le-va del kam-byo
grease (to)	ingrassare	een-gras-sar-eh
handbrake	il freno a mano	fre-no a ma-no
headlights	i fari/fanali	fa-ree/fa-na-lee
heater	il riscaldamento	rees-kal-da-men-to
horn	il clacson	klak-son
hose	il tubo	too-bo
ignition	l'accensione *f*	a-chen-syo-neh
ignition key	la chiavetta dell'accensione	kya-vet-ta del-la-chen-syo-neh
indicator	l'indicatore *m*/la freccia	een-dee-ka-tor-eh/fre-cha
jack	il martinetto/il cricco	mar-tee-net-to/kreek-ko

lights – head/rear/side	**i fanali anteriori/ posteriori/di posizione**	fa-na-lee an-ter-yor-ee/ pos-ter-yor-ee/dee po- zeet-syo-neh
lock/catch	**la serratura**	ser-ra-too-ra
mirror	**lo specchietto**	spek-kyet-to
number plate	**la targa**	tar-ga
nut	**il dado**	da-do
oil	**l'olio** *m*	ol-yo
parking lights	**le luci di posizione**	loo-chee dee po-zeet- syo-neh
petrol	**la benzina**	bend-zee-na
petrol can	**il bidone di benzina**	bee-do-neh dee bend- zee-na
piston	**il pistone**	pees-to-neh
plug	**la candela**	kan-de-la
pump	**la pompa**	pom-pa
radiator	**il radiatore**	ra-dya-tor-eh
rear axle	**il ponte posteriore**	pon-teh pos-ter-yor-eh
rear lights	**le luci posteriori**	loo-chee pos-ter-yor-ee
reverse (to)	**fare marcia indietro**	fa-reh mar-cha een-dye- tro
reverse	**la retromarcia**	ret-ro-mar-cha
reversing lights	**le luci della retromarcia**	loo-chee del-la ret-ro- mar-cha
seat	**il sedile**	se-dee-leh
screwdriver	**il cacciavite**	ka-cha-vee-teh
shock absorber	**l'ammortizzatore** *m*	am-mor-teed-za-tor-eh
silencer	**il silenziatore**	see-lent-sya-tor-eh

spanner	la chiave inglese	kya-veh een-gle-zeh
spare tyre	la gomma di scorta	gom-ma dee skor-ta
spares	i pezzi di ricambio	pet-see dee ree-kam-byo
sparking plug	la candela	kan-de-la
speed	la velocità	ve-lo-chee-ta
speedometer	il tachimetro	ta-kee-me-tro
spring	la molla	mol-la
stall (to)	fermarsi a scosse	fair-mar-see a skos-seh
starter motor	il motorino d'avviamento	mo-to-ree-no dav-vya-men-to
steering	lo sterzo	stert-so
steering wheel	il volante	vo-lan-teh
suspension	la sospensione	sos-pen-syo-neh
tank	il serbatoio	sair-ba-to-yo
tappets	le punterie	poon-ter-ee-eh
transmission	la trasmissione	tras-mees-syo-neh
tyre pressure	la pressione delle gomme	pres-syo-neh del-leh gom-meh
tyres	le gomme	gom-meh
valve	la valvola	val-vo-la
wheel – back/front/ spare	la ruota posteriore/ anteriore/di scorta	rwo-ta pos-ter-yor-eh/ an-ter-yor-eh/dee skor-ta
window	il vetro	ve-tro
windscreen	il parabrezza	pa-ra-bred-za
windscreen washers	gli spruzzatori	sproot-sa-tor-ee
windscreen wipers	i tergicristalli	tair-jee-krees-tal-lee

CYCLING

Where can I hire a bicycle?	**Dove posso affittare una bicicletta?**	Do-veh pos-so af-feet-tar-eh oon-a bee-chee-klet-ta
Do you have a bicycle with gears?	**Ha una bicicletta con cambi?**	A oon-a bee-chee-klet-ta kon kam-bee
The saddle is too high/too low	**La sella è troppo alta/bassa**	La sel-la eh trop-po al-ta/bas-sa
Where is the cycle shop?	**Dov'è il negozio ciclistico?**	Dov-eh eel ne-got-syo chee-klees-tee-ko
Do you repair bicycles?	**Si ripara le biciclette qui?**	See ree-pa-ra leh bee-chee-klet-teh kwee
The brake isn't working	**Il freno non funziona**	Eel fre-no non foont-syo-na
Could you tighten/loosen the brake cable?	**Può aggiustare il cavo del freno?**	Pwo ad-joos-tar-eh eel ka-vo del fre-no
A spoke is broken	**Si è rotto un raggio**	See eh rot-to oon rad-jo

The tyre is punctured	Il pneumatico è forato	Eel pne-oo-ma-tee-ko eh fo-ra-to
The gears need adjusting	Bisogna aggiustare i cambi	Bee-zon-ya ad-joos-tar-eh ee kam-bee
Could you straighten the wheel?	Potrebbe raddrizzare la ruota?	Pot-reb-beh rad-dreet-sar-eh la rwo-ta
The handlebars are loose	Il manubrio si è allentato	Eel ma-noob-ryo see eh al-len-ta-to
Could you please lend me a spanner?	Mi potrebbe imprestare una chiave fissa?	Mee pot-reb-beh eem-pres-tar-eh oon-a kya-veh fees-sa

PARTS OF A BICYCLE

axle	l'asse *m*	as-seh
bell	il campanello di bicicletta	kam-pa-nel-lo dee bee-chee-klet-ta
brake (front/rear)	il freno (anteriore/posteriore)	fre-no (an-ter-yor-eh/pos-ter-yor-eh)
brake cable	il cavo del freno	ka-vo del fre-no
brake lever	la leva del freno	le-va del fre-no
bulb	la lampadina	lam-pa-dee-na
chain	la catena	ka-te-na
dynamo	la dinamo	dee-na-mo
frame	il telaio	te-la-yo
gear lever	la leva del cambio	le-va del kam-byo
gears	i cambi	kam-bee
handlebars	il manubrio	ma-noob-ryo

inner tube	la camera d'aria	ka-mair-a dar-ya
light – front/rear	il fanale/il fanalino posteriore	fa-na-leh/fa-na-lee-no pos-ter-yor-eh
mudguard	il parafango	pa-ra-fan-go
panniers	i cestini	ches-tee-nee
pedal	il pedale	pe-da-leh
pump	la pompa	pom-pa
reflector	il catarifrangente	ka-ta-reef-ran-jen-teh
rim	il cerchione	chair-kyo-neh
saddle	la sella	sel-la
saddlebag	la borsa porta-attrezzi	bor-sa por-ta-at-tret-see
spoke	il raggio	rad-jo
tyre	il pneumatico	pne-oo-ma-tee-ko
valve	la valvola	val-vo-la
wheel	la ruota	rwo-ta

HOTELS & GUEST HOUSES

BOOKING A ROOM

Rooms to let/vacancies	*Affittasi/camere da affittare	Af-fee-ta-see/ka-mair-eh da af-fee-tar-eh
No vacancies	*Tutto occupato	Toot-to ok-koo-pa-to
Have you a room for the night?	Ha una camera per stanotte?	A oon-a ka-mair-a pair sta-not-teh
I've reserved a room; my name is ...	Ho riservato una camera. Mi chiamo ...	O ree-zair-va-to oon-a ka-mair-a. Mee kya-mo ...
Do you know another hotel?	Può indicarmi un altro albergo?	Pwo een-dee-kar-mee oon al-tro al-bair-go
I want a single room with a shower	Vorrei una camera ad un letto con doccia	Vor-ray oon-a ka-mair-a ad oon let-to kon do-cha

We want a room with a double bed and a bathroom/a private toilet	Vorremmo una camera matrimoniale con bagno/un gabinetto privato	Vo-rem-mo oon-a ka-mair-a mat-ree-mon-ya-leh kon ban-yo/oon ga-bee-net-to pree-va-to
Have you a room with twin beds?	Ha una camera con due letti?	A oon-a ka-mair-a kon doo-eh let-tee
How long will you be staying	*Quanto tempo rimane (rimangono pl)?	Kwan-to tem-po ree-man-eh (ree-man-go-no)
Is it for one night only?	*Rimane (rimangono pl) solo una notte?	Ree-man-eh (ree-man-go-no) so-lo oon-a not-teh
I want a room	Vorrei una camera	Vor-ray oon-a ka-mair-a
for two or three days	per due o tre giorni	pair doo-eh o treh jor-nee
for a week	per una settimana	pair oon-a set-tee-ma-na
until Friday	fino a venerdì	fee-no a ven-air-dee
What floor is the room on?	A che piano è questa camera?	A keh pya-no eh qwes-ta ka-mair-a
Is there a lift/elevator?	C'è l'ascensore?	Cheh la-shen-sor-eh
Are there facilities for the disabled?	Può accomodare gli handicappati	Pwo ak-ko-mo-dar-eh lyee han-dee-kap-pa-tee
Have you a room on the first floor?	Ha una camera al primo piano?	A oon-a ka-mair-a al pree-mo pya-no
May I see the room?	Posso vedere la camera?	Pos-so ve-dair-eh la ka-mair-a

I like this room, I'll take it	Questa camera mi piace, la prendo	Kwes-ta ka-mair-a mee pya-cheh, la pren-do
I don't like this room	Questa camera non mi piace molto	Kwes-ta ka-mair-a non mee pya-cheh mol-to
Have you another one?	Ne ha un'altra?	Neh a oon-al-tra
I want a quiet room/a bigger room	Vorrei una camera molto tranquilla/una camera più grande	Vor-ray oon-a ka-mair-a mol-to tran-kweel-la/oon-a ka-mair-a pyoo gran-deh
There's too much noise	C'è troppo rumore	Cheh trop-po roo-mor-eh
I'd like a room with a balcony	Vorrei una camera con balcone	Vor-ray oon-a ka-mair-a kon bal-ko-neh
Have you a room looking on to the street/sea?	Ha una camera che dà sulla strada/sul lungomare?	A oon-a ka-mair-a keh da sool-la stra-da/sool loon-go-mar-eh
Is there	C'è	Cheh
a telephone?	il telefono?	eel te-le-fo-no
a radio?	la radio?	la ra-dyo
a television?	la televisione?	la te-le-vee-zyo-neh
We've only a double room	*Abbiamo solo una camera matrimoniale	Ab-bya-mo so-lo oon-a ka-mair-a mat-ree-mon-ya-leh
This is the only room vacant	*Questa è l'unica camera libera	Kwes-ta eh loo-nee-ka ka-mair-a lee-bair-a
We shall have another room tomorrow	*Avremo un altra camera libera domani	Av-re-mo oon al-tra ka-mair-a lee-bair-a do-ma-nee

The room is only available tonight	*Possiamo darle questa camera solo per stanotte	Pos-sya-mo dar-leh kwes-ta ka-mair-a so-lo pair sta-not-teh
How much is the room per night?	Quanto costa questa camera per notte?	Kwan-to kos-ta kwes-ta ka-mair-a pair not-teh
Have you nothing cheaper?	Non ha niente di meno costoso?	Non a nyen-teh dee me-no kos-to-zo
What do we pay for the children?	I ragazzi, quanto pagano	Ee ra-gat-see, kwan-to pa-ga-no
Could you put a cot/an extra bed in the room, please?	Può mettere una culla/un letto in più per piacere?	Pwo met-tair-eh oon-a kool-la/oon let-to een pyoo pair pya-chair-eh
Are service and tax included?	Il servizio e le tasse sono compresi nel prezzo?	Eel sair-veet-syo eh leh tas-seh so-no kom-pre-zee nel pret-so
How much is the room without meals?	Quanto è la camera senza i pasti?	Kwan-to eh la ka-mair-a send-za ee pas-tee
How much is full board/half board?	Quanto è la pensione completa/la mezza pensione?	Kwan-to eh la pen-syo-neh kom-ple-ta/la med-za pen-syo-neh
Is breakfast included in the price?	La prima colazione è compresa nel prezzo?	La pree-ma ko-lat-syo-neh eh kom-pre-za nel pret-so
Do you have a weekly rate?	Fa dei prezzi settimanali?	Fa day pret-see set-tee-ma-nal-ee
What is the weekly rate?	Qual'è il prezzo settimanale?	Kwal-eh eel pret-so set-tee-ma-na-leh
It's too expensive	E troppo caro	Eh trop-po ka-ro

Please fill in the registration form	*Vuol compilare la scheda di registrazione, per cortesia?	Vwol kom-pee-lar-eh la ske-da dee re-jees-trat-syo-neh, pair kor-te-zee-a
Please leave your passport	*Vuol lasciare il passaporto, per favore?	Vwol la-shar-eh eel pas-sa-por-to, pair fa-vor-eh

IN YOUR ROOM

chambermaid	la cameriera	ka-mair-yair-a
room service	servizio di camera	sair-veet-syo dee ka-mair-a
Could we have breakfast in our room?	Potremmo avere la prima colazione in camera?	Pot-rem-mo a-vair-eh la pree-ma ko-lat-syo-neh een ka-mair-a
I'd like some ice cubes	Vorrei dei cubetti di ghiaccio	Vor-ray day koo-bet-tee dee gya-cho
Please wake me at 8.30	Mi può svegliare alle otto e mezza, per favore	Mee pwo zvel-yar-eh al-leh ot-to eh med-za, pair fa-vor-eh
There's no ashtray in my room	Non ci sono portaceneri in camera mia	Non chee so-no por-ta-che-nair-ee een ka-mair-a mee-a
Can I have more hangers, please?	Posso avere qualche altra gruccia?	Pos-so a-vair-eh kwal-keh al-tra groo-cha
Is there a point for an electric razor?	C'è una presa per rasoio elettrico?	Cheh oon-a pre-za pair ra-zo-yo el-et-tree-ko
What's the voltage?	Che voltaggio ha?	Cheh vol-tad-jo a

Where is the bathroom/the lavatory?	Dov'è il bagno/il gabinetto	Dov-eh eel ban-yo/eel ga-bee-net-to
Is there a shower?	C'è la doccia?	Cheh la do-cha
There are no towels in my room	In camera mia non ci sono asciugamani	Een ka-mair-a mee-a non cee so-no a-shoo-ga-ma-nee
There's no soap	Non c'è sapone	Non cheh sa-po-neh
There's no (hot) water	Non c'è acqua (calda)	Non cheh ak-wa (kal-da)
There's no plug in my washbasin	Nel mio lavandino non c'è tappo	Nel mee-o la-van-dee-no non cheh tap-po
There's no toilet paper in the lavatory	Nel gabinetto non c'è carta igienica	Nel ga-bee-net-to non cheh kar-ta ee-jen-ee-ka
The lavatory won't flush	Lo sciacquone non funziona	Lo sha-kwo-neh non foont-syo-na
The bidet leaks	Il bidè perde	Eel bee-deh pair-deh
The light doesn't work	La luce non funziona	La loo-cheh non foont-syo-na
The lamp is broken	La lampada è rotta	La lam-pa-da eh rot-ta
The blind is stuck	La persiana è bloccata	La pair-sya-na eh blok-ka-ta
The curtains won't close	Non si può chiudere le tendine	Non see pwo kyoo-dair-eh le ten-dee-neh
May I have the key to the bathroom, please?	Posso avere la chiave del bagno, per favore?	Pos-so a-vair-eh la kya-veh del ban-yo, pair fa-vor-eh

May I have another blanket/another pillow?	Posso avere un'altra coperta/un altro cuscino?	Pos-so a-vair-eh oon-al-tra ko-pair-ta/oon al-tro koo-shee-no
These sheets are dirty	Queste lenzuola sono sporche	Kwes-teh lend-zwo-la so-no spor-keh
I can't open my window, please open it	Non posso aprire la finestra. Vuole aprirla lei, per favore?	Non pos-so ap-reer-eh la fee-nes-tra. Vwo-leh ap-reer-la lay, pair fa-vor-eh
It's too hot/cold	Fa troppo caldo/freddo	Fa trop-po kal-do/fred-do
Can the heating be turned up/turned down/turned off?	Può aprire/abbassare/chiudere il riscaldamento?	Pwo ap-reer-eh/ab-bas-sar-eh/kyoo-dair-eh eel ree-skal-da-men-to
Is the room air-conditioned?	Questa camera è ad aria condizionata?	Kwes-ta ka-mair-a eh ad ar-ya kon-deet-syo-na-ta
The air conditioning doesn't work	Il condizionamento aria non funziona	Eel kon-deet-syo-na-men-to ar-ya non foont-syo-na
Come in!	Entri/avanti!	En-tree/a-van-tee
Put it on the table, please	Lo metta sulla tavola, per favore	Lo met-ta sool-la ta-vo-la, pair fa-vor-eh
How long will the laundry take?	Quando sarà pronta la lavanderia?	Kwan-do sa-ra pron-ta la la-van-de-ree-a
Have you a needle and thread?	Ha mica ago e filo?	A mee-ka a-go eh fee-lo
Would you clean these shoes, please?	Mi può lucidare le scarpe, per favore?	Mee pwo loo-chee-dar-eh leh skar-peh, pair fa-vor-eh

Would you clean this dress, please?	Mi può pulire questo abito, per favore?	Mee pwo poo-leer-eh kwes-to a-bee-to, pair fa-vor-eh
Would you press this suit, please?	Mi può stirare questo abito, per favore?	Mee pwo stee-rar-eh kwes-to a-bee-to, pair fa-vor-eh
When will it be ready?	Quando sarà pronto?	Kwan-do sa-ra pron-to
It will be ready tomorrow	*Sarà pronto domani	Sa-ra pron-to do-ma-nee

OTHER SERVICES

porter	il facchino	fak-kee-no
hall porter	il portiere	port-yair-eh
page	il fattorino	fat-tor-ee-no
manager	il direttore	dee-ret-tor-eh
telephonist	la centralinista	chen-tra-lee-nees-ta
My key, please	La chiave, per favore	La kya-veh, pair fa-vor-eh
Can you keep this in your safe?	Può tenere questo nella cassaforte?	Pwo te-nair-eh kwes-to nel-la kas-sa-for-teh
Are there any letters for me?	C'è posta per me?	Cheh pos-ta pair meh
Are there any messages for me?	Ci sono messaggi per me?	Chee so-no mes-sad-jee pair meh
Please post this	Mi potrebbe imbucare questo?	Mee pot-reb-beh eem-boo-kar-eh kwes-to
Is there a telex?	C'è un telex?	Cheh oon telex

Can I dial direct to England/America?	Si può chiamare l'Inghilterra/ l'America direttamente?	See pwo kya-mar-eh leen-geel-ter-ra/la-me-ree-ka dee-ret-ta-men-teh
If anyone phones, tell them I'll be back at 4.30	Se qualcuno telefona, dica che sarò di ritorno alle quattro e mezza	Seh kwal-koo-no te-le-fo-na, dee-ka keh sa-ro dee ree-tor-no al-leh kwat-tro e med-za
No one telephoned	*Non ci sono state telefonate per lei	Non chee so-no sta-teh te-le-fo-na-teh pair lay
There's a lady/ gentleman to see you	*C'è una signora/un signore che desidera vederla	Cheh oon-a seen-yor-a/ oon seen-yor-eh keh de-zee-dair-a ve-dair-la
Please ask her/him to come up	Le/gli dica di salire, per favore	Leh/lyee dee-ka dee sa-leer-eh, pair fa-vor-eh
I'm coming down	Scendo subito	Shen-do soo-bee-to
Can I borrow a typewriter?	Potrei usare una macchina da scrivere?	Pot-ray oo-zar-eh oon-a mak-kee-na da skree-ver-eh
Have you	Ha	A
any writing paper?	della carta da lettere?	del-la kar-ta da let-tair-eh
any envelopes?	delle buste?	del-le boos-teh
any stamps?	dei francobolli?	day fran-ko-bol-lee
Please send the chambermaid/the waiter	Può mandare la cameriera/il cameriere, per favore	Pwo man-dar-eh la ka-mair-yair-a/eel ka-mair-yair-eh, pair fa-vor-eh

I need a guide/an interpreter	**Vorrei una guida/un interprete**	Vor-ray oon-a gwee-da/ oon een-tair-pre-teh
Does the hotel have a baby-sitting service?	**C'è un servizio baby-sitting nell'albergo**	Cheh oon sair-veet-syo baby-sitting nel-lal-bair-go
Where is the toilet/the cloakroom?	**Dov'è il gabinetto/il guardaroba?**	Dov-eh eel ga-bee-net-to/eel gwarda-ro-ba
Where is the dining room?	**Dov'è il ristorante?**	Dov-eh eel rees-tor-an-teh
What time is breakfast/lunch/ dinner?	**A che ora è la prima colazione/la colazione/la cena?**	A keh or-a eh la pree-ma ko-lat-syo-neh/la ko-lat-syo-neh/la che-na
Is there a garage?	**C'è un garage?**	Cheh oon ga-raj
Where can I park the car?	**Dove posso parcheggiare la macchina?**	Do-veh pos-so par-ked-jar-eh la mak-kee-na
Is the hotel open all night?	**Rimane aperto tutta la notte questo albergo?**	Ree-ma-neh a-pair-to toot-ta la not-teh kwes-to al-bair-go
What time does it close?	**A che ora chiude?**	A keh or-a kyoo-deh

DEPARTURE

I have to leave tomorrow	**Devo partire domani**	De-vo par-teer-eh do-ma-nee
Can you make up my bill?	**Può prepararmi il conto?**	Pwo pre-pa-rar-mee eel kon-to
Do you accept credit cards?	**Accetta le carte di credito?**	A-chet-ta leh kar-teh dee kre-dee-to

There is a mistake on the bill	C'è un errore nel conto	Cheh oon er-ror-eh nel kon-to
I shall be coming back on ...; can I book a room for that date?	Ritornerò il ...; può riservarmi una camera per questa data?	Ree-tor-nair-o eel ...; pwo ree-zair-var-mee oon-a ka-mair-a pair kwes-ta data
Could you have my luggage brought down?	Può far portare giù i bagagli?	Pwo far por-tar-eh joo ee ba-gal-yee
Please store the luggage, we will be back at ...	Tenga i bagagli in deposito, per favore. Torneremo alle ...	Ten-ga ee ba-gal-yee een de-po-zee-to, pair fa-vor-eh. Tor-ne-re-mo al-le ...
Please call a taxi for me	Per favore, vuol chiamare un taxi	Pair fa-vor-eh, vwol kya-mar-eh oon taxi
Thank you for a pleasant stay	Grazie di tutto. E stato un soggiorno molto piacevole	Gra-zyeh dee toot-to. Eh sta-to oon sod-jor-no mol-to pya-che-vo-leh

CAMPING

Is there a camp site nearby?	C'è un camping qui vicino?	Cheh oon camping kwee vee-chee-no
May we camp here?	Si può campeggiare qui?	See pwo kam-ped-jar-eh kwee
in your field?	nel suo campo?	nel soo-o kam-po
on the beach?	sulla spiaggia?	sul-la spyad-ja
Where should we put our tent/caravan?	Dove dovremmo mettere la nostra tenda/roulotte?	Do-veh dov-rem-mo met-tair-eh la nos-tra ten-da/roo-lot
Can I park the car next to the tent?	Posso parcheggiare la macchina accanto alla tenda?	Pos-so par-ked-jar-eh la mak-kee-na ak-kan-to al-la ten-da
Is there drinking water/electricity?	C'è l'acqua potabile/l'elettricità?	Cheh lak-wa po-ta-bee-leh/le-let-tree-chee-ta
Are there showers/toilets?	Ci sono le docce/i gabinetti?	Chee so-no le do-cheh/ee ga-bee-net-tee

What does it cost	Quanto costa	Kwan-to kos-ta
per night?	la notte?	la not-teh
per week?	la settimana?	la set-tee-ma-na
per person?	per persona?	pair pair-so-na
Is there	C'è	Cheh
a shop?	un mercato?	oon mair-ka-to
a swimming pool?	una piscina?	oon-a pee-shee-na
a playground?	un campo di ricreazione?	oon kam-po dee ree-kre-at-syo-neh
a restaurant?	un ristorante?	oon rees-tor-an-teh
a launderette?	una lavanderia automatica?	oon-a la-van-dair-ee-a ow-to-ma-tee-ka
Can I buy ice?	Si può comprare del ghiaccio?	See pwo kom-prar-eh del gya-cho
Where can I buy paraffin/butane gas?	Dove posso comprare della paraffina/del gas butano?	Do-veh pos-so kom-prar-eh del-la pa-raf-fee-na/del gaz boo-ta-no
Where do I put rubbish?	Dove si buttano le immondizie?	Do-veh see boot-ta-no le eem-mon-deet-syeh
Where can I wash up?	Dove si lava i piatti?	Do-veh see la-va ee pyat-tee
Where can I wash clothes?	Dove si fa il bucato?	Do-veh see fa eel boo-ka-to
Is there somewhere to dry clothes/equipment?	Dove si può asciugare i panni/le cose?	Do-veh see pwo a-shoo-gar-eh ee pan-nee/leh ko-zeh
My camping gas has run out	Il mio camping gas è esaurito	Eel mee-o camping gaz eh ez-ow-ree-to

The toilet is blocked	Il gabinetto è otturato	Eel ga-bee-net-to eh ot-too-ra-to
The shower doesn't work/is flooded	La doccia non funziona/è inondata	La do-cha non foont-syo-na/eh een-on-da-ta
What is the voltage?	Che voltaggio ha?	Keh vol-tad-jo a
Please prepare the bill, we are leaving today	Prepari il conto, per favore. Partiamo oggi	Pre-pa-ree eel kon-to, pair fa-vor-eh. Par-tya-mo od-jee
How long do you want to stay?	*Quanto tempo rimane?	Kwan-to tem-po ree-ma-neh
What is your car registration number?	*Qual'è il suo numero di targa?	Kwal-eh eel swo noo-mair-o dee tar-ga
I'm afraid the camp site is full	*Purtroppo il camping e pieno	Poor-trop-po eel camping eh pye-no
No camping	*Vietato campeggiare	Vye-ta-to kam-ped-jar-eh

YOUTH HOSTELLING

Is there a youth hostel here?	C'è un ostello della gioventù qui?	Cheh oon os-tel-lo del-la jo-ven-**too** kwee
Have you a room/bed for the night?	Si può avere una camera/un letto stanotte?	See pwo a-vair-eh oon-a ka-mair-a/oon let-to sta-not-teh
How many days can we stay?	Si può rimanere per quanti giorni?	See pwo ree-ma-nair-eh pair kwan-tee jor-nee
Here is my membership card	Ecco la mia tessera di socio	Ek-ko la mee-a tes-sair-a dee so-cho
Do you serve meals?	Si servono pasti?	See sair-vo-no pas-tee
Can I use the kitchen?	Posso servirmi della cucina?	Pos-so sair-veer-mee del-la koo-chee-na
Is there somewhere cheap to eat nearby?	C'è una trattoria non costosa qui vicino?	Cheh oon-a trat-tor-ee-a non kos-to-za kwee vee-chee-no
I want to rent a sheet for my sleeping bag	Vorrei noleggiare una lenzuola per il mio sacco a pelo	Vor-ray no-led-jar-eh oon-a lend-zwo-la pair eel mee-o sak-ko a pe-lo

RENTING OR OWNING A PLACE

We have rented an apartment/villa	Abbiamo affittato un appartamento/una villa	Ab-bya-mo af-feet-ta-to oon ap-par-ta-men-to/oon-a veel-la
Here is our reservation	Ecco la nostra riservazione	Ek-ko la nos-tra ree-zair-vat-syo-neh
Please show us round	Ci faccia vedere la casa, per favore	Chee fa-cha ve-dair-eh la ka-za, pair fa-vor-eh
Does the cost include electricity/the gas cylinder?	E compresa l'elettricità/la bombola?	Eh kom-pre-za le-let-tree-cee-ta/la bom-bo-la
Is there a spare gas cylinder	C'è un'altra bombola di gas?	Cheh oon-al-tra bom-bo-la dèe gaz
Do gas cylinders get delivered?	Si consegna le bombole di gas?	See kon-sen-ya leh bom-bo-leh dee gaz
Please show me how this works	Vuol mostrarmi come funziona questo?	Vwol mos-trar-mee ko-meh foont-syo-na kwes-to

Is the cost of the maid included?	È compreso il servizio della cameriera?	Eh kom-pre-zo eel sair-veet-syo del-la ka-mair-yair-a
Which days does the maid come?	Quali giorni viene la cameriera?	Kwal-ee jor-nee vye-neh la ka-mair-yair-a
For how long?	Quanto tempo rimane?	Kwan-to tem-po ree-ma-neh
Where is	Dov'è	Dov-eh
the electricity mains switch?	l'interruttore della rete?	leen-tair-root-tor-eh del-la re-teh
the water mains stopcock?	il rubinetto di arresto?	eel roo-bee-net-to dee ar-res-to
the light switch?	l'interruttore?	leen-tair-root-tor-eh
the power point?	la presa?	la pre-za
the fuse box?	la scatola delle valvole?	la ska-to-la del-leh val-vo-leh
How does the heating/hot water work?	Come funziona il riscaldamento/l'acqua calda?	Ko-meh foont-syo-na eel res-kal-da-men-to/lak-wa kal-da
Is there a fly-screen?	C'è un paramosche?	Cheh oon pa-ra-mos-keh
When is rubbish collected?	Quando c'è la levata delle immondizie?	Kwan-do cheh la le-va-ta del-leh eem-mon-deet-syeh
Where can we buy logs for the fire?	Dove si può comprare ceppi per il fuoco?	Do-veh see pwo komp-rar-eh chep-pee pair eel fwo-ko
Is there a barbecue?	C'è una griglia?	Cheh oon-a greel-ya
Please give me another set of keys	Mi dia un'altro mazzo di chiavi, per favore	Mee dee-a oon-al-tro mat-so dee kya-vee, pair fa-vor-eh

We have replaced the broken ...	Abbiamo sostituito il ... che abbiamo rotto	Ab-bya-mo sos-tee-twee-to eel ... che ab-bya-mo rot-to
Here is the bill	Ecco il conto	Ek-ko il kon-to
Please return my deposit against breakages	Mi restituisca la cauzione contro i danni, per favore	Mee res-tee-twees-ka la cowt-syo-neh kon-tro ee dan-nee, pair fa-vor-eh

PROBLEMS

The drain ...	Il tubo di scarico ...	Eel too-bo dee ska-ree-ko ...
The pipe ...	Il tubo ...	Eel too-bo ...
The sink ... is blocked	L'acquaio ... è otturato	Lak-wa-yo ... eh ot-too-ra-to
The toilet doesn't flush	Il gabinetto non funziona	Eel ga-bee-net-to non foont-syo-na
There is no water	Non c'è acqua	Non cheh ak-wa
We can't turn the water off/shower on	Non riusciamo a chiudere l'acqua/ ad aprire la doccia	Non ryoo-sha-mo a kyoo-dair-eh lak-wa/ad ap-reer-eh la do-cha
There is a leak/a broken window	C'è una fuga/una finestra rotta	Cheh oon-a foo-ga/oon-a fee-nes-tra rot-ta
The shutters won't close	Non si chiudono le persiane	Non see kyoo-do-no le pair-sya-neh
The window won't open	Non si apre la finestra	Non see ap-re la fee-nes-tra

The electricity has gone off	**Manca l'elettricità**	Man-ka le-let-tree-chee-ta
The heating ...	**Il riscaldamento ...**	Eel rees-kal-da-men-to ...
The cooker ...	**Il fornello ...**	Eel for-nel-lo ...
The refrigerator ...	**Il frigorifero ...**	Eel free-go-ree-fair-o ...
The water heater ... doesn't work	**Il riscaldamento acqua ... non funziona**	Eel rees-kal-da-men-to ak-wa ... non foont-syo-na
The lock is stuck	**La serratura è bloccata**	La ser-ra-too-ra eh blok-ka-ta
This is broken	**Questo è guasto**	Kwes-to-eh gwas-to
This needs repairing	**Bisogna riparare questo**	Bee-zon-ya ree-pa-rar-eh kwes-to
The apartment/villa has been burgled	**Il domicilio è stato violato**	Eel do-mee-cheel-yo eh sta-to vee-o-la-to

PARTS OF THE HOUSE

balcony	**il balcone**	bal-ko-neh
bathroom	**il bagno**	ban-yo
bedroom	**la camera da letto**	ka-mair-a da let-to
ceiling	**il soffitto**	sof-feet-to
chimney	**il camino**	ka-mee-no
corridor	**il corridoio**	kor-ree-do-yo
door	**la porta**	por-ta
fence	**il recinto**	re-cheen-to
fireplace	**il caminetto**	ka-mee-net-to

floor	**il pavimento**	pa-vee-men-to
garage	**il garage**	ga-raj
gate	**il cancello**	kan-chel-lo
hall	**l'entrata**	en-tra-ta
kitchen	**la cucina**	koo-chee-na
living room	**il salotto**	sa-lot-to
patio	**il cortile**	kor-tee-leh
roof	**il tetto**	tet-to
shutters	**le imposte**	eem-pos-teh
stairs	**la scala**	ska-la
terrace	**la terrazza**	ter-rat-sa
wall	**la mura**	moo-ra
window	**la finestra**	fee-nes-tra

FURNITURE AND FITTINGS

armchair	**la poltrona**	pol-tro-na
barbecue	**la griglia**	greel-ya
bath	**il bagno**	ban-yo
bed	**il letto**	let-to
blanket	**la coperta**	ko-pair-ta
bolt (*for door*)	**il chiavistello**	kya-vee-stel-lo
broom	**la scopa**	sko-pa
brush	**la spazzola**	spat-so-la
bucket	**il secchio**	sek-kyo

cassette player	**il registratore a cassetta**	re-jees-tra-tor-eh a kas-set-ta
chair	**la sedia**	se-dya
charcoal	**il carbone di legno**	kar-bo-neh dee len-yo
clock	**l'orologio**	o-ro-lo-jo
cooker	**il fornello**	for-nel-lo
cupboard	**l'armadio**	ar-ma-dyo
cushions	**i cuscini**	koo-shee-nee
curtains	**le tende**	ten-deh
deckchair	**la sedia a sdraio**	se-dya a zdra-yo
door	**la porta**	por-ta
doorbell	**il campanello**	kam-pa-nel-lo
doorknob	**la maniglia della porta**	ma-neel-ya del-la por-ta
dustbin	**la pattumiera**	pat-toom-yair-a
dustpan	**la paletta per la spazzatura**	pa-let-ta pair la spat-sa-too-ra
hinge	**il cardine**	kar-dee-neh
immersion heater	**il riscaldatore a immersione**	ree-skal-da-tor-eh a eem-mair-syo-neh
iron	**il ferro**	fer-ro
lamp	**la lampada**	lam-pa-da
lampshade	**il paralume**	pa-ra-loo-meh
light bulb	**la lampadina**	lam-pa-dee-na
lock	**la serratura**	ser-ra-too-ra
mattress	**il materasso**	ma-tair-as-so
mirror	**lo specchio**	spek-kyo

mop	la scoba di filacci	sko-ba dee fee-la-chee
padlock	il lucchetto	look-ket-to
pillow	il guanciale	gwan-cha-leh
pipe	il tubo	too-bo
plug (*electric*)	la presa	pre-za
(*bath*)	il tappo	tap-po
radio	la radio	ra-dyo
refrigerator	il frigorifero	free-go-ree-fair-o
sheet	la lenzuola	lend-zwo-la
shelf	lo scaffale	skaf-fa-leh
shower	la doccia	do-cha
sink	l'acquaio	ak-wa-yo
sofa	il sofà	so-fa
stool	lo sgabello	zga-bel-lo
sun lounger	il lettino	let-tee-no
table	la tavola	ta-vo-la
tap	il rubinetto	roo-bee-net-to
toilet	il gabinetto	ga-bee-net-to
towel	l'asciugamano	a-shoo-ga-ma-no
vacuum cleaner	l'aspirapolvere *m*	as-peer-a-pol-vair-eh
washbasin	il lavandino	la-van-dee-no
washing machine	la lavatrice	la-va-tree-cheh
window catch	la fermafinestre	fair-ma-fee-nes-treh
window sill	il davanzale	da-vand-za-leh

KITCHEN EQUIPMENT

bleach	il candeggiante	kan-de-jan-teh
bottle opener	l'apribottiglie *m*	ap-ree-bot-teel-yeh
bowl	la ciotola	cho-to-la
can opener	l'apriscatole *m*	a-pree-ska-to-leh
candles	le candele	kan-de-leh
clothes line	la corda del bucato	kor-da del boo-ka-to
clothes peg	la molletta da bucato	mol-let-ta da boo-ka-to
chopping board	il tagliere	tal-yair-eh
coffee pot	la macchina del caffè	mak-kee-na del kaf-feh
colander	il collino	kol-lee-no
coolbox	la ghiacciaia	gya-cha-ya
corkscrew	il cavatappi	ka-va-tap-pee
cup	la tazza	tat-sa
detergent	il detersivo	de-tair-see-vo
fork	la forchetta	for-ket-ta
frying pan	la padella	pa-del-la
glass	il bicchiere	beek-kyair-eh
ice pack	la borsa per ghiaccio	bor-sa pair gya-cho
ice tray	il vassoio da ghiaccio	vas-so-yo da gya-cho
kettle	il bollitore	bol-lee-tor-eh
knife	il coltello	kol-tel-lo
matches	i fiammiferi	fyam-mee-fair-ee
pan	la pentola	pen-to-la

plate	il piatto	pyat-to
scissors	le forbici	for-bee-chee
sieve	il setaccio	se-ta-cho
spoon	il cucchiaio	kook-kya-yo
teatowel	il canovaccio	ka-no-va-cho
torch	la torcia elettrica	tor-cha e-let-tree-ka
washing powder	il detersivo in polvere	de-tair-see-vo een pol-vair-eh
washing-up liquid	il detersivo	de-tair-see-vo

ODD JOBS[1]

bracket	la mensola	men-so-la
hammer	il martello	mar-tel-lo
iron	il ferro	fer-ro
lacquer	la vernice trasparente	ver-nee-cheh tras-pa-ren-teh
metal	il metallo	me-tal-lo
nails	i chiodi	kyo-dee
paint	la vernice	ver-nee-cheh
paint brush	il penello	pe-nel-lo
plastic	la plastica	plas-tee-ka
pliers	le pinze	peent-seh

1. See also SHOPPING & SERVICES (p. 114).

saw	**la sega**	se-ga
screwdriver	**il cacciavite**	ka-cha-vee-teh
screws	**le vite**	vee-teh
spanner	**la chiave fissa**	kya-veh fees-sa
steel	**l'acciaio** *m*	a-cha-yo
tile	**la mattonella**	mat-to-nel-la
wire	**il filo metallico**	fee-lo me-tal-lee-ko
wood	**il legno**	len-yo

MEETING PEOPLE

How are you?	**Come sta (state *pl*)?**	Ko-meh sta (sta-teh)
Fine, thank you; and you?	**Bene, grazie; e lei?**	Be-neh, gra-zyeh; eh lay
What is your name?	**Come si chiama?**	Ko-meh see kya-ma
May I introduce myself?	**Posso presentarmi?**	Pos-so pre-zen-tar-mee
May I introduce ...?	**Posso presentarle ...?**	Pos-so pre-zen-tar-leh ...
My name is ...	**Mi chiamo ...**	Mee kya-mo ...
This is ...	**Questo/questa è ...**	Kwes-to/kwes-ta eh ...
Have you met ...?	**Conosce ...?**	Ko-no-sheh ...
Glad to meet you	**Lieto di conoscerla**	Lye-to dee ko-no-shair-la
Am I disturbing you?	**La disturbo?**	La dees-toor-bo
Go away	**Se ne vada**	Seh neh va-da
Leave me alone	**Mi lasci in pace**	Mee la-shee een pa-cheh
Sorry to have troubled you	**Mi scusi per il disturbo**	Mee skoo-zee pair eel dees-toor-bo

MAKING FRIENDS

Are you on holiday?	E qui in vacanza?	Eh kwee een va-kant-sa
Do you travel a lot?	Viaggia molto?	Vyad-ja mol-to
We've been here a week	Siamo qui da una settimana	Sya-mo kwee da oon-a set-tee-ma-na
Is this your first time here?	E la prima volta che lei è qui?	Eh la pree-ma vol-ta keh lay eh kwee
Do you like it here?	Le piace da queste parti?	Leh pya-cheh da kwes-teh par-tee
Are you on your own?	E solo/sola?	Eh so-lo/so-la
I am with	Sono qui con	So-no kwee kon
my husband	mio marito	mee-o ma-ree-to
my wife	mia moglie	mee-a mol-yeh
my parents	i miei genitori	ee myay je-nee-tor-ee
my family	la famiglia	la fa-meel-ya
a friend	un amico/a	oon a-mee-ko/ka
I am travelling alone	Viaggio da solo	Vyad-jo da so-lo
Which part of Italy do you come from?	Da che parte d'Italia viene?	Da keh par-teh dee-tal-ya vye-neh
I come from ...	Vengo da .../Sono di ...	Ven-go da .../So-no dee ...
What do you do?	Quale è la sua occupazione?	Kwal-eh eh la soo-a ok-koo-pat-syo-neh
What are you studying?	Cosa studia?	Ko-za stoo-dya
I'm on holiday/a business trip	Sono in vacanza/in giro d'affari	So-no een va-kant-sa/een jee-ro daf-far-ee

Are you married?	E sposato?	Eh spo-za-to
Do you have children?	Ha dei bambini?	A day bam-bee-nee
Have you been to England/America?	E stato in Inghilterra/ America?	Eh sta-to een een-geel-ter-ra/a-me-ree-ka
I hope to see you again	Spero di rivederla	Spe-ro dee ree-ve-dair-la
Do you smoke?	Lei fuma?	Lay foo-ma
No, I don't, thanks	No, non fumo, grazie	No, non foo-mo, gra-zyeh
Help yourself	Si serva	See sair-va
Do you mind if I smoke?	Ti da fastidio se fumo?	Tee da fas-teed-yo seh foo-mo
Can I get you a drink?	Posso offrirle qualcosa da bere?	Pos-so of-freer-leh kwal-ko-za da be-reh
I'd like a ... please	Prenderei volentieri un ...	Pren-dair-ay vo-len-tyair-eh oon ...

INVITATIONS

Would you like to have lunch tomorrow?	Ci incontriamo per pranzo domani?	Chee een-kon-trya-mo pair prand-zo do-ma-nee
I'd love to come	Sarei lieto di venire	Sa-ray lye-to dee ve-neer-eh
I'm sorry, I can't come	Mi dispiace, non posso venire	Mee dees-pya-cheh, non pos-so ve-neer-eh
Can you come to dinner?	Può venire a cena?	Pwo ve-neer-eh a che-na

We are giving a party, would you like to come?	Noi diamo un ricevimento, vuol venire?	Noy dya-mo oon ree-che-vee-men-to, vwol ve-neer-eh
May I bring a friend?	Posso portare anche un amico *m*/un' amica *f*?	Pos-so por-tar-eh an-keh oon a-mee-ko/oon-a-mee-ka
Thank you for the invitation	Grazie dell'invito	Gra-zyeh del-leen-vee-to
Are you doing anything tonight/tomorrow afternoon	Ha già dei programmi per stasera/domani pomeriggio?	A ja day pro-gram-mee pair sta-se-ra/do-ma-nee po-mair-eed-jo
Could we have coffee/a drink together?	Potremmo prendere un caffè/bere qualcosa insieme?	Pot-rem-mo pren-dair-eh oon kaf-feh/be-reh kwal-ko-za een-sye-meh
Shall we go to the cinema/theatre/beach?	Vogliamo andare al cinema/al teatro/al mare?	Vol-ya-mo an-dar-eh al chee-ne-ma/al te-at-ro/al mar-eh
Would you like to go dancing?	Vuole andare a ballare?	Vwol-eh an-dar-eh a bal-lar-eh
Would you like to go for a drive?	Vuole fare un giro in macchina?	Vwol-eh far-eh oon jee-ro een mak-kee-na
Do you know a good disco/restaurant?	Conosce una buona discoteca/un buon ristorante?	Ko-no-sheh oon-a bwo-na dees-ko-te-ka/oon bwon rees-tor-an-teh
Where shall we meet?	Dove ci troviamo?	Do-veh cee tro-vya-mo
What time shall I/we come?	A che ora devo/dobbiamo venire?	A keh or-a de-vo/dob-bya-mo ve-neer-eh

Could you meet me at ...?	Possiamo trovarci a ...?	Pos-sya-mo tro-var-chee a ...
May I see you home?	Posso accompagnarla a casa?	Pos-so ak-kom-pan-yar-la a ka-za
Can we give you a lift home/to your hotel?	Possiamo darle un passaggio fino a casa/all'albergo?	Pos-sya-mo dar-leh oon pas-sad-jo fee-no a ka-za/al-lal-bair-go
Can we meet again?	Possiamo vederci di nuovo?	Pos-sya-mo ve-dair-chee dee nwo-vo
Where do you live?	Dove abita?	Do-veh a-bee-ta
Would you give me your telephone number?	Vuol darmi il suo numero di telefono?	Vwol dar-mee eel soo-o noo-mair-o dee te-le-fo-no
Thank you for a pleasant evening	Grazie per la bellissima serata	Gra-zyeh pair la bel-lees-see-ma se-ra-ta
I hope to see you again soon	Spero di rivederla presto	Sper-o dee ree-ve-dair-la pres-to
See you soon/later/ tomorrow	A presto/a più tardi/a domani	A pres-to/a pyoo tar-dee/a do-ma-nee

GOING TO A RESTAURANT

Can you suggest	**Mi può indicare**	Mee pwo een-dee-kar-eh
a good restaurant?	**un buon ristorante?**	oon bwon rees-tor-an-teh
a cheap restaurant?	**un ristorante a buon mercato?**	oon rees-tor-an-teh a bwon mair-ka-to
a vegetarian restaurant?	**un ristorante vegetariano?**	oon rees-tor-an-teh ve-je-tar-yan-o
I'd like to book a table for four at 1 p.m.	**Vorrei riservare un tavolo per quattro persone per l'una**	Vor-ray ree-zair-var-eh oon ta-vo-lo pair kwat-tro pair-so-neh pair loo-na
I've reserved a table; my name is …	**Ho riservato un tavolo, sono …**	O ree-zair-va-to oon ta-vo-lo, so-no …
We did not make a reservation	**Non abbiamo riservato un tavolo**	Non ab-bya-mo ree-zair-va-to oon ta-vo-lo
Is there a table free on the terrace/by the window/in a corner?	**Ha un tavolo sulla veranda/vicino alla finestra/in un angolo?**	A oon ta-vo-lo sool-la ve-ran-da/vee-chee-no al-la fee-nes-tra/een oon an-go-lo

Have you a table for three?	**Ha un tavolo per tre?**	A oon ta-vo-lo pair treh
This way, please	***Da questa parte, per favore**	Da kwes-ta par-teh, pair fa-vor-eh
Is there a non-smoking area?	**C'è una zona per non fumatori?**	Cheh oon-a dzo-na pair non foo-ma-tor-ee
You would have to wait about ... minutes	***Dovrebbe aspettare circa ... minuti**	Dov-reb-beh as-pet-tar-eh cheer-ka ... mee-noo-tee
We shall have a table free in half an hour	***Avremo un tavolo libero tra mezz'ora**	Av-re-mo oon ta-vo-lo lee-bair-o tra med-zor-a
We don't serve lunch until 12.30	***Cominciamo a servire il pranzo alle dodici e mezzo**	Ko-meen-chya-mo a sair-veer-eh eel prand-zo al-leh do-dee-chee eh med-zo
We don't serve dinner until 8 p.m.	***Cominciamo a servire la cena alle otto**	Ko-meen-chya-mo a sair-veer-eh la che-na al-leh ot-to
We stop serving at 11 o'clock	***Smettiamo di servire alle undici**	Smet-tya-mo dee sair-veer-eh al-leh oon-dee-chee
Sorry, the kitchen is closed	**Mi dispiace, è chiusa la cucina**	Mee dees-pya-cheh, eh kyoo-za la koo-chee-na
Where is the cloakroom?	**Dov'è la toilette?**	Dov-eh la twa-let
It is downstairs/ upstairs	***E al piano di sotto/ al piano di sopra**	Eh al pya-no dee so-to/al pya-no dee sop-ra

ORDERING

Service and VAT (not) included	*Servizio e IVA (non) sono compresi	Sair-veet-syo eh ee-va (non) so-no kom-pre-zee
Cover charge	*Coperto	Ko-pair-to
Waiter/waitress	Cameriere/cameriera	Ka-mair-yair-eh/ka-mair-yair-a
May I see the menu/ the wine list, please?	Posso vedere il menù/la lista dei vini, per favore?	Pos-so ve-dair-eh eel me-noo/la lees-ta day vee-nee
Is there a set menu for lunch?	Ha un pranzo a prezzo fisso?	A oon prand-zo a pret-so fees-so
We are in a hurry	Abbiamo fretta	Ab-bya-mo fret-ta
Do you serve snacks?	Si può fare uno spuntino?	See pwo far-eh oon-o spoon-tee-no
I want something light	Vorrei qualcosa di leggero	Vor-ray kwal-ko-za dee led-jair-o
Could we have a small helping?	Potremmo avere una mezza porzione?	Pot-rem-mo a-vair-eh oon-a med-za port-syo-neh
What is the dish of the day?	Cos'è il piatto del giorno?	Koz-eh eel pyat-to del jor-no
What do you recommend?	Cosa raccomanda lei?	Ko-za rak-ko-man-da lay
Can you tell me what this is?	Mi può dire che cos'è questo piatto?	Mee pwo deer-eh keh koz-eh kwes-to pyat-to

Do you have any local dishes/vegetarian dishes?	Ha delle specialità regionali/dei piatti vegetariani?	A del-leh spe-cha-lee-ta re-jo-na-lee/day pyat-tee ve-je-tar-ya-nee
What are the specialities of the restaurant/of the region?	Quali sono le specialità di questo ristorante/questa regione?	Kwal-ee so-no leh spe-cha-lee-ta dee kwes-to rees-tor-an-teh/kwes-ta re-jo-neh
Would you like to try ...?	*Vuol provare ...?	Vwol pro-var-eh ...
There's no more ...	*Non abbiamo più ...	Non ab-bya-mo pyoo ...
I'd like ...	Vorrei ...	Vor-ray ...
May I have peas instead of beans?	Posso avere piselli invece di fagioli?	Pos-so a-vair-eh pee-zel-lee een-ve-cheh dee fa-jo-lee
I don't want any oil/sauce with it	Lo voglio senza olio/senza salsa	Lo vol-yo send-za ol-yo/send-za sal-sa
Some more bread, please	Ancora del pane, per favore	An-kor-a del pa-neh, pair fa-vor-eh
A little more, please	Un po' di più, per favore	Oon po dee pyoo, pair fa-vor-eh
Is it hot or cold?	E un piatto caldo o freddo?	Eh oon pyat-to kal-do o fred-do

COMPLAINTS

| Where are our drinks? | Non ci ha ancora portato da bere | Non chee a an-kor-a por-ta-to da ber-eh |
| Why does it take so long? | Perchè bisogna aspettare tanto? | Per-keh bee-zon-ya as-pet-tar-eh tan-to |

This isn't what I ordered, I want ...	Non ho ordinato questo, io voglio ...	Non o or-dee-na-to kwes-to, ee-o vol-yo ...
That's enough, thank you	Basta così, grazie	Bas-ta ko-zee, gra-zyeh
This is	Questo è	Kwes-to eh
bad	cattivo	kat-tee-vo
uncooked	poco cotto	po-ko kot-to
stale	andato a male	an-da-to a ma-leh
cold	freddo	fred-do
too salty	troppo salato	trop-po sa-la-to
overcooked	stracotto	stra-kot-to
This isn't fresh	Questo non è fresco	Kwes-to non eh fres-ko
This plate/knife/ spoon/glass is not clean	Questo piatto/ coltello/ cucchiaio/bicchiere è sporco	Kwes-to pyat-to/kol-tel-lo/koo-kya-yo/bee-kyair-eh eh spor-ko
I'd like to see the headwaiter	Mi fa vedere il capocameriere	Mee fa ve-dair-eh eel ka-po-ka-mair-yair-eh

PAYING

The bill, please	Il conto, prego	Eel kon-to, pre-go
Does it include service?	Il servizio è compreso?	Eel sair-veet-syo eh kom-pre-zo
Please check the bill – I don't think it's correct	Vuol controllare il conto. Non mi sembra esatto	Vwol kon-trol-lar-eh eel kon-to. Non mee sem-bra e-zat-to

Can I pay with travellers' cheques/a credit card?	Posso pagare con i travellers' cheques/una carta di credito?	Pos-so pa-gar-eh kon ee travellers' cheques/oon-a kar-ta dee kre-dee-to
I didn't have soup	Non ho preso la minestra	Non o pre-zo la mee-nes-tra
I had chicken, not steak	Ho preso pollo, non bistecca	O pre-zo pol-lo, non bees-tek-ka
May we have separate bills?	Ci faccia il conto separato	Chee fa-cha eel kon-to se-pa-ra-to
Keep the change	Tenga il resto	Ten-ga eel res-to
It was very good	Era molto buono	Er-a mol-to bwo-no
We enjoyed it, thank you	Ci ha piaciuto, grazie	Chee a pya-choo-to, gra-zyeh

BREAKFAST AND TEA

Breakfast	La prima colazione	La pree-ma ko-lat-syo-neh
What time is breakfast served?	A che ora servono la prima colazione?	A keh or-a sair-vo-no la pree-ma ko-lat-syo-neh
A large white coffee, please	Un cappuccino, per favore	Oon kap-poo-chee-no, pair fa-vor-eh
A black/espresso coffee	Un caffè nero/espresso	Oon kaf-feh ne-ro/es-pres-so
I would like decaffinated coffee/a herb tea	Vorrei un caffè Hag/una tisana	Vor-ray oon kaf-feh Hag/oon-a tee-za-na

A cup of tea, please	Una tazza di tè, per favore	Oon-a tat-sa dee teh, pair fa-vor-eh
I'd like tea with milk/lemon	Vorrei tè con latte/al limone	Vor-ray teh kon lat-teh/al lee-mo-neh
A cup of chocolate	Una tazza di cioccolata	Oon-a tat-sa dee cho-ko-la-ta
Hot/cold milk	Latte caldo/freddo	Lat-teh kal-do/fred-do
May we have some sugar, please?	Lo zucchero, per favore	Lo tsoo-ke-ro, pair fa-vor-eh
Do you have artificial sweeteners?	Ha dei dolcificanti?	A day dol-chee-fee-kan-tee
A roll and butter	Un panino con burro	Oon pa-nee-no kon boor-ro
Bread	Il pane	Pa-neh
Toast	Il pane tostato	Pa-neh tos-ta-to
We'd like more butter, please	Vorremmo ancora del burro, per favore	Vor-rem-mo an-kor-a del boor-ro, pair fa-vor-eh
Have you some jam/marmalade?	Ha della marmellata/marmellata d'aranci?	A del-la mar-mel-la-ta/mar-mel-la-ta dar-an-chee
A hard-boiled/soft-boiled egg	Un uovo sodo/à la coque	Oon wo-vo so-do/a la kok
I'd like fried eggs/scrambled eggs	Vorrei delle uova fritte/strapazzate	Vor-ray del-leh wo-va freet-teh/stra-pat-sa-teh
Bacon and eggs, please	Uova e pancetta, per favore	Wo-va eh pan-chet-ta, pair fa-vor-eh

Ham	Il prosciutto cotto	Eel pro-shoot-to kot-to
What fruit juices do you have?	Che succhi di frutta ha?	Keh sook-kee dee froot-ta a
Orange/grapefruit/ tomato juice	Un succo d'arancio/ di pompelmo/di pomodoro	Oon sook-ko dar-an-cho/dee pom-pel-mo/ dee po-mo-do-ro
Yogurt	Yogurt	Yo-goort
Cereal	I fiocchi d'avena	Fyok-kee da-ve-na
Fresh fruit	La frutta fresca	Froot-ta fres-ka
Help yourself at the buffet	Servitevi al buffet	Sair-vee-te-vee al buffet

SNACKS AND PICNICS

Can I have a ... sandwich, please?	Mi dia un sandwich di ... per favore	Mee dee-a oon sandwich dee ... pair fa-vor-eh
What are those?	Cos'è questo?	Koz-eh kwes-to
What are they made of?	Di cosa sono fatti?	Dee ko-za so-no fat-tee
What is in them?	Cosa c'è dentro?	Ko-za cheh den-tro
I'll have one of these, please	Me ne dia uno, per favore	Meh neh dee-a oon-o, pair fa-vor-eh
It's to take away	E da portar via	Eh da por-tar vee-a
biscuits	i biscotti	bees-kot-tee
bread	il pane	pa-neh
butter	il burro	boor-ro
cheese	il formaggio	for-mad-jo

chips	le patatine fritte	pa-ta-tee-neh freet-teh
chocolate bar	la tavoletta di cioccolata	ta-vo-let-ta dee cho-ko-la-ta
egg/eggs	l'uovo/uova *m*	wo-vo/wo-va
ham (*cooked*)	il prosciutto cotto	pro-shoot-to kot-to
ice-cream	il gelato	je-la-to
pancakes	le frittelle	freet-tel-leh
parma ham	il prosciutto crudo	pro-shoot-to kroo-do
pastries	le paste	pas-teh
pickles	i sottaceti	sot-ta-che-tee
pizza with tomato, anchovies, olives, capers and mozzarella	pizza alla napoletana	peet-sa al-la na-po-let-an-a
pizza with salami or ham, anchovies, tomato, olives and mozzarella	pizza alla siciliana	peet-sa al-la see-cheel-yan-a
roll	il panino	pa-nee-no
salad	l'insalata *f*	een-sa-la-ta
sausage	la salsiccia	sal-see-cha
snack	lo spuntino	spoon-tee-no
snack bar	la tavola calda	ta-vo-la kal-da
soup	la minestra	mee-nes-tra
tomato	il pomodoro	po-mo-do-ro
waffles	le cialde	chal-deh

DRINKS[1]

What will you have to drink?	*Cosa desidera bere?	Ko-za de-zee-dair-a be-reh
A bottle of the local wine, please	Una bottiglia di vino locale, per favore	Oon-a bot-teel-ya dee vee-no lo-ka-leh, pair fa-vor-eh
Do you serve wine by the glass?	Vende vino a bicchieri?	Ven-deh vee-no a beek-kyair-ee
Carafe/glass	Una carafa/un bicchiere	Oon-a ka-ra-fa/oon beek-kyair-eh
Bottle/half bottle	Una bottiglia/una mezza bottiglia	Oon-a bot-teel-ya/oon-a med-za bot-teel-ya
Do you serve cocktails?	Si serve i cocktail?	See sair-veh ee cocktail
Two glasses of beer, please	Due birre, per favore	Doo-eh beer-reh, pair fa-vor-eh
Do you have draught beer?	Ha birra alla spina?	A beer-ra al-la spee-na
Two more beers	Altre due birre	Al-treh doo-eh beer-reh
A large/small beer	Una birra grande/piccola	Oon-a beer-ra gran-deh/peek-ko-la
I'd like	Vorrei	Vor-ray
a long soft drink with ice	una bibita analcolica con ghiaccio	oon-a bee-bee-ta a-nal-ko-lee-ka kon gya-cho
a soft drink	un analcolico	oon a-nal-ko-lee-ko

1. For the names of beverages, see p.110.

an apple juice	un succo di mela	oon sook-ko dee me-la
an orange juice	un succo di arancia	oon sook-ko dee a-ran-cha
a fruit juice	un succo di frutta	oon sook-ko dee froot-ta
a milk shake	un frullato/un frappé	oon frool-la-to/oon frap-peh
iced coffee	un caffè freddo	oon kaf-feh fred-do
hot chocolate	un cioccolato	oon chok-ko-la-to
iced tea	un tè freddo	oon teh fred-do
China tea	un tè di China	oon teh dee chee-na
Indian tea	un tè d'India	oon teh deen-dya
Neat	Liscio	Lee-sho
On the rocks	Con ghiaccio	Kon gya-cho
With soda water	... e soda	... eh so-da
With water	... e acqua	... eh ak-wa
Mineral water (fizzy/ still)	Acqua minerale (gassata/non gassata)	Ak-wa meen-air-al-eh (gaz-za-ta/non gaz-za-ta)
I'd like another glass of water, please	Vorrei un altro bicchiere d'acqua, per favore	Vor-ray oon al-tro beek-kyair-eh dak-wa, pair fa-vor-eh
The same again, please	Lo stesso, per favore	Lo stes-so, pair fa-vor-eh
Three black coffees and one with cream	Tre caffè neri e uno con panna	Treh kaf-feh ne-ree eh oon-o kon pan-na
May we have an ashtray?	Si può avere un portacenere?	See pwo a-vair-eh oon por-ta-che-nair-eh

RESTAURANT VOCABULARY

artificial sweetener	il dolcificante	dol-chee-fee-kan-teh
ashtray	il portacenere	por-ta-che-nair-eh
bill	il conto	kon-to
bowl	la scodella	sko-del-la
cigarettes	le sigarette	see-ga-ret-teh
cloakroom	il guardaroba	gwar-da-ro-ba
course (dish)	la portata/il piatto	por-ta-ta/eel pyat-to
cup	la tazza	tat-sa
fork	la forchetta	for-ket-ta
glass	il bicchiere	beek-kyair-eh
hungry (to be)	aver fame	avair fa-meh
knife	il coltello	kol-tel-lo
matches	i fiammiferi	fyam-mee-fair-ee
menu	il menù	me-noo
mustard	la senape	se-na-peh
napkin	la salvietta	sal-vyet-ta
oil	l'olio m	ol-yo
pepper	il pepe	pe-peh
plate	il piatto	pyat-to
salt	il sale	sa-leh
salt-cellar	la saliera	sal-yair-a
sauce	la salsa	sal-sa
saucer	il piattino	pyat-tee-no

service	**il servizio**	sair-veet-syo
spoon	**il cucchiaio**	kook-kya-yo
table	**la tavola**	ta-vo-la
tablecloth	**la tovaglia**	to-val-ya
thirsty (*to be*)	**aver sete**	a-vair se-teh
tip	**la mancia**	man-cha
toothpick	**lo stuzzicadenti**	stoot-see-ka-den-tee
vegetarian	**vegetariano**	ve-je-tar-ya-no
vinegar	**l'aceto** *m*	a-che-to
waiter	**il cameriere**	ka-mair-yair-eh
waitress	**la cameriera**	ka-mair-yair-a
water	**l'acqua** *f*	ak-wa
wine list	**la lista dei vini**	lees-ta day vee-nee

THE MENU

MINESTRE

brodetto	fish soup
brodo di manzo	consommé
brodo di pollo	chicken broth
crema di piselli	cream of pea soup
crema di pollo	cream of chicken soup
fettuccine in brodo	noodle soup
minestra di cipolle	onion soup
minestra di fagioli	bean soup
minestra di lenticchie	lentil soup
minestra di pomodoro	tomato soup
minestra di riso	rice soup
minestrone	vegetable soup with noodles

pasta e fagioli	pasta and beans in broth
pasta in brodo	pasta in broth
stracciatella	broth with beaten egg and cheese
taglierini in brodo	thin noodles in broth
zuppa di cozze	mussel soup
zuppa pavese	consommé with fried bread, poached egg and grated cheese
zuppa di verdura	vegetable soup

ANTIPASTI

acciughe/alici	anchovies
affettati	cold cuts
antipasto misto	mixed hors d'œuvres
bresaola	dried beef, thinly sliced
calamaretti	small squid
carciofini sott'olio	artichokes in olive oil
carpaccio	raw beef, thinly sliced
coppa	raw smoked ham
cozze	mussels
crostini di mare	shellfish on fried bread
datteri di mare	date-shell mussels
finocchiona	fennel-flavoured salami
frutti di mare	shellfish salad
funghi sott'olio	mushrooms in olive oil
granchio	crab

insalata di finocchi e cetrioli	fennel and cucumber salad
insalata di frutti di mare	seafood salad
insalata di funghi	salad of raw mushrooms
insalata di riso e scampi	salad of rice and scampi
insalata di tonno	tuna fish salad
lumache	snails
olive	olives
ostriche	oysters
peperoni con alici e capperi	peppers with anchovies and capers
peperoni sott'olio	peppers in oil
pomodori con tonno	tomatoes stuffed with tuna fish
prosciutto e melone	parma ham and melon
prosciutto e fichi	parma ham and figs
salame	salami
scampi	prawns
sardine	sardines
seppie	cuttlefish
tonno	tuna fish
totani	squid
uova sode agli spinaci	eggs florentine
uova tonnate	hard boiled eggs in tuna sauce

PASTA ASCIUTTA

cannelloni al forno	large tubes of pasta, stuffed and browned in the oven

cappelletti	rings of pasta filled with minced meat
fettuccine alla marinara	ribbon noodles with tomato sauce
gnocchi alla piemontese	little balls of semolina and egg
gnocchi di patate	little balls of potato, flour and egg
lasagne (verdi) al forno	large strips of pasta (with spinach) cooked in a sauce in the oven
maccheroni	macaroni
pappardelle al sugo di lepre	strips of pasta with hare sauce
penne/rigatoni	large macaroni
ravioli/tortellini	squares of pasta with a stuffing (meat or spinach and cream cheese)
spaghetti alla bolognese	spaghetti with meat sauce
spaghetti al pomodoro	spaghetti with tomato sauce
spaghetti alle vongole	spaghetti with clam sauce
tagliatelle alla bolognese	ribbon noodles with meat sauce
tortellini al sugo di carne	small ravioli with meat sauce

RISO

risi e bisi	rice with green peas
riso ai gamberi	rice with shrimps
riso e ceci	a broth of rice and chick-peas with tomatoes and spices
riso alla genovese	rice with a sauce of minced beef or veal with vegetables

risotto alla milanese	rice with butter, saffron, beef marrow and parmesan
risotto alla sbirraglia	rice with chicken
risotto alla veronese	rice and ham with mushrooms
risotto di frutti di mare	rice with shellfish
risotto di peoci	rice with mussels
risotto alla romana	rice with lamb and tomatoes
supplì di riso	rice croquettes filled with ham and cheese

PESCE

anguille	eel
aragosta	rock lobster
baccalà	salt cod
burrida	fish stew
calamari	squid
cappon magro	a pyramid of vegetables and fish
cefalo/muggine	grey mullet
cernia	grouper
coda di rospo	monkfish
cozze	mussels
fritto misto	mixed fried fish (squid, octopus and cuttlefish)
gamberi	shrimps
granchio di mare	crab

merluzzo	hake
nasello	whiting
pagro	sea bream
pesce alla griglia	grilled fish
pesce arrosto	baked or roast fish
pesce fritto	fried fish
pesce San Pietro	John Dory
pesce spada	swordfish
polipi	octopus
ricci	sea urchins
salmone	salmon
sarde/sardine	sardines
scampi	prawns
seppie	cuttlefish
sgombro	mackerel
sogliola	sole
spigola	sea bass
storione	sturgeon
tonno	tuna
totani	squid
triglia	red mullet
trota	trout
ventresca	white meat tuna
vongole	small clams

CARNE

abbacchio/agnello	lamb
animelle alla salvia	sweetbreads with sage
arista	roast loin of pork
bistecca alla pizzaiola	steak with tomato and garlic sauce
bollito	variety of boiled meats
braciola	rib steak
braciola di maiale	pork chop
capretto	kid
cervella	brain
cotechino	spicy pork/sausage
cotoletta alla bolognese	fried veal cutlet with ham and tomato
cotoletta alla milanese	veal cutlet coated in egg and breadcrumbs and fried
fegato (alla veneziana)	liver (with onions)
filetto	fillet
girello	rump
lingua	tongue
maiale	pork
manzo	beef
manzo stufato al vino rosso	beef stewed in red wine
ossobuco alla milanese	stewed shin of veal with tomatoes, garlic and white wine
piccata di vitello	veal cooked with lemon and parsley

polpette	meat balls
polpettone	meat roll
porchetta	roast suckling pig
prosciutto affumicato	gammon
rognoncini al vino bianco	kidneys in white wine sauce
salsicce di maiale	pork sausages
saltimbocca alla romana	rolls of veal with ham
scaloppa milanese	escalope coated in egg and breadcrumbs, and fried
scaloppa napoletana	escalope coated in breadcrumbs and fried, with tomato sauce
scaloppine al marsala	small escalopes in marsala sauce
scaloppine al vino bianco	small escalopes in white wine sauce
spezzatino di vitello	veal stew
stracotto	beef stew with pork sausage
trippa	tripe
vitello	veal
vitello tonnato	cold veal with tuna fish sauce
zampone di maiale	stuffed pig's trotter

POLLAME E CACCIAGONE

anitra	duck
beccaccia	woodcock
cervo	venison
cinghiale	boar

coniglio	rabbit
fagiano	pheasant
faraona	guinea-fowl
lepre	hare
oca	goose
pernice	partridge
petto di pollo	chicken breast
piccione	pigeon
pollo	chicken
quaglie	quails
tacchino	turkey
tordi	thrush
uccelletti	small birds of all kinds

CONTORNI

acetosella	sorrel
aglio	garlic
arugula	rocket
asparagi	asparagus
barbabietola	beetroot
bietola	chard
caponata	cold dish of aubergines, peppers, courgettes and tomatoes
carciofi	artichokes
carote	carrots

castagne	chestnuts
cavolfiore	cauliflower
cavoli	cabbage
cavolini di bruxelles	brussels sprouts
ceci	chick-peas
cetriolo	cucumber
cipolla	onion
fagioli	dried white beans
fagiolini	green beans
fave	broad beans
finocchio	fennel
funghi	mushrooms
insalata verde	green salad
lattuga	lettuce
lenticchie	lentils
melanzane	aubergine, egg plant
patate	potatoes
peperonata	tomatoes, peppers and onions stewed together
peperoni	peppers
piselli	peas
polenta	cornmeal
pomodoro	tomato
porro	leek
radicchio	red chicory
ravanelli	radishes

rape	turnip
scarola	endive
sedano	celery
spinaci	spinach
zucchini	courgettes/baby marrows

UOVA

frittata	omelette
frittata al pomodoro	tomato omelette
frittata al prosciutto	ham omelette
frittata con spinaci	spinach omelette
uova al tegame con formaggio	fried eggs with cheese
uova mollette	soft boiled eggs
uova sode	hard boiled eggs
uova strapazzate	scrambled eggs

DOLCI

amaretti	macaroons
budino alla toscana	cream cheese with raisins, almonds, sugar and egg yolks
cassata alla siciliana	ice cream with candied fruit
gelato di cioccolato	chocolate ice cream
gelato di fragola	strawberry ice cream
gelato di limone	lemon ice cream

macedonia di frutta	fruit salad
Mont Blanc	puree of chestnuts with whipped cream
panettone	spiced cake with sultanas
panna montata	whipped cream
ricotta al maraschino	curd cheese with maraschino
tartufi di cioccolata	chocolate truffles
torrone	nougat
torta	gateau, cake
torta di cioccolata	chocolate cake
tortiglione	almond cakes
torta di mele	apple tart
zabaione	zabaglione
zuppa inglese	trifle

FRUTTA E NOCI

albicocche	apricots
arancia	orange
banana	banana
ciliege	cherries
cocomero/anguria	watermelon
datteri	dates
fichi	figs
fragole	strawberries
fragole di bosco	wild strawberries

lamponi	raspberries
mandarini	tangerines
mandorle	almonds
mela	apple
melone	melon
noci	walnuts
pera	pear
pesca	peach
pompelmo	grapefruit
prugna	plum
uva	grape

BEVANDE

acqua minerale	mineral water
amaro	bitters
aranciata	orangeade
birra	beer
alla spina	draught
bionda	light
in bottiglia	bottled
in lattina	in a can
scura	dark
brandy	brandy
caffè nero/espresso	black coffee

caffè e latte/cappuccino	white coffee
caffè con panna	coffee with cream
cioccolato	hot chocolate
fullato/frappé	milk shake
grappa	spirit made from grape pressings
limonata	lemonade
succo di frutta	fruit juice
succo di arancia	orange juice
succo di mela	apple juice
succo di pomodoro	tomato juice
succo di pompelmo	grapefruit juice
succo di uva	grape juice
tè di China	China tea
tè d'India	Indian tea
tisana	herb tea
al cinorrode	rose hip
al tiglio	lime
alla menta	mint
camomilla	camomile
vino	wine
bianco	white
rosso	red
dolce	sweet
secco	dry
spumante	sparkling

WAYS OF COOKING

a vapore	steamed
affumicato	smoked
al agrodolce	with a dressing of vinegar or lemon juice and sugar
al burro	with butter
al forno	baked
al pesto	with basil, oil and garlic sauce
al ragù	stewed with vegetables
al sugo	with sauce
alla bolognese	with meat sauce
alla griglia	grilled
alla napoletana	with tomato sauce
alla panna	with cream
alla pizzaiola	with tomato and garlic sauce
arrosto	roast
bollito	boiled
carne – al sangue	meat – rare
media	medium
ben cotta	well done
casalinga	home made
con aglio	with garlic
con bagna cauda	hot sauce of olive oil, garlic and anchovy for dipping raw vegetables

con pomodoro	with tomato
crudo	raw
fritto	fried
in camicia	poached
in padella	fried
in umido	stewed
marinato	marinated
passato	puréed
ripieno	stuffed
salsa verde	sauce made from oil, lemon juice, capers, parsley and garlic
stufato	braised
trifolato	with truffles

SHOPPING[1] & SERVICES

WHERE TO GO

Where are the best department stores?	Dove sono i migliori magazzini?	Do-veh so-no ee meel-yor-ee ma-gad-zee-nee
Where is the market?	Dov'è il mercato?	Dov-eh eel mair-ka-to
Is there a market every day?	C'è mercato ogni giorno?	Cheh mair-ka-to on-yee jor-no
Where's the nearest chemist?	Dov'è la farmacia più vicina?	Dov-eh la far-ma-chee-a pyoo vee-chee-na
Can you recommend a ...?	Mi può raccomandare un ...?	Mee pwo rak-ko-man-dar-eh oon ...

1. Shops generally close at mid-day in Italy, and re-open at some point in the afternoon. The length of the mid-day break varies considerably from region to region, but is longer in the south than in the north.

| Where can I buy ...? | **Dove posso comprare ...?** | Do-veh pos-so kom-prar-eh ... |
| When do the shops open/close? | **A che ora aprono/ chiudono i negozi?** | A keh or-a **ap**-ro-no/ **kyoo**-do-no ee ne-got-see |

SHOPS AND SERVICES

baker	**il panettiere**	pa-net-tyair-eh
bank	**la banca**	ban-ka
barber	**il barbiere**	bar-byair-eh
bookshop	**la libreria**	lee-brair-ee-a
builder	**il costruttore edile**	kos-troot-tor-eh- **e**-dee-leh
butcher	**la macelleria**	ma-chel-lair-ee-a
cake shop	**la pasticceria**	pas-tee-chair-ee-a
camera shop	**il negozio fotografico**	ne-got-syo fo-to-**gra**-fee-ko
camping equipment	**l'equipaggiamento da campeggio**	e-kee-pad-ja-men-to da kam-ped-jo
carpenter	**il falegname**	fa-len-ya-meh
chemist	**la farmacia**	far-ma-chee-a
dairy	**la latteria**	lat-tair-ee-a
decorator/painter	**il pittore**	peet-tor-eh
dentist	**il dentista**	den-tees-ta
department stores	**i grandi magazzini**	gran-dee ma-gad-zee-nee
delicatessen	**la salumeria**	sa-loo-mair-ee-a

doctor	il medico	me-dee-ko
dry cleaner	la pulitura a secco	poo-lee-too-ra a sek-ko
electrician	l'elettricista *m*	e-let-tree-chees-ta
electrical appliances	gli elettrodomestici	e-let-tro-do-mes-tee-chee
fishmonger	il pescivendolo	pe-shee-ven-do-lo
florist	il fiorista	fyor-ees-ta
gardener	il giardiniere	jar-deen-yair-eh
greengrocer	il fruttivendolo	froot-tee-ven-do-lo
grocer	la drogheria	dro-gair-ee-a
haberdashery	la merceria	mer-chair-ee-a
hairdresser	il parrucchiere	par-rook-kyair-eh
hardware shop	il negozio di ferramenta	ne-got-syo dee fer-ra-men-ta
hypermarket	l'ipermercato *m*	ee-pair-mair-ka-to
ironmonger	il negozio di ferramenta	ne-got-syo dee fer-ra-men-ta
jeweller	la gioielleria	joy-el-lair-ee-a
launderette/laundry	la lavanderia	la-van-dair-ee-a
market	il mercato	mair-ka-to
newsagent	il giornalaio	jor-na-la-yo
notary	il notaio	no-ta-yo
odd job man	l'uomo tuttofare *m*	wo-mo toot-to-far-eh
optician	l'ottico *m*	ot-tee-ko
pastry shop	la pasticceria	pas-tee-chair-ee-a
photographer	il fotografo	fo-to-gra-fo

plasterer	l'intonacatore *m*	een-to-na-ka-tor-eh
plumber	l'idraulico *m*	eed-row-lee-ko
police	la polizia/i carabinieri	pol-eet-see-a/ka-ra-been-yair-ee
post office	l'ufficio postale	oof-fee-cho pos-ta-leh
shoe repairer	il calzolaio	kalt-so-la-yo
shoe shop	il negozio di calzature	ne-got-syo dee kalt-sa-too-reh
sports shop	il negozio sportivo	ne-got-syo spor-tee-vo
stationer	la cartoleria	kar-to-lair-ee-a
sweet shop	il negozio di dolciumi	ne-got-syo dee dol-choo-mee
tobacconist	la tabaccheria	ta-bak-kair-ee-a
travel agent	l'agenzia di viaggi	a-jent-see-a dee vyad-jee
wine merchant	la rivendita di vino	ree-ven-dee-ta dee vee-no
toy shop	il negozio di giocattoli	ne-got-syo dee jo-kat-to-lee

IN THE SHOP

Self-service	*Self-service	Self-service
Sale (clearance)	*La svendita	Sven-dee-ta
Cash desk	*Cassa	Kas-sa
Shop assistant	Commesso/ commessa	Ko-mes-so/ko-mes-sa

Manager	**Direttore**	Dee-ret-tor-eh
Can I help you?	*In cosa posso servirla?	Een ko-za pos-so sair-veer-la
I want to buy …	Vorrei comprare …	Vor-ray kom-prar-eh …
Do you sell …?	Vende …?	Ven-deh …
I just want to look round	Vorrei solo dare un'occhiata in giro	Vor-ray solo dar-eh oon-ok-kya-ta een jee-ro
I don't want to buy anything now	Non compro niente adesso	Non kom-pro nyen-teh a-des-so
Could you show me …?	Può farmi vedere …?	Pwo far-mee ve-dair-eh …
I don't like this	Questo non mi piace	Kwes-to non mee pya-cheh
I'll have this	Prendo pure questo	Pren-do poo-reh kwes-to
You'll find them at the counter	*Li troverà a quel banco	Lee tro-vair-a a kwel ban-ko
We've sold out but we'll have more tomorrow	*Sono finiti ma li riceveremo domani	So-no fee-nee-tee ma lee ree-che-ve-re-mo do-ma-nee
Anything else?	*Nient'altro?	Nyen-tal-tro
That will be all	Questo è tutto	Kwes-to eh toot-to
Will you take it with you?	*Lo prende adesso?	Lo pren-deh a-des-so
Please send them to this address/X hotel	Per favore li mandi a questo indirizzo/all'albergo X	Pair fa-vor-eh lee man-dee a kwes-to een-dee-reet-so/al-lal-bair-go X

CHOOSING

I want something in leather/green	Vorrei qualcosa in pelle/di color verde	Vor-ray kwal-lo-za een pel-leh/dee ko-lor vair-deh
I need it to match this	Voglio che vada bene con questo	Vol-yo keh va-da be-neh kon kwes-to
What colour do you want?	*Che colore desidera?	Keh ko-lor-eh de-zee-dair-a
I don't like this colour	Non mi piace questo colore	Non mee pya-cheh kwes-to ko-lor-eh
I like the colour but I want a different style	Il colore va bene ma vorrei uno stile diverso	Eel ko-lor-eh va be-neh ma vor-ray oon-o stee-leh dee-vair-so
I like the one in the window	Mi piace quello in vetrina	Mee pya-cheh kwel-lo een vet-ree-na
I want a darker/lighter shade	Vorrei una tinta più scura/più chiara	Vor-ray oon-a teen-ta pyoo skoo-ra/pyoo kya-ra
I need something warmer/thinner	Vorrei qualcosa di più pesante/più leggero	Vor-ray kwal-ko-za dee pyoo pe-zan-teh/pyoo led-je-ro
Do you have one in another colour/size?	Ha niente in un colore diverso/di un'altra taglia?	A nyen-teh een oon ko-lor-eh dee-vair-so/dee oon-al-tra tal-ya
Have you anything better/cheaper?	Vorrei qualcosa di meglio/meno costoso	Vor-ray kwal-ko-za dee mel-yo/me-no kos-to-zo
Could I see that one, please?	Posso vedere quello, per favore?	Pos-so ve-dair-eh kwel-lo, pair fa-vor-eh

How much is this?	**Quanto costa?**	Kwan-to kos-ta
I am sorry, that's too much for me	**Mi dispiace, costa troppo**	Mee dees-pya-cheh, kos-ta trop-po
For how long is it guaranteed?	**Per quanto tempo è garantito?**	Pair kwan-to tem-po eh ga-ran-tee-to
Can I try it on?	**Posso provarlo?**	Pos-so pro-var-lo
It's too	**E troppo**	Eh-trop-po
short	**corto**	kor-to
long	**lungo**	loon-go
tight	**stretto**	stret-to
loose	**largo**	lar-go
Have you a larger/smaller one?	**Ne ha uno più grande/più piccolo?**	Neh a oon-o pyoo gran-deh/pyoo **peek**-ko-lo
What size?[1]	***Di che misura?**	Dee keh mee-zoo-ra
I want size ...	**Voglio la misura ...**	Vol-yo la mee-zoo-ra ...
The English/American size is ...	**La misura inglese/americana è ...**	La mee-zoo-ra een-gle-zeh/a-me-ree-ka-na eh ...
The collar size is ...	**Il numero di colletto è ...**	Eel noo-mair-o dee ko-let-to eh ...
My chest measurement is ...	**Il mio numero di petto è ...**	Eel mee-o **noo**-mair-o dee pet-to eh ...
My waist measurement is ...	**Il mio numero di cintura è ...**	Eel mee-o **noo**-mair-o dee cheen-toor-a eh ...
Is there a mirror?	**Cè uno specchio?**	Cheh oon-o-spek-kyo

1. See p. 129 for Continental sizes.

Is it colourfast?	**E di colore solido?**	Eh dee ko-lor-eh **so-lee-do**
Is it machine washable?	**E lavabile in lavatrice?**	Eh la-va-bee-leh een la-va-tree-cheh
Will it shrink?	**Si restringerà?**	See res-treen-jair-a
Is it handmade?	**E fatto a mano?**	Eh fat-to a ma-no
What's it made of?	**Di cosa è fatto?**	Dee ko-za eh fat-to

MATERIALS

cotton	**il cotone**	ko-to-neh
lace	**il merletto**	mair-let-to
leather	**il cuoio**	kwo-yo
linen	**il lino**	lee-no
plastic	**la plastica**	plas-tee-ka
silk	**la seta**	se-ta
suede	**la pelle scamosciata**	pel-leh ska-mo-sha-ta
synthetic	**sintetico**	seen-te-tee-ko
wool	**la lana**	la-na

COLOURS

beige	**beige**	beige
black	**nero**	ne-ro
blue	**blu**	bloo
brown	**marrone**	mar-ro-neh

gold	**oro**	or-o
green	**verde**	vair-deh
grey	**grigio**	gree-jo
mauve	**malva**	mal-va
orange	**arancione**	a-ran-cho-neh
pink	**rosa**	ro-za
purple	**porpora**	por-por-a
red	**rosso**	ros-so
silver	**argento**	ar-jen-to
white	**bianco**	byan-ko
yellow	**giallo**	jal-lo

COMPLAINTS

I want to see the manager	**Desidero vedere il direttore**	De-zee-dair-o ve-dair-eh eel dee-ret-tor-eh
It doesn't work	**Non funziona**	Non foont-syo-na
It does not fit	**Non è la misura giusta**	Non eh la mee-zoo-ra joos-ta
This is	**E**	Eh
dirty	**sporco**	spor-ko
stained	**macchiato**	mak-kya-to
torn	**strappato**	strap-pa-to
broken	**rotto**	rot-to
cracked	**spaccato**	spak-ka-to
I bought this yesterday	**L'ho comprato ieri**	Lo kom-pra-to yair-ee

I want to return this	**Voglio scambiare questo**	Vol-yo skam-byar-eh kwes-to
Will you change it, please?	**Lo può cambiare, per favore?**	Lo pwo kam-byar-eh, pair fa-vor-eh
Will you refund my money?	**Mi può restituire il denaro?**	Mee pwo res-tee-tweer-eh eel de-na-ro
Here is the receipt	**Ecco la ricevuta**	Ek-ko la ree-che-voo-ta

PAYING

That's 6,000 lire, please	***Costa sei mila lire**	Kos-ta say mee-la leer-eh
They are 100 lire each	***Costano cento lire l'uno**	Kos-ta-no chen-to leer-eh loo-no
It's too expensive	**E troppo caro**	Eh trop-po ka-ro
Don't you have anything cheaper?	**Non ha niente di meno costoso?**	Non a nyen-teh de me-no kos-to-zo
Will you take English/ American currency?	**Posso pagare in sterline/in dollari?**	Pos-so pa-gar-eh een stair-lee-neh/een dol-lar-ee
Do you take travellers' cheques?	**Accetta travellers' cheques?**	A-chet-ta travellers' cheques
Do I have to pay VAT?	**Devo pagare l'IVA**	De-vo pa-gar-eh lee-va
Please pay the cashier	***Si accomodi alla cassa, per favore**	See ak-ko-mo-dee al-la kas-sa, pair fa-vor-eh
May I have a receipt, please?	**Mi può rilasciare una ricevuta, per favore?**	Mee pwo ree-la-shar-eh oon-a ree-che-voo-ta, pair fa-vor-eh

You've given me too little/too much change	**Mi ha dato meno di resto/mi ha dato troppo**	Mee a da-to me-no dee res-to/mee a da-to trop-po
How much does that come to?	**Quanto è tra tutto?**	Kwan-to eh tra toot-to
That will be ...	***Fa .../Sono ...**	Fa .../So-no ...

CHEMIST[1]

Can you prepare this prescription for me, please?	**Mi può preparare questa ricetta, per favore?**	Mee pwo pre-par-ar-eh kwes-ta ree-chet-ta, pair fa-vor-eh
Have you a small first-aid kit?	**Ha una valigetta di pronto soccorso?**	Ha oon-a va-lee-jet-ta dee pron-to sok-kor-so
A bottle of aspirin, please	**Una boccetta di aspirine, per favore**	Oon-a bo-chet-ta dee as-pee-ree-neh, pair fa-vor-eh
A tin of adhesive plasters	**Una scatolina di cerotti**	Oon-a ska-to-lee-na dee chair-ot-tee
Can you suggest something for	**Mi può indicare qualcosa contro**	Mee pwo een-dee-kar-eh kwal-ko-za kon-tro
indigestion?	**l'indigestione?**	leen-dee-jes-tyo-neh
constipation?	**la stitichezza?**	la stee-tee-ket-sa
diarrhoea?	**la diarrea?**	la dee-ar-re-a
I want something for insect bites	**Voglio qualcosa contro i morsi degli insetti**	Vol-yo kwal-ko-za kon-tro ee mor-see del-yee een-set-tee

1. See also AT THE DOCTOR'S (p. 179).

Can you give me something for sunburn?	Mi può dare qualcosa contro le bruciature di sole?	Mee pwo dar-eh kwal-ko-za kon-tro leh broo-cha-too-reh dee so-leh
I want some throat/cough lozenges	Vorrei delle pasticche per la gola/per la tosse	Vor-ray del-leh pas-teek-keh pair la go-la/pair la tos-seh
I need something for a hangover/sea sickness	Vorrei qualcosa contro il mal di testa/il mal di mare	Vor-ray kwal-ko-za kon-tro eel mal dee tes-ta/eel mal dee mar-eh
I want some antiseptic cream/lipsalve	Vorrei della crema antisettica/della pomata per le labbra	Vor-ray del-la kre-ma an-tee-set-tee-ka/del-la po-ma-ta pair le lab-bra
I want	Desidero	De-zee-dair-o
a disinfectant	del disinfettante	del dee-zeen-fet-tan-teh
a mouthwash	un disinfettante per la bocca	oon dee-zeen-fet-tan-teh pair la bok-ka
some nose drops	delle gocce per il naso	del-leh go-cheh pair eel na-zo
Do you sell contraceptives?	Si vende degli antifecondativi?	See ven-deh del-yee an-tee-fe-kon-da-tee-vee

TOILET ARTICLES

| A packet of razor blades, please | Un pacchetto di lamette da barba, per favore | Oon pak-ket-to dee la-met-teh da bar-ba, pair fa-vor-eh |

Do you have an after-shave lotion?	Ha una lozione per barba?	A oon-a lot-syo-neh pair bar-ba
How much is this lotion?	Quanto costa questa lozione?	Kwan-to kos-ta kwes-ta lot-syo-neh
A tube of toothpaste, please	Un dentifricio, per favore	Oon den-tee-free-cho, pair fa-vor-eh
Give me a box of paper handkerchiefs, please	Mi dia una scatola di fazzoletti di carta, per favore	Mee dee-a oon-a ska-to-la dee fat-so-let-tee dee kar-ta, pair fa-vor-eh
I want some eau-de-cologne/perfume	Vorrei dell'acqua di Colonia/un profumo	Vor-ray del-lak-wa dee ko-lon-ya/oon pro-foo-mo
What kinds of soap do you have?	Che tipi di sapone avete?	Keh tee-pee dee sa-po-neh a-ve-teh
A bottle/sachet of shampoo for normal/dry/greasy hair	Una bottiglia/una bustina di shampoo per capelli normali/secchi/grassi	Oon-a bo-teel-ya/oon-a boos-tee-na dee sham-poo pair ka-pel-lee nor-ma-lee/sek-kee/gras-see
Do you sell sanitary towels/tampons/cotton wool?	Vende assorbenti igienici/tamponi/cotone?	Ven-deh as-sor-ben-tee ee-jen-ee-chee/tam-po-nee/ko-to-neh
Do you have any suntan oil/cream?	Ha qualche lozione/crema abbronzante?	A kwal-keh lot-syo-neh/kre-ma ab-brond-zan-teh
I'd like some	Vorrei	Vor-ray
cleansing cream/lotion	una crema/una lozione detergente	oon-a kre-ma/oon-a lot-syo-neh de-tair-jen-teh
hair conditioner	un balsamo	oon bal-sa-mo

hand cream	**una crema per le mani**	oon-a kre-ma pair le ma-nee
moisturizer	**una crema idratante**	oon-a kre-ma eed-ra-tan-teh
sun cream for children	**crema solare per ragazzi**	kre-ma so-lar-eh pair ra-gat-see
toilet paper	**carta igienica**	kar-ta ee-jen-ee-ka

CLOTHES AND SHOES[1]

I want a hat/sunhat	**Vorrei un cappello/un cappello da sole**	Vor-ray oon kap-pel-lo/oon kap-pel-lo da so-leh
I'd like a pair of white cotton gloves/black leather gloves	**Vorrei un paio di guanti di filo bianco/di pelle nera**	Vor-ray oon pa-yo dee gwan-tee dee fee-lo byan-ko/dee pel-leh ne-ra
May I see some dresses, please?	**Potrei vedere qualche abito, per favore?**	Pot-ray ve-dair-eh kwal-keh a-bee-to, pair fa-vor-eh
Where's the coat department?	**Dove sono i soprabiti?**	Do-veh so-no ee sop-ra-bee-tee
Where are beach clothes?	**Dove sono gli abiti da spiaggia?**	Do-veh so-no lyee a-bee-tee da spyad-ja
The men's department is on the second floor	***Le confezioni per uomo sono al secondo piano**	Le kon-fet-syo-nee pair wo-mo so-no al se-kon-do pya-no

1. See also CLOTHING SIZES (p. 129).

Where can I find stockings/socks?	Dov'è che vendono calze/calzini?	Dov-eh keh ven-do-no kalt-seh/kalt-see-nee
I am looking for	Cerco	Chair-ko
a blouse	una blusa	oon-a bloo-za
a bra	un reggipetto	oon red-jee-pet-to
a dress	un vestito	oon ves-tee-to
a sweater	una maglietta	oon-a mal-yet-ta
I need	Ho bisogno di	O bee-zon-yo dee
a coat	un soprabito	oon sop-ra-bee-to
a raincoat	un impermeabile	oon eem-pair-mee-a-bee-leh
a jacket	una giacchetta	oon-a jak-ket-ta
a pair of trousers	un paio di calzoni	oon pa-yo dee kalt-so-nee
I want a short-/long-sleeved shirt, collar size …	Voglio una camicia a maniche corte/lunghe, colletto numero …	Vol-yo oon-a ka-mee-cha a ma-nee-keh kor-teh/loon-geh, kol-let-to noo-mair-o …
Do you sell	Vende	Ven-deh
buttons?	bottoni?	bot-to-nee
elastic?	elastico?	e-las-tee-ko
zips?	cerniere?	chair-nyair-eh
This doesn't fit	Non va bene	Non va be-neh
I don't know the Italian size	Non conosco le misure italiane	Non ko-nos-ko leh mee-zoo-reh ee-tal-ya-neh
Can you measure me?	Può prendermi le misure?	Pwo pren-dair-mee leh mee-zoo-reh

It's for a three-year old	E per un bambino di tre anni	Eh pair oon bam-bee-no dee treh an-nee
I need a pair of walking shoes	Ho bisogno di un paio di scarpe da passeggio	O bee-zon-yo dee oon pa-yo dee skar-peh da pas-sed-jo
I need a pair of beach sandals/black shoes	Ho bisogno di un paio di sandali da spiaggia/scarpe nere	O bee-zon-yo dee oon pa-yo dee san-da-lee da spyad-ja/skar-peh ne-reh
These heels are too high/too low	Questi tacchi sono troppo alti/troppo bassi	Kwes-tee tak-kee so-no trop-po al-tee/trop-po bas-see

CLOTHING SIZES

WOMEN'S DRESSES, ETC

British	10	12	14	16	18	20
American	8	10	12	14	16	18
Italian	42	44	46	48	50	52

MEN'S SUITS

British and American	36	38	40	42	44	46
Continental	46	48	50	52	54	56

MEN'S SHIRTS

British and American	14	14½	15	15½	16	16½	17
Continental	36	37	38	39	41	42	43

STOCKINGS

British and American	8	8½	9	9½	10	10½	11
Continental	0	1	2	3	4	5	6

SOCKS

British and American	9½	10	10½	11	11½
Continental	38–39	39–40	40–41	41–42	42–43

WAIST, CHEST/BUST AND HIPS

Inches	24	26	28	30	32	34	36	38
Centimetres	61	66	71	76	81	87	92	97
Inches	40	42	44	46	48	50	52	54
Centimetres	102	107	112	117	122	127	132	137

SHOES

British	1	2	3	4	5	6	7	8	9	10	11	12
American	2½	3½	4½	5½	6½	7½	8½	9½	10½	11½	12½	13½
Continental	33	34–5	36	37	38	39–40	41	42	43	44	45	46

FOOD[1]

Give me a kilo/half a kilo of ..., please	Vuol darmi un chilo/mezzo chilo di ..., per favore	Vwol dar-mee oon kee-lo/med-zo kee-lo dee ... pair fa-vor-eh
I want some sweets/chocolate, please	Vorrei dei dolciumi/una cioccolata, per favore	Vor-ray day dol-choo-mee/oon-a cho-ko-la-ta, pair fa-vor-eh
A bottle of milk	Una bottiglia di latte	Oon-a bot-teel-ya dee lat-teh
Is there anything back on the bottle?	C'è un rimborso sulla bottiglia?	Cheh oon reem-bor-so sool-la bot-teel-ya
A litre/half a litre of wine	Un litro/mezzo litro di vino	Oon leet-ro/med-zo leet-ro dee vee-no
A bottle of beer	Una bottiglia di birra	Oon-a bot-teel-ya dee beer-ra
I want	Vorrei	Vor-ray
a jar	un barattolo	oon ba-rat-to-lo
a can	una scatola	oon-a ska-to-la
a packet of ...	un pacchetto di ...	oon pak-ket-to dee ...
... slices of ham please	... fette di prosciutto cotto/crudo, per favore	... fet-teh dee pro-shoot-to kot-to/kroo-do, pair fa-vor-eh
Is it fresh or frozen?	E fresco o congelato?	Eh fres-ko o kon-je-la-to

1. See also the various MENU sections (p. 98 onwards) and WEIGHTS AND MEASURES (p. 205).

Do you sell frozen food?	Vende cibi congelati?	Ven-deh chee-bee kon-je-la-tee
These pears are too hard/soft	Queste pere non sono ancora mature/sono troppo mature	Kwes-teh pe-reh non so-no an-kor-a ma-too-reh/so-no trop-po ma-too-reh
Is it fresh?	È fresco?	Eh fres-ko
Are they ripe?	Sono mature?	So-no ma-too-reh
This is bad/stale	Questa è marcia/andata a male	Kwes-ta eh mar-cha/an-da-ta a ma-leh
A loaf of bread, please	Un filone di pane, per favore	Oon fee-lo-neh dee pa-neh, pair fa-vor-eh
How much a kilo/a litre?	Quanto costa al chilo/al litro?	Kwan-to kos-ta al kee-lo/al leet-ro
Will you mince it/bone it?	Me lo potrebbe tritare/disossare (meat)/spinare (fish)?	Me lo pot-reb-beh tree-tar-eh/dees-os-sar-eh/spee-nar-eh
Will you clean the fish?	Mi potrebbe pulire il pesce?	Mee pot-reb-beh poo-leer-eh eel pe-sheh
Leave/take off the head	Vuole lasciare/staccare la testa	Vwo-leh la-shar-eh/stak-kar-eh la tes-ta
Please fillet the fish	Mi potrebbe filettare il pesce?	Mee po-treb-beh fee-let-tar-eh eel pe-sheh
I'll take the bones	Mi dia le ossa, per favore	Mee dee-a leh os-sa, pair fa-vor-eh
Is there any shellfish?	Ci sono dei frutti di mare?	Chee so-no day froot-tee dee ma-reh
Shall I help myself?	Mi posso servire?	Mee pos-so sair-veer-eh

HAIRDRESSER AND BARBER · 133

HAIRDRESSER AND BARBER

May I make an appointment for tomorrow/this afternoon?	Posso fissare un appuntamento per domani/per questo pomeriggio?	Pos-so fees-sar-eh oon ap-poon-ta-men-to pair do-ma-nee/pair kwes-to po-mair-eed-jo
What time?	A che ora?	A keh or-a
I want my hair cut/ trimmed	Mi vuol tagliare/ spuntare i capelli, per favore	Mee vwol tal-yar-eh/ spoon-tar-eh ee ka- pel-lee, pair fa-vor-eh
I want my hair trimmed just a little	Vorrei solo una spuntatina	Vor-ray so-lo oon-a spoon-ta-tee-na
Shorter on top	Più corti in cima	Pyoo kor-tee een chee-ma
Not too short at the sides	Non troppo corti ai lati	Non trop-po kor-tee ay la-tee
I'll have it shorter at the back, please	Può farmeli un po' più corti sul collo?	Pwo far-me-lee oon po pyoo kor-tee sool kol-lo
That's fine	Va bene così	Va be-neh ko-zee
No shorter	Basta così	Bas-ta ko-zee
My hair is greasy/dry/ normal	Ho i capelli grassi/ secchi/normali	O ee ka-pel-lee gras- see/sek-kee/nor-ma-lee
I want a shampoo	Vorrei uno shampoo	Vor-ray oon-o sham-poo
Please use conditioner	Vorrei del balsamo, per favore	Vor-ray del bal-sa-mo, pair fa-vor-eh
I want my hair washed, styled and blow-dried	Vorrei lo shampoo, il taglio e la piega a phon	Vor-ray lo sham-poo, eel tal-yo eh la pye-ga a fon

I want my hair washed and set	Vorrei lavare i capelli e fare la messa in piega, per favore	Vor-ray la-var-eh ee ka-pel-lee e far-eh la mes-sa een pye-ga, pair fa-vor-eh
I want a dark rinse	Vorrei un colore scuro	Vor-ray oon ko-lor-eh skoo-ro
I'd like to see a colour chart	Vorrei vedere la gamma delle tinte	Vor-ray ve-dair-eh la gam-ma del-leh teen-teh
I want my hair tinted	Vorrei farmi tingere i capelli	Vor-ray far-mee teen-jair-eh ee ka-pel-lee
I want a darker/lighter shade	Vorrei una tinta più scura/più chiara	Vor-ray oon-a teen-ta pyoo skoo-ra/pyoo kya-ra
I want my hair permed/waved	Vorrei la permanente/capelli ondulati	Vor-ray la per-ma-nen-teh/ka-pel-lee on-doo-la-tee
I'd like it set this way, please	Vorrei una messa in piega così, per favore	Vor-ray oon-a mes-sa een pye-ga ko-zee, pair fa-vor-eh
Have you any lacquer?	Ha una lacca?	A oon-a lak-ka
The water is too cold	L'acqua è troppo fredda	Lak-wa eh trop-po fred-da
The dryer is too hot	Il casco è troppo caldo	Eel kas-ko eh trop-po kal-do
Thank you, I like it very much	Grazie, mi piace moltissimo	Gra-zyeh, mee pya-cheh mol-tees-see-mo
I want a shave/manicure	Vuol farmi la barba, per favore/vorrei la manicure	Vwol far-mee la bar-ba, pair fa-vor-eh/vor-ray la ma-nee-koo-reh

| Shave and hair cut | Barba e capelli | Barba eh ka-pel-lee |
| Please trim my beard/ my moustache | Vuole spuntarmi la barba/i baffi, per favore | Vwo-leh spoon-tar-mee la bar-ba/ee baf-fee, pair fa-vor-eh |

HARDWARE[1]

Where is the camping equipment?	Dove sono le attrezzature da campeggio?	Do-veh so-no leh at-tret-sa-too-reh da kam-ped-jo
Where can I get butane gas/paraffin?	Dove posso trovare del gas butano/ della paraffina?	Do-veh pos-so tro-var-eh del gaz boo-ta-no/del-la pa-raf-fee-na
I need	Mi occorre	Mee ok-kor-reh
a bottle-opener	un apribottiglie	oon ap-ree-bot-teel-yeh
a tin-opener	un apriscatole	oon ap-ree-ska-to-leh
a corkscrew	un cavatappi	oon ka-va-tap-pee
I'd like some candles and a box of matches	Vorrei delle candele ed una scatola di fiammiferi	Vor-ray del-leh kan-de-leh ed oon-a ska-to-la dee fyam-mee-fair-ee
I want	Vorrei	Vor-ray
a flashlight	una torcia elettrica	oon-a tor-cha e-let-tree-ka
a knife	un coltello	oon kol-tel-lo
a pair of scissors	un paio di forbici	oon pa-yo dee for-bee-chee

1. See also CAMPING (p. 66) and RENTING OR OWNING A PLACE (p. 70).

a small/large screwdriver	un cacciavite grande/piccolo	oon ka-cha-vee-teh gran-deh/peek-ko-lo
Do you have a battery for this?	Ha una batteria per questo?	A oon-a bat-tair-ee-a pair kwes-to
Do you sell string/rope?	Vende dello spago/della corda?	Ven-deh del-lo spa-go/del-la kor-da
Where can I find washing-up liquid/soap?	Dove posso trovare un detersivo per i piatti/del sapone?	Do-veh pos-so tro-var-eh oon de-tair-see-vo pair ee pyat-tee/del sa-po-neh
Do you have a dishcloth/broom?	Ha uno strofinaccio/una scopa?	A oon-o stro-fee-na-cho/oon-a sko-pa
I want a bucket/frying pan	Mi occorre un secchiello/una padella	Mee ok-kor-reh oon sek-kyel-lo/oon-a pa-del-la
I want to buy a barbecue	Vorrei comprare una griglia	Vor-ray kom-prar-eh oon-a greel-ya
Do you sell charcoal?	Vende il carbone di legno?	Ven-deh eel kar-bo-neh dee len-yo
adaptor	la presa multipla	pre-za mool-tee-pla
basket	il cestino	ches-tee-no
duster	lo straccio	stra-cho
electrical flex	il cordoncino elettrico	kor-don-chee-no e-let-tree-ko
extension lead	una prolunga	pro-loon-ga
fuse	la valvola fusibile	val-vo-la foo-zee-bee-leh
fuse wire	il fusibile	foo-zee-bee-leh
insulating tape	il nastro isolante	nas-tro ee-zo-lan-teh

penknife	il temperino	tem-pe-ree-no

LAUNDRY AND DRY CLEANING

Where is the nearest launderette/dry cleaner?	Dov'è la più vicina lavanderia automatica/ lavanderia a secco?	Dov-eh la pyoo vee-chee-na la-van-dair-ee-a ow-to-ma-tee-ka/la-van-dair-ee-a a sek-ko
I want to have these things washed/ cleaned	Vorrei far lavare/ pulire a secco queste cose	Vor-ray far la-var-eh/ poo-leer-eh a sek-ko kwes-teh ko-zeh
Can you get this stain out?	Può togliere questa macchia?	Pwo tol-yair-eh kwes-ta mak-kya
It is	E	Eh
coffee	caffè	kaf-feh
wine	vino	vee-no
grease	grasso	gras-so
These stains won't come out	*Queste macchie non vanno via	Kwes-teh mak-kyeh non van-no vee-a
It only needs to be pressed	Ha solo bisogno di essere stirato	A so-lo bee-zon-yo dee es-sair-eh stee-ra-to
This is torn; can you mend it?	Questo è rotto. Può rammendarlo?	Kwes-to eh rot-to. Pwo ram-men-dar-lo
Do you do invisible mending?	Può fare un rammendo invisibile?	Pwo far-eh oon ram-men-do een-vee-zee-bee-leh
There's a button missing	Ci manca un bottone	Chee man-ka oon bot-to-neh

Can you sew on a button here, please?	Può attaccare un bottone qui, per favore?	Pwo at-ta-kar-eh oon bot-to-neh kwee, pair fa-vor-eh
When will they be ready?	Quando saranno pronti?	Kwan-do sa-ran-no pron-tee
I need them by this evening/tomorrow	Ne ho bisogno per questa sera/domani	Neh o bee-zon-yo pair kwes-ta se-ra/do-ma-nee
Call back at 5 o'clock	*Torni alle cinque	Tor-nee al-leh cheen-kweh
We can do it by Tuesday	*Possiamo farlo per martedì	Pos-sya-mo far-lo pair mar-te-dee
It will take three days	*Ci vorranno tre giorni	Chee vor-ran-no treh jor-nee
This isn't mine	Questo non è mio	Kwes-to non eh mee-o
I've lost my ticket	Ho perso il mio biglietto	O pair-so eel mee-o beel-yet-to

HOUSEHOLD LAUNDRY

bath towel	il telo da bagno	te-lo da ban-yo
blanket	la coperta	ko-pair-ta
napkin	il tovagliolo	to-val-yo-lo
pillow case	la federa	fe-dair-a
sheet	il lenzuolo	lend-zwo-lo
table cloth	la tovaglia	to-val-ya
tea towel	il canovaccio per asciugare i piatti	ka-no-va-cho pair a-shoo-gar-eh ee pyat-tee
towel	l'asciugamano *m*	a-shoo-ga-ma-no

NEWSPAPERS, BOOKS AND WRITING MATERIALS

Do you sell English/ American newspapers?	**Vende giornali inglesi/americani?**	Ven-deh jor-na-lee een-gle-zee/a-me-ree-ka-nee
Can you get this magazine for me?	**Può ordinare questa rivista per me?**	Pwo or-dee-nar-eh kwes-ta ree-vees-ta pair meh
I want a map of the city	**Vorrei una mappa della città**	Vor-ray oon-a map-pa del-la cheet-ta
Do you have any English books?	**Vende libri inglesi?**	Ven-deh lee-bree een-gle-zee
Have you any novels by ...?	**Ha qualche romanzo di ...?**	A kwal-keh ro-man-zo dee ...
I want some picture postcards/plain postcards	**Vorrei delle cartoline illustrate/cartoline postali**	Vor-ray del-leh kar-to-lee-neh eel-loos-tra-teh/kar-to-lee-neh pos-ta-lee
Do you sell souvenirs/toys?	**Vende dei ricordi/ giocattoli?**	Ven-deh day ree-kor-dee/jo-kat-to-lee
ballpoint	**la biro**	bee-ro
calculator	**il calcolatore**	kal-ko-la-tor-eh
dictionary	**il dizionario**	deet-syo-nar-yo
drawing paper	**la carta da disegno**	kar-ta da dee-zen-yo
drawing pin	**la puntina da disegno**	poon-tee-na da dee-zen-yo
elastic band	**l'elastico** *m*	e-las-tee-ko

envelope	**la busta**	boos-ta
felt-tip pen	**il pennarello**	pen-na-rel-lo
glue	**la colla**	kol-la
greetings card	**il biglietto d'auguri**	beel-yet-to dow-goo-ree
guide book	**la guida**	gwee-da
ink	**l'inchiostro** *m*	een-kyos-tro
notebook	**il taccuino**	tak-kwee-no
paperclip	**il fermaglio**	fair-mal-yo
pen	**la penna**	pen-na
(coloured) pencil	**la matita (colorata)**	ma-tee-ta (ko-lo-ra-ta)
pencil sharpener	**il temperino**	tem-pe-ree-no
postcard	**la cartolina**	kar-to-lee-na
rubber	**la gomma**	gom-ma
sellotape	**il nastro adesivo**	nas-tro a-de-zee-vo
string	**lo spago**	spa-go
writing paper	**la carta da scrivere**	kar-ta da **skree**-vair-eh

OPTICIAN

I have broken my glasses. Can you repair them?	**Ho rotto gli occhiali. Me li può riparare?**	O rot-to lyee ok-kya-lee. Meh lee pwo ree-pa-rar-eh
Can you give me a new pair of glasses to the same prescription?	**Posso avere degli occhiali nuovi con la stessa prescrizione?**	Pos-so a-vair-eh del-yee ok-kya-lee nwo-vee kon la stes-sa pres-kreet-syo-neh

I have difficulty with reading/with long-distance vision	Mi risulta difficile leggere/vedere da lontano	Mee ree-zool-ta deef-fee-chee-leh led-jair-eh/ve-dair-eh da lon-ta-no
Please test my eyes	Vuole misurarmi la vista	Vwol-eh mee-zoo-rar-mee la vees-ta
I have lost one of my contact lenses	Ho perso una delle mie lenti a contatto	O pair-so oon-a del-leh mee-eh len-tee a kon-tat-to
I should like to have contact lenses	Desidero delle lenti a contatto	De-zee-dair-o del-leh len-tee a kon-tat-to
short-sighted	miope	myo-peh
long-sighted	presbite	prez-bee-teh

PHOTOGRAPHY

I want to buy a camera	Vorrei comprare una macchina fotografica	Vor-ray kom-prar-eh oon-a mak-kee-na fo-to-gra-fee-ka
Do you have a film/cartridge for this camera?	Ha una pellicola/un rotolo per questa macchina?	A oon-a pel-lee-ko-la/oon ro-to-lo pair kwes-ta mak-kee-na
A 100/400/1000 ASA film, please	Una pellicola di cento/quattrocento/mille ASA, per favore	Oon-a pel-lee-ko-la dee chen-to/kwat-tro-chen-to/meel-leh ASA, pair fa-vor-eh
What is the fastest film you have?	Qual'è la pellicola la più rapida che avete?	Kwal-eh la pel-lee-ko-la la pyoo ra-pee-da keh a-ve-teh

Film for slides/prints	Una pellicola per diapositive/stampe	Oon-a pel-lee-ko-la pair dee-a-po-zee-tee-veh/stam-peh
A 120 ... film, please	Una pellicola di cento venti ..., per favore	Oon-a pel-lee-ko-la dee chen-to ven-tee ..., pair fa-vor-eh
Give me a 35 mm colour film with 20/36 exposures	Mi dia una pellicola a colori di trentacinque millimetri con venti/trentasei esposizioni	Mee dee-a oon-a pel-lee-ko-la a ko-lor-ee dee tren-ta-cheen-kweh meel-lee-met-ree kon ven-tee/tren-ta-say es-poz-eet-syo-nee
I want a colour film/black and white film	Voglio una pellicola per fotografie a colori/in bianco e nero	Vol-yo oon-a pel-lee-ko-la pair fo-to-gra-fee-eh a ko-lor-eh/een byan-ko eh ne-ro
Would you fit the film in the camera for me, please?	Può aggiustarmi la pellicola nella macchina, per favore?	Pwo ad-joos-tar-mee la pel-lee-ko-la nel-la mak-kee-na, pair fa-vor-eh
Do you sell flash cubes?	Ha lampi al magnesio?	A lam-pee al mag-nez-yo
How much is it?	Quanto è?	Kwan-to eh
Does the price include processing?	Lo sviluppo è compreso nel prezzo?	Lo zvee-loop-po eh kom-pre-zo nel pret-so
I'd like this film developed and printed	Vorrei far sviluppare e stampare queste fotografie	Vor-ray far zvee-loop-par-eh eh stam-par-eh kwes-teh fo-to-gra-fee-eh

Can I have … prints/ enlargements of this negative?	Vorrei … stampe/ ingrandimenti di questo negativo	Vor-ray … stam-peh/ een-gran-dee-men-tee dee kwes-to ne-ga- tee-vo
When will they be ready?	Quando saranno pronte?	Kwan-do sa-ran-no pron-teh
Will they be done tomorrow?	Saranno pronte per domani?	Sa-ran-no pron-teh pair do-ma-nee
My camera's not working. Can you mend it?	La mia macchina non funziona. Può accomodarla?	La mee-a mak-kee-na non foont-syo-na. Pwo ak-ko-mo-dar-la
There is something wrong with the shutter/light meter	L'otturatore/il fotometro non funziona bene	Lot-too-ra-tor-eh/eel fo- to-met-ro non foont- syo-na be-neh
There is something wrong with the flash	La lampada flash non funziona bene	La lam-pa-da flash non foont-syo-na be-neh
The film is jammed	La pellicola non scorre	La pel-lee-ko-la non skor-reh
battery	la batteria	bat-te-ree-a
cine film	il filmino per cinecamera	feel-mee-no pair chee- ne-ka-mair-a
filter	il filtro	feel-tro
lens	la lente	len-teh
lens cap	il copriobiettivo	kop-ree-ob-yet-tee-vo
video camera	l'apparecchio video m	ap-pa-rek-kyo vee-de-o

RECORDS AND CASSETTES

Do you have any records/cassettes of local music?	Ha dei dischi/delle cassette di musica locale?	A day dees-kee/del-leh kas-set-teh dee moo-zee-ka lo-ka-leh
Are there any new records by ...?	Ci sono dei dischi nuovi di ...?	Chee so-no day dees-kee nwo-vee dee ...
Do you sell compact discs/video cassettes?	Ha dei compact discs/delle video-cassette?	A day compact discs/del-le vee-de-o-kas-set-teh

TOBACCONIST

Do you stock English/American cigarettes?	Vende sigarette inglesi/americane?	Ven-deh see-ga-ret-teh een-gle-zee/a-me-ree-ka-neh
What English cigarettes do you have?	Che sigarette inglesi ha?	Keh see-ga-ret-teh een-gle-zee a
A packet of ..., please	Un pacchetto di ..., per favore	Oon pak-ket-to dee ..., pair fa-vor-eh
I want some	Vorrei delle	Vor-ray del-le
filter-tip cigarettes	sigarette con filtro	see-ga-ret-teh kon feel-tro
cigarettes without filter	sigarette senza filtro	see-ga-ret-teh send-za feel-tro
menthol cigarettes	sigarette mentolate	see-ga-ret-teh men-to-la-teh

A box of matches, please	Una scatola di fiammiferi, per favore	Oon-a ska-to-la dee fyam-mee-fair-ee, pair fa-vor-eh
Do you have cigarette papers/pipe cleaners?	Ha cartine per sigarette/qualcosa per pulire la pipa?	A kar-tee-neh pair see-ga-ret-teh/kwal-ko-za pair poo-leer-eh la pee-pa
I want to buy a lighter	Vorrei comprare un accendisigaro	Vor-ray kom-prar-eh oon a-chen-dee-see-ga-ro
Do you sell lighter fuel/flints?	Vende benzina/pietrine per accendisigari?	Ven-deh bend-zee-na/pyet-ree-neh pair a-chen-dee-see-ga-ree
I want a gas refill for this lighter	Vorrei una bomboletta di gas per questo accendisigaro	Vor-ray oon-a bom-bo-let-ta dee gaz pair kwes-to a-chen-dee-see-ga-ro

REPAIRS

This is broken. Could you mend it?	Questo è rotto. Può ripararlo?	Kwes-to eh rot-to. Pwo ree-pa-rar-lo
I want these shoes soled (with leather)	Vorrei far risuolare queste scarpe (in cuoio)	Vor-ray far ree-swo-lar-eh kwes-teh skar-peh (een kwo-yo)
Can you heel these shoes (with rubber)?	Può mettere dei tacchi (di gomma) a queste scarpe?	Pwo met-tair-eh day tak-kee (dee gom-ma) a kwes-teh skar-peh
I have broken the heel. Can you put on a new one?	Il tacco è rotto. Può metterne uno nuovo?	Eel tak-ko eh rot-to. Pwo met-tair-neh oon-o nwo-vo

My watch is broken	Mi si è rotto l'orologio	Mee see eh rot-to lo-ro-lo-jo
My watch is always fast/slow	Il mio orologio va sempre avanti/indietro	Eel mee-o o-ro-lo-jo va sem-preh a-van-tee/een-dye-tro
Can you repair it?	Può ripararlo?	Pwo ree-pa-rar-lo
I've broken the strap	Mi si è rotto il cinturino	Mee see eh rot-to eel cheen-too-ree-no
The fastener/clip/chain is broken	La chiusura/la molletta/la catena è rotta	La kyoo-zoo-ra/la mol-let-ta/la ka-te-na rot-ta
The charm has come loose	Il ciondolo si è allentato	Eel chon-do-lo see eh al-len-ta-to
The stone is loose	La gemma non è ben fissa	La jem-ma non eh ben fees-sa
I have broken my glasses/the frame	Mi si sono rotti gli occhiali/mi si è rotta la montatura	Mee see so-no rot-tee lyee ok-kya-lee/mee see eh rot-ta la mon-ta-too-ra
How much will it cost?	Quanto mi verrà a costare?	Kwan-to mee ver-ra a kos-tar-eh
How much will a new one cost?	Quanto costerebbe nuovo?	Kwan-to kos-te-reb-beh nwo-vo
It can't be repaired	*Non si può riparare	Non see pwo ree-pa-rar-eh
You need a new one	*Deve comprarne uno nuovo	De-veh kom-prar-neh oon-o nwo-vo
Can you do it while I wait?	Può farlo mentre aspetto?	Pwo far-lo men-tre as-pet-to

When should I pick them up?	Quando devo venire a ritirarli?	Kwan-do de-vo ve-neer-eh a ree-teer-ar-lee

POST OFFICE

Where's the main post office?	Dov'è l'ufficio postale centrale?	Dov-eh loof-fee-cho pos-ta-leh chen-tra-leh
Where's the nearest post office?	Dov'è l'ufficio postale più vicino?	Dov-eh loof-fee-cho pos-ta-leh pyoo vee-chee-no
What time does the post office open/close?	A che ora apre/chiude l'ufficio postale?	A keh or-a a-preh/kyoo-deh loof-fee-cho pos-ta-leh
Where's the post box?	Dov'è una buca per le lettere?	Dov-eh oon-a boo-ka pair le let-tair-eh
Which counter do I go to for	Qual'è lo sportello per	Kwal-eh lo spor-tel-lo pair
telegrams	i telegrammi	ee te-le-gram-mee
stamps	i francobolli	ee fran-ko-bol-lee
money orders?	mandare vaglia postali?	man-dar-eh val-ya pos-ta-lee

LETTERS AND TELEGRAMS

How much is a letter to England?	Che francobolli ci vuole per l'Inghilterra?	Keh fran-ko-bol-lee chee vwo-leh pair leen-geel-ter-ra
How much is an airmail letter to the USA?	Quanto costa una lettera per via aerea per gli Stati Uniti?	Kwan-to kos-ta oon-a let-tair-a pair vee-a a-air-e-a pair lyee sta-tee oo-nee-tee
It's inland	Per l'interno	Pair leen-tair-no
Give me three ... lire stamps, please	Vorrei tre francobolli da ... lire	Vor-ray treh fran-ko-bol-lee da ... leer-eh
I want to send this letter express	Voglio mandare questa lettera espresso	Vol-yo man-dar-eh kwes-ta let-tair-a es-pres-so
I want to register this letter	Voglio mandare questa lettera raccomandata	Vol-yo man-dar-eh kwes-ta let-tair-a rak-ko-man-da-ta
Two airmail forms, please	Due moduli per posta aerea, per favore	Doo-eh mo-doo-lee pair pos-ta a-air-e-a, pair fa-vor-eh
Where is the poste restante section?	Dov'è lo sportello del Fermo Posta?	Dov-eh lo spor-tel-lo del fair-mo pos-ta
Are there any letters for me?	Vi sono lettere per me?	Vee so-no let-tair-eh pair me
What is your name?	*Il suo nome, per favore	Eel soo-o no-meh, pair fa-vor-eh
Have you any means of identification?	*Ha qualche documento d'identità?	A kwal-keh do-koo-men-to dee-den-tee-ta

I want to send a parcel	**Vorrei spedire un pacco**	Vor-ray spe-deer-eh oon pak-ko
I want to send a telegram/a reply-paid telegram/an overnight telegram	**Voglio mandare un telegramma/un telegramma con risposta pagata/un telegramma ELT**	Vol-yo man-dar-eh oon te-le-gram-ma/oon te-le-gram-ma kon rees-pos-ta pa-ga-ta/oon te-le-gram-ma eh el-le teh
How much does it cost per word?	**Quanto costa a parola?**	Kwan-to kos-ta a pa-ro-la
Write the message here and your own name and address	***Scriva qui il testo con il suo nome e indirizzo**	Skree-va kwee eel tes-to kon eel soo-o no-meh eh een-dee-reet-so
Can I send a telex?	**Potrei mandare un telex?**	Pot-ray man-dar-eh oon telex

TELEPHONING

Where's the nearest phone box?	**Dov'è la cabina telefonica la più vicina?**	Dov-eh la ka-bee-na te-le-fo-nee-ka la pyoo vee-chee-na
I want to make a phone call	**Voglio fare una telefonata**	Vol-yo far-eh oon-a te-le-fo-na-ta
May I use your phone?	**Posso usare questo telefono?**	Pos-so oo-zar-eh kwes-to te-le-fo-no
Do you have a telephone directory for ...?	**Ha l'elenco telefonico di ...?**	A le-len-ko te-le-fo-nee-ko dee ...
Please give me ... tokens	**Può darmi ... gettoni, per favore**	Pwo dar-mee ... jet-to-nee, pair fa-vor-eh

Please get me Milan ...	Desidero chiamare Milano ...	De-zee-dair-o kya-mar-eh mee-la-no ...
I want to telephone England	Voglio telefonare l'Inghilterra	Vol-yo te-le-fo-nar-eh leen-geel-ter-ra
What do I dial to get the international operator?	Qual'è il numero del centralino internazionale?	Kwal-eh eel noo-mair-o del chen-tra-lee-no een-tair-nat-syo-na-leh
What is the code for ...?	Qual'è il prefisso per ...?	Kwal-eh eel pre-fees-so pair ...
I want to make a personal call	Voglio fare una chiamata personale	Vol-yo far-eh oon-a kya-ma-ta pair-so-na-leh
Could you tell me how much it costs?	Può dirmi quanto costa?	Pwo deer-mee kwan-to kos-ta
I want to reverse the charges/call collect	Vorrei fare una rovesciata	Vor-ray far-eh oo-na ro-ve-sha-ta
We were cut off. Can you reconnect me?	Ci hanno interrotto. Può rimettermi in linea?	Chee han-no een-tair-rot-to. Pwo ree-met-tair-mee een lee-ne-a
Hallo	Pronto	Pron-to
I want extension ...	Voglio parlare con l'interno ...	Vol-yo par-lar-eh kon leen-tair-no ...
May I speak to ...	Posso parlare con ...	Pos-so par-lar-eh kon ...
Who's speaking?	Chi parla?	Kee par-la
Hold the line, please	*Rimanga in linea, prego	Ree-man-ga een lee-ne-a, pre-go
Put the receiver down	*Abbassi il ricevitore	Ab-bas-see eel ree-che-vee-tor-eh
He's not here	*Non è qui	Non eh kwee
He's at ...	*E a ...	Eh a ...

When will he be back?	Quando sarà di ritorno?	Kwan-do sa-ra dee ree-tor-no
Will you take a message?	Posso lasciare un messaggio?	Pos-so la-shar-eh oon mes-sad-jo
Tell him that ... phoned	Gli dica che gli ha telefonato ...	Lyee dee-ka keh lyee a te-le-fo-na-to ...
Please ask him to phone me	Per favore, gli dica di telefonarmi	Pair fa-vor-eh, lyee dee-ka dee te-le-fo-nar-mee
What's your number?	*Qual'è il suo numero?	Kwal-eh eel soo-o noo-mair-o
My number is ...	Il mio numero è ...	Eel mee-o noo-mair-o eh ...
I can't hear you	Non sento	Non sen-to
The number is out of order	*Il numero è guasto	Eel noo-mair-o eh gwas-to
The line is engaged	*La linea è occupata	La lee-ne-a eh ok-koo-pa-ta
There's no reply	*Non c'è risposta	Non cheh rees-pos-ta
You have the wrong number	*Il suo numero è sbagliato	Eel soo-o noo-mair-o eh zbal-ya-to

SIGHTSEEING[1]

Where is the tourist office?	Dov'è l'ufficio turistico?	Dov-eh loof-fee-cho too-rees-tee-ko
What should we see here?	Cosa c'è di interessante da vedere qui?	Ko-za cheh dee een-tair-es-san-teh da ve-dair-eh kwee
Is there a map/plan of the places to visit?	C'è una mappa/una pianta con le cose da vedere?	Cheh oon-a map-pa/ oon-a pyan-ta kon leh ko-zeh da ve-dair-eh
I want a good guidebook	Vorrei una buona guida	Vor-ray oon-a bwo-na gwee-da
Is there a good sightseeing tour?	C'è un bel giro turistico?	Cheh oon bel jee-ro too-rees-tee-ko
Does the coach stop at ... hotel?	Si ferma l'autobus all'albergo ...?	See fair-ma low-to-bus al-lal-bair-go ...
Is there an excursion to ...?	C'è una escursione per ...?	Cheh oon-a es-koor-syo-neh pair ...

1. See also TRAVEL (p. 16) and DIRECTIONS (p. 34).

How long does the tour take?	Quanto tempo dura il giro?	Kwan-to tem-po doo-ra eel jee-ro
Are there guided tours of the museum?	Ci sono giri organizzati del museo?	Chee so-no jee-ree or-ga-neet-sa-tee del moo-se-o
Does the guide speak English?	Parla inglese la guida?	Par-la een-gle-zeh la gwee-da
We don't need a guide	Non abbiamo bisogno di una guida	Non ab-bya-mo bee-zon-yo dee oon-a gwee-da
I would prefer to go round alone; is that all right?	Preferisco girare da solo; va bene?	Pre-fe-rees-ko jee-rar-eh da so-lo; va be-neh
How much does the tour cost?	Quanto costa il giro?	Kwan-to kos-ta eel jee-ro
Are all admission fees included?	Sono compresi tutti gli ingressi?	So-no kom-pre-zee toot-tee lyee een-gres-see
Does it include lunch?	E compreso il pranzo?	Eh kom-pre-zo eel pran-zo

MUSEUMS AND ART GALLERIES

When does the museum open/close?	A che ora apre/chiude il museo?	A keh or-a ap-reh/kyoo-deh eel moo-se-o
Is it open every day?	E aperto ogni giorno?	Eh a-pair-to on-yee jor-no
The gallery is closed on Mondays	*La galleria è chiusa il lunedì	La gal-lair-ee-a eh kyoo-za eel loo-ne-dee

How much does it cost?	Quanto costa l'ingresso?	Kwan-to kos-ta leen-gres-so
Are there reductions for	Ci sono riduzioni per	Chee so-no ree-doot-syo-nee pair
children?	ragazzi?	ra-gat-see
students?	studenti?	stoo-den-tee
the elderly?	gli anziani?	lyee an-zya-nee
Are admission fees lower on any special day?	Ci sono prezzi ridotti certi giorni?	Chee so-no pret-see ree-dot-tee chair-tee jor-nee
Admission free	*Ingresso libero	Een-gres-so lee-bair-o
Have you got a ticket?	*Ha il biglietto?	A eel beel-yet-to
Where do I buy a ticket?	Dove si comprano i biglietti?	Do-veh see kom-pra-no ee beel-yet-tee
Please leave your bag in the cloakroom	*Lasci la cartella nel guardaroba, per favore	La-shee la kar-tel-la nel gwar-da-ro-ba, pair fa-vor-eh
It's over there	*E da quella parte	Eh da kwel-la par-teh
Where is the ... collection/exhibition?	Dov'è la collezione/ l'esposizione ...?	Dov-eh la kol-let-syo-neh/les-po-zeet-syo-neh ...
Can I take photographs?	Si può fare delle fotografie?	See pwo far-eh del-leh fo-to-gra-fee-eh
Can I use a tripod?	Posso servirmi del treppiede?	Pos-so sair-veer-mee del trep-pye-deh
Photographs are not allowed	*Vietato fotografare	Vye-ta-to fo-to-gra-far-eh
I want to buy a catalogue	Vorrei comprare un catalogo	Vor-ray kom-prar-eh oon ka-ta-lo-go

Will you make photocopies?	Si fa le fotocopie?	See fa leh fo-to-kop-yeh
Could you make me a transparency of this painting?	Vuole farmi una diapositiva di questa pittura?	Vwol-eh far-mee oon-a dya-po-zee-tee-va dee kwes-ta peet-too-ra
How long will it take?	Quando sarà pronta?	Kwan-do sa-ra pron-ta

HISTORICAL SITES

We want to visit ...; can we get there by car?	Vogliamo visitare ...; ci si arriva in macchina?	Vol-ya-mo vee-zee-tar-eh ...; chee see ar-ree-va-een mak-kee-na
Is it far to walk?	E lungo a piedi?	Eh loon-go a pye-dee
Is it an easy walk?	E facile arrivarci a piedi?	Eh fa-chee-leh ar-ree-var-chee a pye-dee
Is there access for wheelchairs?	Ci si può entrare con le sedie a rotelle?	Chee see pwo en-trar-eh kon le se-dyeh a ro-tel-leh
Is it far to	E distante	Eh dees-tan-teh
the aqueduct?	l'acquedotto?	lak-weh-dot-to
the castle?	il castello?	eel kas-tel-lo
the fort?	la fortezza?	la for-tet-sa
the fortifications?	le fortificazioni?	leh for-tee-fee-cat-syo-nee
the fountain?	la fontana?	la fon-ta-na
the gate?	il cancello?	eel kan-chel-lo
the walls?	le mura?	leh moo-ra
When was it built?	Quando fu costruito?	Kwan-do foo kost-rwee-to

Who built it?	Chi lo costruì?	Kee lo kost-**rwee**
Where is the old part of the city?	Dov'è il centro storico?	Dov-eh eel chen-tro sto-ree-ko
What is this building?	Cos'è quest' edificio?	Koz-eh kwes-te-dee-fee-cho
Where is	Dov'è	Dov-eh
the house of ...?	la casa di ...?	la ka-za dee ...
the church of ...?	la chiesa di ...?	la kye-za dee ...
the cemetery of ...?	il cimitero di ...?	eel chee-mee-te-ro dee ...

GARDENS, PARKS AND ZOOS

Where is the botanical garden/zoo?	Dov'è il giardino botanico/lo zoo?	Dov-eh eel jar-dee-no bo-ta-nee-ko/lo zoo
How do I get to the park?	Qual'è la strada per il parco?	Kwal-eh la stra-da pair eel par-ko
Can we walk there?	Si può fare una passeggiata lì?	See pwo far-eh oon-a pas-sed-ja-ta lee
Can we drive through the park?	Si può girare a macchina nel parco?	See pwo jee-rar-eh a mak-kee-na nel par-ko
Are the gardens open to the public?	Il giardino è aperto al pubblico?	Eel jar-dee-no eh a-pair-to al poob-blee-ko
What time do the gardens close?	A che ora chiude il giardino?	A keh or-a kyoo-deh eel jar-dee-no
Is there a plan of the gardens?	C'è una pianta dei giardini?	Cheh oon-a pyan-ta day jar-dee-nee

| Who designed the gardens? | Chi creò i giardini? | Kee kre-o ee jar-dee-nee |
| Where is the tropical plant house/lake? | Dov'è la serra delle piante tropicali/il lago? | Dov-eh la ser-ra del-leh pyan-teh tro-pee-ka-lee/eel la-go |

EXPLORING

I'd like to walk around the old town	Vorrei fare un giro per il centro storico	Vor-ray far-eh oon jee-ro pair eel chen-tro sto-ree-ko
Is there a good street plan showing the buildings?	C'è una bella pianta con gli edifici indicati?	Cheh oon-a bel-la pyan-ta kon lyee e-dee-fee-chee een-dee-ka-tee
We want to visit	Vogliamo visitare	Vol-ya-mo vee-zee-tar-eh
the cathedral	la cattedrale	la kat-ted-ra-leh
the fortress	la fortezza	la for-tet-sa
the library	la biblioteca	la beeb-lyo-te-ka
the monastery	il monastero	eel mo-nas-te-ro
the palace	il palazzo	eel pa-lat-so
the ruins	le rovine	leh ro-vee-neh
May we walk around the walls/go up the tower?	Si può fare il giro delle mura a piedi/salire la torre?	See pwo far-eh eel jee-ro del-leh moo-ra a pye-dee/sa-leer-eh la tor-reh

| Where is the antiques market/flea market? | Dov'è il mercato delle antichità/il mercato delle pulci? | Dov-eh eel mair-ka-to del-leh an-tee-kee-ta/ eel mair-ka-to del-leh pool-chee |

GOING TO CHURCH

Is there	C'è	Cheh
a Catholic church?	una chiesa cattolica?	oon-a kye-za kat-to-lee-ka
a Protestant church?	una chiesa protestante?	oon-a kye-za pro-tes-tan-teh
a mosque?	una moschea?	oon-a mos-ke-a
a synagogue?	una sinagoga?	oon-a see-na-go-ga
What time is mass/the service?	A che ora è la messa/la funzione?	A cheh or-a eh la mes-sa/la foont-syo-neh
I'd like to look round the church	Vorrei fare il giro della chiesa	Vor-ray far-eh eel jee-ro del-la kye-za
When was the church built?	Quando fu costruita la chiesa?	Kwan-do foo kost-rwee-ta la kye-za
Should women cover their heads?	Le donne dovrebbero mettersi qualcosa in testa?	Leh don-neh dov-reb-be-ro met-tair-see kwal-ko-za een tes-ta

ENTERTAINMENT

Is there an entertainment guide?	C'è una guida degli spettacoli?	Cheh oon-a gwee-da del-yee spet-ta-ko-lee
What's on at the theatre/cinema?	Cosa danno al teatro/al cinema?	Ko-za dan-no al te-at-ro/al **chee**-ne-ma
Is there a concert on this evening?	C'è un concerto stasera?	Cheh oon kon-chair-to sta-se-ra
Can you recommend	Può consigliarmi	Pwo kon-seel-yar-mee
a good ballet?	un bel balletto?	oon bel bal-let-to
a good film?	un bel film?	oon bel film
a good musical?	un bell'operetta?	oon bel-lo-pe-ret-ta
Who is directing/conducting?	Chi è il direttore/il maestro?	Kee eh eel dee-ret-tor-eh/eel ma-es-tro
Who is singing?	Chi canta?	Kee kan-ta
I want two seats for tonight/the matinée tomorrow	Due posti per stasera/per la matinée di domani	Doo-eh pos-tee pair sta-se-ra/pair la ma-tee-neh dee do-ma-nee

I want to book seats for Thursday	Vorrei riservare dei posti per giovedì	Vor-ray ree-zair-var-eh day pos-tee pair jo-ve-dee
Is the matinée sold out?	E tutto esaurito per la matinée?	Eh toot-to e-zow-ree-to pair la ma-tee-neh
I'd like seats in	Desidero	De-zee-dair-o
the stalls	poltrone	pol-tro-neh
the circle	posti in galleria	pos-tee een gal-lair-ee-a
the gallery	posti in loggione	pos-tee een lod-jo-neh
The cheapest seats please	I posti meno cari, per favore	Ee pos-tee me-no ka-ree, pair fa-vor-eh
We've sold out (for this performance)	*Tutto esaurito (per questa rappresentazione)	Toot-to ez-ow-ree-to (pair kwes-ta rap-pre-zen-tat-syo-neh)
Where are these seats?	Dove si trovano questi posti?	Do-veh see tro-va-no kwes-tee pos-tee
What time does the performance start?	A che ora comincia lo spettacolo?	A keh or-a ko-meen-cha lo spet-ta-ko-lo
What time does it end?	A che ora finisce?	A keh or-a fee-nee-sheh
Where is the cloakroom?	Dov'è il guardaroba?	Dov-eh eel gwar-da-ro-ba
This is your seat	*Ecco il suo posto	Ek-ko eel soo-o pos-to
A programme, please	Un programma, per favore	Oon pro-gram-ma, pair fa-vor-eh
Where are the best nightclubs?	Dove sono i migliori locali notturni?	Do-veh so-no ee meel-yor-ee lo-ka-lee not-toor-nee

What time is the floorshow/the cabaret?	A che ora comincia lo spettacolo/il cabaret?	A keh or-a ko-meen-cha lo spet-ta-ko-lo/eel ka-bar-eh
Where can we go dancing?	Dove si può andare a ballare?	Do-veh see pwo an-dar-eh a bal-lar-eh
Where is the best disco?	Dov'è la discoteca migliore?	Dov-eh la dees-ko-te-ka meel-yor-eh
Would you like to dance?	Vuole ballare?	Vwo-leh bal-lar-eh
Can you recommend a good show?	Può raccomandarmi un buon spettacolo?	Pwo rak-ko-man-dar-mee oon bwon spet-ta-ko-lo

SPORTS & GAMES

Where is the nearest tennis court/golf course?	Dov'è il più vicino campo da tennis/campo di golf?	Dov-eh eel pyoo vee-chee-no kampo da tennis/kampo dee golf
What is the charge per	Quanto si paga	Kwan-to see pa-ga
game?	per partita?	pair par-tee-ta
hour?	all'ora?	al-lor-a
day?	a giornata?	a jor-na-ta
Is it a club?	E un'associazione?	Eh oon-as-so-chat-syo-neh
Do I need temporary membership?	Ci vuole l'iscrizione provvisorio?	Chee vwo-leh lees-kreet-syo-neh prov-vee-zor-yo
Where can we go swimming/fishing?	Dove si può andare per far il bagno/per pescare?	Do-veh see pwo an-dar-eh pair far-eh eel ban-yo/pair pes-kar-eh
Can I hire	Si può noleggiare	See pwo no-led-jar-eh

a racket?	una racchetta?	oon-a rak-ket-ta
clubs?	mazze da golf?	mat-seh da golf
fishing tackle?	arnesi da pesca?	ar-ne-zee da pes-ka
Do I need a permit?	Occorre un permesso speciale?	Ok-kor-reh oon pair-mes-so spe-cha-leh
Where do I get a permit?	Chi rilascia questo permesso?	Kee ree-la-sha kwes-to pair-mes-so
Can we swim in the river?	Si può fare il bagno nel fiume?	See pwo far-eh eel ban-yo nel fyoo-meh
Is there an open-air/indoor swimming pool?	C'è una piscina all'aperto/coperta?	Cheh oon-a pee-shee-na al-la-pair-to/ko-pair-ta
Is it heated?	E riscaldata?	Eh rees-kal-da-ta
Is there a skating rink?	C'è una pista per pattinaggio?	Cheh oon-a pees-ta pair pat-tee-nad-jo
Can I hire skates/skiing equipment?	Posso noleggiare i pattini/l'attrezzatura da sci?	Pos-so no-led-jar-eh ee pat-tee-nee/lat-tret-sa-too-ra da shee
I've never skied before	Non ho mai sciato	Non o ma-ee shee-a-to
Are there ski runs for beginners/average skiers?	Ci sono delle piste per principianti/sciatori medii?	Chee so-no del-leh pees-teh pair preen-chee-pyan-tee/shee-a-tor-ee me-dee
I'd like to go cross-country skiing	Vorrei fare lo sci di fondo	Vor-ray far-eh lo shee dee fon-do
Are there ski lifts?	Vi sono sciovie?	Vee so-no sho-vee-eh
Can I take lessons here?	Danno anche lezioni?	Dan-no an-keh let-syo-nee

Where is the stadium?	Dov'è lo stadio?	Dov-**eh** lo sta-dyo
Are there any seats left in the grandstand?	Ci sono ancora posti in tribuna?	Chee so-no an-**kor**-a pos-tee een tree-**boo**-na
Can you get us tickets?	Può procurarci dei biglietti?	Pwo pro-koo-**rar**-chee day beel-**yet**-tee
How much are the cheapest seats?	Quanto costano i posti meno cari?	Kwan-to **kos**-ta-no ee pos-tee **me**-no ka-ree
How much are they?	Quanto costano?	Kwan-to **kos**-ta-no
Which are the cheapest seats?	Quali sono i posti meno costosi?	Kwal-ee so-no ee pos-tee **me**-no kos-**to**-zee
Are the seats in the sun/shade?	Questi posti sono al sole/all'ombra?	Kwes-tee pos-tee so-no al **so**-leh/al-**lom**-bra
We want to go to a football match/the tennis tournament	Vogliamo andare ad una partita di calcio/al torneo di tennis	Vol-**ya**-mo an-**dar**-eh ad oon-a par-**tee**-ta dee **kal**-cho/al tor-**ne**-o dee tennis
Who's playing?	Chi gioca?	Kee **jo**-ka
When does it start?	Quando comincia?	Kwan-do ko-meen-cha
What is the score?	Qual'è il punteggio?	Kwal-**eh** eel poon-**ted**-jo
Who's winning?	Chi vince?	Kee **veen**-cheh
I'd like to ride	Vorrei andare a cavallo	Vor-**ray** an-**dar**-eh a ka-**val**-lo
Is there a riding stable nearby?	C'è una scuderia qui vicino?	Cheh oon-a skoo-de-**ree**-a kwee vee-**chee**-no
Do you give lessons?	Si da lezioni?	See da let-**syo**-nee
I am an inexperienced rider	Non ho molta esperienza	Non o **mol**-ta es-per-**yen**-sa
I am a good rider	Cavalco bene	Ka-**val**-ko **be**-neh

Where's the racecourse?	Dove sono le corse di cavalli?	Do-veh so-no le kor-seh dee ka-val-lee
When's the next meeting?	Quando sarà il prossimo incontro?	Kwan-do sa-ra eel pros-see-mo een-kon-tro
Which is the favourite?	Chi è il favorito?	Kee eh eel fa-vo-ree-to
Who's the jockey?	Chi è il fantino?	Kee eh eel fan-tee-no
What are the odds?	Qual'è la posta?	Kwal-eh la pos-ta
Do you play cards?	Gioca a carte?	Jo-ka a kar-teh
Would you like a game of chess?	Ha voglia di fare una partita a scacchi?	A vol-ya dee far-eh oon-a par-tee-ta a skak-kee
I'll give you a game of checkers if you like	Posso fare una partita a dama, se vuole	Pos-so far-eh oon-a par-tee-ta a da-ma, seh vwo-leh
I'd like to try waterskiing	Vorrei fare dello sci nautico	Vor-ray far-eh del-lo shee now-tee-ko
I haven't waterskied before	Non ho mai fatto lo sci nautico	Non o ma-ee fat-to lo shee now-tee-ko
Can I rent/borrow a wetsuit?	Posso noleggiare/ imprestare una muta subacquea?	Pos-so no-led-jar-eh/ eem-pres-tar-eh oon-a moo-ta soob-ak-we-a
Should I wear a life jacket?	Dovrei mettermi un giubbotto di salvataggio?	Dov-ray met-tair-mee oon joob-bot-to dee sal-va-tad-jo
Can I hire	Si può noleggiare	See pwo no-led-jar-eh
a rowing boat?	una barca a remi?	oon-a bar-ka a re-mee
a motor boat?	una barca a motore?	oon-a bar-ka a mo-tor-eh
a wind surfer?	un windsurf?	oon windsurf

a surf board?	un sandolino?	oon san-do-lee-no
Is there a map of the river?	C'è una mappa del fiume?	Cheh oon-a map-pa del fyoo-meh
Are there many locks to pass?	Ci sono tante serrande da chiusa?	Chee so-no tan-teh ser-ran-deh da kyoo-za
Can we get fuel here?	Si può comprare il carburante qui?	See pwo kom-prar-eh eel kar-boo-ran-teh kwee

ON THE BEACH[1]

Where are the best beaches?	Dove sono le migliori spiagge?	Do-veh so-no leh meel-yor-ee spyad-jeh
Is there a quiet beach near here?	C'è una spiaggia tranquilla qui vicino?	Cheh oon-a spyad-ja tran-kweel-la kwee vee-chee-no
Can we walk or is it too far?	Ci si può andare a piedi o è troppo lontana?	Chee see pwo an-dar-eh a pye-dee o eh trop-po lon-ta-na
Is there a bus to the beach?	C'è un autobus per andare alla spiaggia?	Cheh oon ow-to-bus pair an-dar-eh al-la spyad-ja
Is the beach sand or shingle?	La spiaggia è sabbia o ghiaia?	La spyad-ja eh sab-bya o gya-ya
Is it dangerous to bathe here?	E pericoloso fare bagni qui?	Eh pair-ee-ko-lo-zo far-eh ban-yee kwee

1. See also SPORTS & GAMES (163).

it safe for swimming?	Si può nuotare senza pericolo?	See pwo nwo-tar-eh sen-za pe-ree-ko-lo
there a lifeguard?	C'è un bagnino?	Cheh oon ban-yee-no
it safe for children?	E sicura questa spiaggia per i ragazzi?	Eh see-koo-ra kwes-ta spyad-ja pair ee ra-gat-see
diving dangerous from these rocks?	E pericoloso tuffarsi da questi scogli?	Eh pair-ee-ko-lo-zo toof-far-see da kwes-tee skol-yee
athing prohibited	*Vietato fare bagni	Vye-ta-to far-eh ban-yee
iving prohibited	*Vietato tuffarsi	Vye-ta-to toof-far-see
's dangerous	*E pericoloso	Eh pair-ee-ko-lo-zo
hat time is high/low tide?	A che ora è la bassa/l'alta marea?	A keh or-a eh la bas-sa/lal-ta ma-re-a
here's a strong current here	*C'è una forte corrente qui	Cheh oon-a for-teh kor-ren-teh kwee
re you a strong swimmer?	*Nuota bene lei?	Nwo-ta be-neh lay
it deep?	E profonda l'acqua qui?	Eh pro-fon-da lak-wa kwee
low's the water? Cold?	Com'è l'acqua? Fredda?	Kom-eh lak-wa. Fred-da
's warm	E tiepida	Eh tye-pee-da
an one swim in the lake/river?	Si può fare un bagno nel lago/nel fiume?	See pwo far-eh oon ban-yo nel la-go/nel fyoo-meh
there an indoor/ outdoor swimming pool?	C'è una piscina coperta/all'aperto?	Cheh oon-a pee-shee-na ko-pair-ta/al-la-pair-to

Is is salt or fresh water?	E acqua salata o dolce?	Eh ak-wa sa-la-ta o dol-cheh
Are there showers?	Ci sono docce?	Chee so-no do-cheh
I want a beach hut for	Vorrei una cabina per	Vor-ray oon-a ka-bee-n pair
the day	oggi soltanto	od-jee sol-tan-to
the morning	stamani	sta-ma-nee
two hours	due ore	doo-eh or-eh
I want to hire a deckchair/sunshade	Vorrei noleggiare una sedia a sdraio/un ombrellone	Vor-ray no-led-jar-eh oon-a se-dya a zdra-yo/oon om-brel-lo-nel
Where can I buy	Dove posso comprare	Do-veh pos-so kom-prar-eh
a snorkel?	un respiratore a tubo?	oon res-pee-ra-tor-eh too-bo
flippers?	delle pinne?	del-leh peen-neh
a bucket and spade?	un secchiello ed una paletta?	oon sek-kyel-lo ed oon-a pa-let-ta
Where's the harbour?	Dov'è il porto?	Dov-eh eel por-to
Can we go out in a fishing boat?	Si può andare in un battello da pesca?	See pwo an-dar-eh een oon bat-tel-lo da pes-
We want to go fishing	Vorremmo andare a pescare	Vor-rem-mo an-dar-eh pes-kar-eh
Is there any underwater fishing?	Si può fare pesca subacquea?	See pwo far-eh pes-ka soob-ak-we-a
Can I hire a boat?	Si può noleggiare una barca?	See pwo no-led-jar-eh oon-a bar-ka
What does it cost by the hour?	Quanto costa all'ora?	Kwan-to kos-ta al-lor-a

ball	il pallone	pal-lo-neh
bat	il bastone	bas-to-neh
boat	la barca	bar-ka
sailing	a vela	a ve-la
motor	a motore	a mo-tor-eh
rowing	a remi	a re-mee
crab	il granchio	gran-kyo
first aid	il pronto soccorso	pron-to sok-kor-so
jelly fish	la medusa	me-doo-za
lifebelt/buoy	la cintura/il gavitello di salvataggio	cheen-too-ra/ga-vee-tel-lo dee sal-va-tad-jo
lighthouse	il faro	fa-ro
rock	la roccia	ro-cha
sand	la sabbia	sab-bya
sandcastle	il castello di sabbia	kas-tel-lo dee sab-bya
sun	il sole	so-leh
sunglasses	gli occhiali da sole	ok-kya-lee da so-leh
swimsuit/swimming trunks	il costume da bagno	kos-too-meh da ban-yo
towel	l'asciugamano m	a-shoo-ga-ma-no
waves	le onde	on-deh

IN THE COUNTRY[1]

Is there a scenic route to …?	C'è una strada panoramica a …?	Cheh oon-a stra-da pa-no-ra-mee-ka a …
Can you give me a lift to …?	Può darmi un passaggio a …?	Pwo dar-mee oon passad-jo a …
Is there a footpath to …?	C'è un sentiero per …?	Cheh oon sen-tyair-o pair …
Is it possible to go across country?	Ci si può arrivare per i campi?	Chee see pwo ar-ree-var-eh pair ee kam-pee
Is there a shortcut?	C'è una scorciatoia?	Cheh oon-a skor-cha-toy-a
Is this a public footpath?	E questo un sentiero autorizzato?	Eh kwes-to oon sen-tyair-o ow-to-reet-sa-to
Is there a bridge across the stream?	C'è un ponte sul torrente?	Cheh oon pon-teh sool tor-ren-teh
Can we walk?	Ci si arriva a piedi?	Chee see ar-ree-va a pye-dee

1. See also DIRECTIONS (p. 34).

THE WEATHER

Is it usually as hot as this?	Fa sempre caldo così?	Fa sem-preh kal-do ko-zee
It's going to be hot/cold today	Farà caldo/freddo oggi	Fa-ra kal-do/fred-do od-jee
The mist will clear later	La nebbia scomparirà più tardi	La neb-bya skom-pa-ree-ra pyoo tar-dee
Will it be fine tomorrow?	Farà bel tempo domani?	Fa-ra bel tem-po do-ma-nee
What is the weather forecast?	Come sono le previsioni del tempo?	Ko-meh so-no le pre-vee-zyo-nee del tem-po
What lovely/awful weather	Che bel/brutto tempo	Keh bel/broot-to tem-po
Do you think it will rain/snow?	Pensa che pioverà/nevicherà?	Pen-sa keh pyo-vair-a/ne-vee-kair-a

TRAVELLING
WITH CHILDREN

Can you put a child's bed/cot in our room?	Può mettere un letto da bambino/una culla nella nostra stanza?	Pwo met-tair-eh oon let-to da bam-bee-no/oon-a kool-la nel-la nos-tra stan-za
Can you give us adjoining rooms?	Può darci stanze contigue?	Pwo dar-chee stan-zeh kon-tee-gweh
Does the hotel have a baby-sitting service?	C'è un servizio baby-sitting nell'albergo?	Cheh oon sair-veet-syo baby-sitting nel-lal-bair-go
Can you find me a baby-sitter?	Può trovarmi un baby-sitter?	Pwo tro-var-mee oon baby-sitter
We shall be out for a couple of hours	Usciamo per un paio d'ore	Oo-sha-mo pair oon pa-yo dor-eh
We shall be back at ...	Torneremo alle ...	Tor-ne-re-mo al-leh ...
Is there a children's menu?	C'è un menù per bambini?	Cheh oon me-noo pair bam-bee-nee

Do you have half portions for children?	Si fa metà porzioni per bambini?	See fa me-ta port-syo-nee pair bam-bee-nee
Have you got a high chair?	Ha un seggiolone?	A oon sed-jo-lo-neh
Are there any organized activities for children?	Ci sono delle attività organizzate per bambini?	Chee so-no del-le at-tee-vee-ta or-ga-neet-sa-teh pair bam-bee-nee
Is there	C'è	Cheh
a paddling pool?	una piscina per bambini?	oon-a pee-shee-na pair bam-bee-nee
a playground?	un campo di ricreazione?	oon kam-po dee ree-kre-at-syo-neh
a games room?	una stanza dei giochi?	oon-a stan-za day jo-kee
Is there	C'è	Cheh
an amusement park	un parco dei divertimenti	oon par-ko day dee-vair-tee-men-tee
a zoo	uno zoo	oon-o zoo
a toyshop nearby?	un negozio di giocattoli qui vicino?	oon ne-got-syo dee jo-kat-to-lee kwee vee-chee-no
I'd like	Vorrei	Vor-ray
a beach ball	un pallone da spiaggia	oon pal-lone da spyad-ja
a bucket and spade	un secchiello ed una paletta	oon sek-kyel-lo ed oon-a pa-let-ta
a doll	una bambola	oon-a bam-bo-la
some flippers	delle pinne	del-leh peen-neh

some goggles	degli occhiali di protezione	del-yee ok-kya-lee dee pro-tet-syo-neh
some playing cards	delle carte da gioco	del-leh kar-teh da jo-ko
some roller skates	dei pattini a rotelle	day pat-tee-nee a ro-tel-leh
a snorkel	un respiratore a tubo	oon res-pee-ra-tor-eh a too-bo
Where can I feed/ change my baby?	Dove posso allattare il bimbo/cambiare il pannolino al bimbo?	Do-veh pos-so al-lat-tar-eh eel beem-bo/kam-byar-eh eel pan-no-lee-no al beem-bo
Can you heat this bottle for me?	Mi potrebbe riscaldare questo poppatoio?	Mee pot-reb-beh rees-kal-dar-eh kwes-to pop-pa-to-yo
I want	Voglio	Vol-yo
some disposable nappies	dei pannolini eliminabile dopo l'uso	day pan-no-lee-nee e-lee-mee-na-bee-leh do-po loo-zo
a feeding bottle	un poppatoio	oon pop-pa-to-yo
some baby food	del cibo per bambini	del chee-bo pair bam-bee-nee
My daughter suffers from travel sickness	Mia figlia soffre di cinetosi	Mee-a feel-ya sof-freh dee chee-ne-to-zee
She has hurt herself	Si è fatta male	See eh fat-ta ma-leh
My son is ill	Mio figlio è malato	Mee-o feel-yo eh ma-la-to
He has lost his toy	Ha perduto il suo giocattolo	A pair-doo-to eel soo-o jo-kat-to-lo
I'm sorry if they have bothered you	Scusa se le hanno annoiato	Skoo-za seh leh an-no an-no-ya-to

BUSINESS MATTERS[1]

I would like to make an appointment with ...	Desidero un appuntamento con ...	De-zee-dair-o oon ap-poon-ta-men-to kon ...
I have an appointment with ...	Ho un appuntamento con ...	O oon ap-poon-ta-men-to kon ...
My name is ...	Mi chiamo ...	Mee kya-mo ...
Here is my card	Ecco il mio biglietto	Ek-ko eel mee-o beel-yet-to
This is our catalogue	Ecco il nostro catalogo	Ek-ko eel nos-tro ka-ta-lo-go
I would like to see your products	Desidero vedere i suoi prodotti	De-zee-dair-o ve-dair-eh ee swo-ee pro-dot-tee
Could you send me some samples?	Mi vuol mandare dei campioni?	Mee vwol man-dar-eh day kam-pyo-nee

1. See also TELEPHONING (p. 150).

Can you provide an interpreter/a secretary?	**Potrebbe farmi avere un interprete/una segretaria?**	Pot-reb-beh far-mee a-vair-eh oon een-tair-pre-teh/oon-a seg-re-tar-ya
Where can I make some photocopies?	**Dove posso far fare delle fotocopie?**	Do-veh pos-so far far-eh del-leh fo-to-kop-yeh

AT THE DOCTOR'S

Is there a doctor's surgery near here?	C'è un ambulatorio medico qui vicino?	Cheh oon am-boo-la-tor-yo me-dee-ko kwee vee-chee-no
I must see a doctor, can you recommend one?	Devo vedere un medico. Può raccomandarmene uno?	De-vo ve-dair-eh oon me-dee-ko. Pwo rak-ko-man-dar-me-ne-oon-o
Please call a doctor	Mi vuol chiamare un medico, per favore?	Mee vwol kya-mar-eh oon me-dee-ko, pair fa-vor-eh
When can the doctor come?	Quando verrà il medico?	Kwan-do ver-ra eel me-dee-ko
Does the doctor speak English?	Parla inglese il medico?	Par-la een-gle-zeh eel me-dee-ko
Can I make an appointment for as soon as possible?	Posso fare un appuntamento urgentemente?	Pos-so far-eh oon ap-poon-ta-men-to oor-jen-te-men-teh

AILMENTS

I am ill	**Mi sento poco bene**	Mee sen-to po-ko be-neh
I have high/low blood pressure	**Soffro di pressione alta/bassa**	Sof-fro dee pres-syo-neh al-ta/bas-sa
I am pregnant	**Sono incinta**	So-no een-cheen-ta
I am allergic to ...	**Sono allergico a ...**	So-no al-lair-jee-ko a ...
I think it is infected	**Credo che sia infetto**	Kre-do keh see-a een-fet-to
I've a pain in my arm	**Ho un dolore al braccio**	O oon do-lor-eh al bra-cho
My wrist hurts	**Ho male al polso**	O ma-leh al pol-so
I think I've sprained/ broken my ankle	**Credo di essermi slogata/rotta la caviglia**	Cre-do dee es-sair-mee zlo-ga-ta/rot-ta la ka-veel-ya
I fell down and hurt my back	**Sono caduto e mi sono fatto male alla schiena**	So-no ka-doo-to eh mee so-no fat-to ma-leh al-la skye-na
My feet are swollen	**Ho i piedi gonfi**	O ee pye-dee gon-fee
I've burned/cut/ bruised myself	**Mi sono bruciato/ tagliato/ ammaccato**	Mee so-no broo-cha-to/ tal-ya-to/am-mak-ka-to
I have an upset stomach	**Ho mal di stomaco**	O mal dee sto-ma-ko
I have indigestion	**Ho preso una indigestione**	O pre-zo oon-a een-dee-jes-tyo-neh
My appetite's gone	**Non ho appetito**	Non o ap-pe-tee-to

I think I've got food poisoning	Credo di aver mangiato del cibo avariato	Kre-do dee a-vair man-ja-to del chee-bo a-var-ya-to
I can't eat/sleep	Non posso mangiare/dormire	Non pos-so man-jar-eh/dor-meer-eh
I am a diabetic	Ho il diabete	O eel dee-a-be-teh
I have a heart condition	Sono ammalato di cuore	So-no am-ma-la-to dee kwo-reh
My nose keeps bleeding	Mi esce sangue dal naso	Mee e-sheh san-gweh dal na-so
I have earache	Ho mal d'orecchi	O mal dor-ek-kee
I have difficulty in breathing	Provo difficoltà a respirare	Pro-vo dee-fee-kol-ta a res-peer-ar-eh
I feel dizzy	Mi gira la testa	Mee jee-ra la tes-ta
I feel sick/shivery	Ho la nausea/mi vengono i brividi	O la naw-ze-a/mee ven-go-no ee bree-vee-dee
I feel sick	Sento nausea	Sen-to naw-ze-a
I keep vomiting	Mi viene spesso di vomitare	Mee vye-neh spes-so dee vo-mee-tar-eh
I think I've caught 'flu	Credo di aver preso l'influenza	Kre-do dee a-vair pre-zo leen-floo-en-za
I've got a heavy cold	Ho un forte raffreddore	O oon for-teh raf-fred-dor-eh
I've had the cold since yesterday	Sono due giorni che ho il raffreddore	So-no doo-eh jor-nee keh o eel raf-fred-dor-eh
I've had it for a few hours	L'ho da alcune ore	Lo da al-koo-neh or-eh
abscess	l'ascesso *m*	a-shes-so
ache	il dolore	do-lor-eh

allergy	l'allergia *f*	al-lair-jee-a
appendicitis	l'appendicite *f*	ap-pen-dee-chee-teh
asthma	l'asma	az-ma
back pain	il mal di schiena	mal dee skye-na
blister	la vescica	ve-shee-ka
boil	il foruncolo	fo-roon-ko-lo
bruise	l'ammaccatura *f*	am-mak-ka-too-ra
burn	la bruciatura	broo-cha-too-ra
chill	il colpo di freddo	kol-po dee fred-do
cold	il raffreddore	raf-fred-dor-eh
constipation	la stitichezza	stee-tee-ket-sa
cough	la tosse	tos-seh
cramp	il crampo	kram-po
diabetic	diabetico	dee-a-be-tee-ko
diarrhoea	la diarrea	dee-ar-re-a
earache	il mal d'orecchi	mal do-rek-kee
fever	la febbre	feb-breh
fracture	la frattura	frat-too-ra
hay fever	la febbre del fieno	feb-breh del fye-no
headache	il mal di testa	mal dee tes-ta
high blood pressure	l'ipertensione *f*	ee-pair-ten-syo-neh
ill, sick	ammalato	am-ma-la-to
illness	la malattia	ma-lat-tee-a
indigestion	l'indigestione *f*	een-dee-jes-tyo-neh
infection	l'infezione *f*	een-fet-syo-neh
influenza	l'influenza *f*	een-floo-en-za

insect bite	la puntura d'insetto	poon-too-ra deen-set-to
insomnia	l'insonnia *f*	een-son-nya
nose bleed	la emorragia nasale	e-mor-ra-jee-a na-za-leh
pain	il dolore	do-lor-eh
rheumatism	il reumatismo	re-oo-ma-teez-mo
sore throat	il mal di gola	mal dee go-la
sting	la puntura	poon-too-ra
stomach ache	il mal di stomaco	mal dee sto-ma-ko
sunburn	la scottatura di sole	skot-ta-too-ra dee so-leh
sunstroke	il colpo di sole	kol-po dee so-leh
swelling	la tumefazione	too-me-fat-syo-neh
toothache	il mal di denti	mal dee den-tee
ulcer	l'ulcera	ool-chair-a
wound	la ferita	fe-ree-ta

TREATMENT

I feel better now	Adesso mi sento meglio	A-des-so mee sen-to mel-yo
Did you take your temperature?	*Si è misurata la temperatura?	See eh mee-zoo-ra-ta la tem-pair-a-too-ra
Does that hurt?	*Le fa male?	Leh fa ma-leh
A lot or a little?	*Tanto o poco?	Tan-to o po-ko
Where does it hurt?	*Dove le fa male?	Do-veh leh fa ma-leh
Have you a pain here?	*Le fa male qui?	Leh fa ma-leh kwee

How long have you had the pain/been suffering from …?	*Da quanto tempo ha questo dolore/ soffre di …?	Da kwan-to tem-po a kwes-to do-lor-eh/sof-freh dee …
Open your mouth	*Vuole aprire la bocca, per favore	Vwol-eh a-preer-eh la bok-ka, pair fa-vor-eh
Put out your tongue	*Mi faccia vedere la lingua	Mee fa-cha ve-dair-eh la leen-gwa
Breathe in	*Respiri	Res-peer-ee
Hold your breath	*Trattenga il respiro	Trat-ten-ga eel res-peer-o
I will need a blood specimen	*Mi occorre un campione del sangue	Mee ok-kor-reh oon kam-pyo-neh del san-gweh
What medicines are you taking?	*Che medicine prende?	Keh me-dee-chee-neh pren-deh
I take this medicine – could you give me another prescription?	Prendo questa medicina. Mi potrebbe fare un'altra ricetta?	Pren-do kwes-ta me-dee-chee-na. Mee pot-reb-beh far-eh oon-al-tra ree-chet-ta
I will give you an antibiotic/a sedative/a painkiller	*Le ordinerò degli antibiotici/un calmante/un antidolorifico	Le or-deen-air-o del-yee an-tee-byo-tee-chee/ oon kal-man-teh/oon an-tee-do-lo-ree-fee-ko
Please lie down	*Si sdrai, per favore	See zdra-ee, pair fa-vor-eh
Take these pills/this medicine	*Prenda queste pillole/questa medicina	Pren-da kwes-teh peel-lo-leh/kwes-ta me-dee-chee-na
Take this prescription to the chemist	*Porti questa ricetta alla farmacia	Por-tee kwes-ta ree-chet-ta al-la far-ma-chee-a

Take this three times a day	*Prenda questa medicina tre volte al giorno	Pren-da kwes-ta me-dee-chee-na treh vol-teh al jor-no
I'll give you an injection	*Le faccio una iniezione	Le fa-cho oon-a een-yet-syo-neh
Roll up your sleeve	*Si tiri su la manica	See tee-ree soo la ma-nee-ka
You should follow a diet for a few days	*Deve stare a dieta per alcuni giorni	De-veh star-eh a dye-ta pair al-koo-nee jor-nee
Come and see me again in two days' time	*Torni da me tra due giorni	Tor-nee da meh tra doo-eh jor-nee
Your leg must be X-rayed	*Deve farsi fare i raggi X a questa gamba	De-veh far-see far-eh ee rad-jee eeks a kwes-ta gam-ba
You must go to hospital	*Deve ricoverarsi in ospedale	De-veh ree-ko-vair-ar-see een os-pe-da-leh
You must stay in bed for a few days	*Deve rimanere a letto per alcuni giorni	De-veh ree-ma-nair-eh a let-to pair al-koo-nee jor-nee
You're hurting me	Mi fa male	Mee fa ma-leh
Must I stay in bed?	Devo rimanere a letto?	De-vo ree-ma-nair-eh a let-to
Will you come and see me again?	Torna di nuovo a farmi una visita?	Tor-na dee nwo-vo a far-mee oon-a vee-zee-ta
When do you think I can leave?	Quando crede che possa partire?	Kwan-do kre-deh keh pos-sa par-teer-eh
You should not travel for at least … days	*Non si metta in viaggio per almeno … giorni	Non see met-ta een vyad-jo pair al-me-no … jor-nee

Nothing to worry about	*Niente di preoccupante	Nyen-teh dee pre-ok-koo-pan-teh
How much do I owe you?	Quanto le devo?	Kwan-to leh de-vo
I'd like a receipt for the health insurance	Vorrei una ricevuta per l'assicurazione	Vor-ray oon ree-che-voo-ta pair las-see-koo-rat-syo-neh
ambulance	l'ambulanza f	am-boo-lant-sa
anaesthetic	l'anestetico m	an-es-te-tee-ko
aspirin	l'aspirina f	as-pee-ree-na
bandage	la fascia	fa-sha
chiropodist	il pedicure	pe-dee-koo-reh
hospital	l'ospedale m	os-pe-da-leh
injection	l'iniezione f	een-yet-syo-neh
laxative	il lassativo	las-sa-tee-vo
nurse	l'infermiera f	een-fair-myair-a
operation	l'operazione f	o-pair-at-syo-neh
optician	l'ottico m	ot-tee-ko
pill	la pastiglia	pas-teel-ya
(adhesive) plaster	il cerotto	chair-ot-to
prescription	la ricetta	ree-chet-ta
X-ray	i raggi X	rad-jee eeks

PARTS OF THE BODY

| ankle | la caviglia | ka-veel-ya |
| arm | il braccio | bra-cho |

back	il dorso	dor-so
bladder	la vescica	ve-shee-ka
blood	il sangue	san-gweh
body	il corpo	kor-po
bone	l'ossa	os-sa
brain	il cervello	chair-vel-lo
breast	il petto	pet-to
cheek	la guancia	gwan-cha
chest	il petto	pet-to
chin	il mento	men-to
ear	l'orecchio *m*	or-rek-kyo
elbow	il gomito	go-mee-to
eye	l'occhio *m*	ok-kyo
face	la faccia	fa-cha
finger	il dito	dee-to
foot	il piede	pye-deh
forehead	la fronte	fron-teh
gum	la gengiva	jen-jee-va
hand	la mano	ma-no
head	la testa	tes-ta
heart	il cuore	kwor-eh
heel	il tallone	tal-lo-neh
hip	il fianco	fyan-ko
jaw	la mascella	ma-shel-la
kidney	il rene	re-neh
knee	il ginocchio	jee-nok-kyo

leg	**la gamba**	gam-ba
lip	**il labbro**	lab-bro
liver	**il fegato**	fe-ga-to
lung	**il polmone**	pol-mo-neh
mouth	**la bocca**	bok-ka
muscle	**il muscolo**	moos-ko-lo
nail	**l'unghia**	oon-gya
neck	**il collo**	kol-lo
nerve	**il nervo**	nair-vo
nose	**il naso**	na-zo
rib	**la costola**	kos-to-la
shoulder	**la spalla**	spal-la
skin	**la pelle**	pel-leh
spine	**la colonna vertebrale**	ko-lon-na vair-te-bra-leh
stomach	**lo stomaco**	sto-ma-ko
thigh	**la coscia**	ko-sha
throat	**la gola**	go-la
thumb	**il pollice**	pol-lee-cheh
toe	**il dito**	dee-to
tongue	**la lingua**	leen-gwa
tonsils	**le tonsille**	ton-seel-leh
tooth	**il dente**	den-teh
vein	**la vena**	ve-na
wrist	**il polso**	pol-so

AT THE DENTIST'S

I must see a dentist	Devo vedere un dentista	De-vo ve-dair-eh oon den-tees-ta
Can I make an appointment with the dentist?	Posso fissare un appuntamento col dentista?	Pos-so fees-sar-eh oon ap-poon-ta-men-to kol den-tees-ta
As soon as possible	Il più presto possibile	Eel pyoo pres-to pos-see-bee-leh
I have toothache	Ho mal di denti	O mal dee den-tee
This tooth hurts	Questo dente mi fa male	Kwes-to den-teh mee fa ma-leh
I have a broken tooth	Ho rotto un dente	O rot-to oon den-teh
I have an abscess	Ho un ascesso	O oon a-shes-so
I've lost a filling	Mi è caduta l'otturazione	Mee eh ka-doo-ta lot-too-rat-syo-neh
Can you fill it?	Può otturarlo?	Pwo ot-too-rar-lo
Can you do it now?	Può farlo adesso?	Pwo far-lo a-des-so
Must you take the tooth out?	Mi deve togliere il dente?	Mee de-veh tol-yair-eh eel den-teh

I do not want the tooth taken out	**Non voglio togliermi il dente**	Non vol-yo tol-yair-mee eel den-teh
Please give me an injection/an anaesthetic	**Per favore, mi faccia una iniezione/un anestetico**	Pair fa-vor-eh, mee fa-cha oon-a een-yet-syo-neh/oon an-es-te-tee-ko
My gums are swollen/keep bleeding	**Le mie gengive sono gonfie/continuano a sanguinare**	Leh mee-yeh jen-jee-veh so-no gon-fyeh/kon-teen-wa-no a san-gwee-nar-eh
I have broken/chipped my dentures	**Mi si è rotta/scheggiata la dentiera**	Mee see eh rot-ta/sked-ja-ta la dent-yair-a
Can you fix it (temporarily)?	**Può aggiustarla (provvisoriamente)?**	Pwo ad-joos-tar-la (prov-vee-zor-ya-men-teh)
You're hurting me	**Mi fa male**	Mee fa ma-leh
How much do I owe you?	**Quanto le devo?**	Kwan-to leh de-vo
When should I come again?	**Quando devo tornare?**	Kwan-do de-vo tor-nar-eh
Please rinse your mouth	***Si sciacqui la bocca, per favore**	See shak-wee la bok-ka, pair fa-vor-eh
I will X-ray your teeth	***Le faccio la radiografia (ai denti)**	Le fa-cho la ra-dyo-gra-fee-a (a-ee den-tee)
You have an abscess	***Ha un ascesso**	A oon a-shes-so
The nerve is exposed	***Il nervo è esposto**	Eel nair-vo eh ez-pos-to
This tooth will have to come out	***Questo dente bisogna toglierlo**	Kwes-to den-teh bee-zon-ya tol-yair-lo

PROBLEMS & ACCIDENTS

Where's the police station[1]?	Dov'è il posto di polizia?	Dov-eh eel pos-to dee po-leet-see-a
Call the police	Chiami la polizia	Kya-mee la po-leet-see-a
It's urgent	E urgente	Eh oor-jen-teh
There's a fire	C'è un fuoco	Cheh oon fwo-ko
Our car has been broken into	Abbiamo avuto un furto in macchina	Ab-bya-mo a-voo-to oon foor-to een mak-kee-na

1. The control of traffic is performed by the **vigili urbani** as well as by **pubblica sicurezza** and the **carabinieri**, who are in fact a branch of the army. The **carabinieri** also perform other police duties, and on entering most towns and villages there is a notice which gives the telephone number of the local police under the words **pronto intervento**. Most other police work is done by officers of the **questura**, who combine some of the functions of a district attorney's department and the CID. Both the **vigili** and the **carabinieri** are empowered to give on-the-spot fines, for which they issue a receipt. These are best paid immediately – to dispute them is often time-consuming and comparatively expensive; but the police usually do no more than warn foreign visitors unless the offence is particularly blatant. In the event of an accident call the police. It is essential to get full details of the other driver's insurance, licence and registration.

My son/daughter is lost	Mio figlio/mia figlia si è perso/a	Mee-o feel-yo/mee-a feel-ya see eh pair-so/a
Where is the British consulate?	Dov'è il consolato britannico?	Dov-eh eel kon-so-la-to bree-tan-nee-ko
Please let the consulate know	Informi il consolato, per favore	Een-for-mee eel kon-so-la-to, pair fa-vor-eh
I've been robbed/ mugged	Mi hanno rubato/ violato	Mee an-no roo-ba-to/ vee-o-la-to
My bag/wallet has been stolen	Mi hanno rubato la borsa/il portafoglio	Mee an-no roo-ba-to la bor-sa/eel por-ta-fol-yo
I found this in the street	Ho trovato questo per la strada	O tro-va-to kwes-to pair la stra-da
I have lost	Ho perso	O pair-so
my luggage	i bagagli	ee ba-gal-yee
my passport	il passaporto	eel pas-sa-por-to
my travellers' cheques	il blocchetto dei travellers' cheques	eel blok-ket-to day travellers' cheques
I have missed my train	Ho perso il treno	O pair-so eel tre-no
My luggage is on board	I miei bagagli sono a bordo	Ee mee-ay ba-gal-yee so-no a bor-do
Call a doctor	Chiami un medico	Kya-mee oon me-dee-ko
Call an ambulance	Chiami un'ambulanza	Kya-mee oon-am-boo-lant-sa
There has been an accident	C'è stato un incidente	Cheh sta-to oon een-chee-den-teh
He's badly hurt	E ferito gravemente	Eh fe-ree-to gra-ve-men-teh
He has fainted	E svenuto	Eh zve-noo-to

He's losing blood	Perde sangue	Pair-deh san-gweh
Her arm is broken	Si è rotta la braccia	See eh rot-ta la bra-cha
Please get some water/a blanket/ some bandages	Porti un po' d'acqua/una coperta/delle fascie, per favore	Por-tee oon po dak-wa/ oon-a ko-pair-ta/del-le fa-sheh, pair fa-vor-eh
I've broken my glasses	Ho rotto gli occhiali	O rot-to lyee ok-kya-lee
I can't see	Non posso vedere	Non pos-so ve-dair-eh
A child has fallen in the water	Un ragazzo è caduto nell'acqua	Oon ra-gat-so eh ka-doo-to nel-lak-wa
First aid, quickly	Il pronto soccorso, subito	Eel pron-to sok-kor-so, soo-bee-to
May I see your insurance certificate?	*Posso vedere il suo certificato d'assicurazione?	Pos-so ve-dair-eh eel swo chair-tee-fee-ka-to das-see-koo-rat-syo-neh
Apply to the insurance company	*Si rivolga alla compagnia d'assicurazione	See ree-vol-ga al-la kom-pan-yee-a das-see-koo-rat-syo-neh
Driving licence	Patente m	Pa-ten-teh
I didn't understand the sign	Non ho capito il cartello	Non o ka-pee-to eel kar-tel-lo
How much is the fine?	Quant'è la multa?	Kwan-teh la mool-ta
I want a copy of the police report	Voglio una copia del verbale di polizia	Vol-yo oon-a ko-pya del vair-ba-leh dee po-leet-see-a
There's a bus strike	*C'è lo sciopero degli autobus	Cheh lo sho-pair-o del-yee ow-to-boos

What are the name and address of the owner?	Qual'è il nome e l'indirizzo del proprietario?	Kwal-eh eel no-meh eh leen-dee-reet-so del prop-rye-tar-yo
Are you willing to act as a witness?	E disposto a far da testimone?	Eh dees-pos-to a far da tes-tee-mo-neh
Can I have your name and address, please?	Vuol darmi il suo nome e indirizzo, per favore?	Vwol dar-mee eel soo-o no-meh eh een-dee-reet-so, pair fa-vor-eh
Can you help me?	Può aiutarmi?	Pwo ay-oo-tar-mee

TIME & DATES

TIME

What time is it?	**Che ore sono?**	Keh or-eh so-no
It's one o'clock	**E l'una**	Eh loon-a
It's two o'clock	**Sono le due**	So-no le doo-eh
It's quarter to ten	**Manca un quarto alle dieci/sono le dieci meno un quarto**	Man-ka oon kwar-to al-leh dye-chee/so-no le dye-chee me-no oon kwar-to
It's twenty to three	**Manca venti alle tre/sono le tre meno venti**	Man-ka ven-tee al-le treh/so-no le treh me-no ven-tee
It's quarter past five	**Sono le cinque e un quarto**	So-no le cheen-kweh eh oon kwar-to
It's half past four	**Sono le quattro e mezza**	So-no le kwat-tro eh med-za

It's five past eight	**Sono le otto e cinque**	So-no le ot-to eh cheen-kweh
second	**il secondo**	se-kon-do
minute	**il minuto**	mee-noo-to
hour	**l'ora** f	or-a
It's early/late	**E presto/tardi**	Eh pres-to/tar-dee
My watch is slow/is fast/has stopped	**Il mio orologio va indietro/va avanti/è fermo**	Eel mee-o o-ro-lo-jo va een-dye-tro/va a-van-tee/eh fair-mo
Sorry I'm late	**Mi scusi per il ritardo**	Mee skoo-zee pair eel ree-tar-do

DATE

What's the date?	**Quanti ne abbiamo?**	Kwan-tee neh ab-bya-mo
It's 9 December[1]	**E il nove dicembre**	Eh eel no-veh dee-chem-breh
We got here on 27 July	**Siamo arrivati qui il ventisette luglio**	Sya-mo ar-ree-va-tee kwee eel ven-tee-set-teh lool-yo
We're leaving on 5 January	**Partiamo il cinque gennaio**	Par-tya-mo eel cheen-kweh jen-na-yo

---

1. In Italian cardinal numbers are used for dates except for *first*, for which **primo** is used.

DAY

morning	**la mattina**	mat-tee-na
this morning	**stamani**	sta-ma-nee
in the morning	**di mattina**	dee mat-tee-na
midday, noon	**mezzogiorno**	med-zo-jor-no
afternoon	**il pomeriggio**	po-mair-eed-jo
yesterday afternoon	**ieri pomeriggio**	yair-ee po-mair-eed-jo
evening	**la sera**	se-ra
tomorrow evening	**domani sera**	do-ma-nee se-ra
midnight	**mezzanotte**	med-za-not-teh
night	**la notte**	not-teh
tonight	**stanotte**	sta-not-teh
sunrise, dawn	**l'alba**	al-ba
sunset	**il tramonto**	tra-mon-to
twilight	**il crepuscolo**	kre-poos-ko-lo
today	**oggi**	od-jee
yesterday	**ieri**	yair-ee
day before yesterday	**ieri l'altro/l'altro ieri**	yair-ee lal-tro/lal-tro yair-ee
tomorrow	**domani**	do-ma-nee
day after tomorrow	**domani l'altro**	do-ma-nee lal-tro
in ten days' time	**fra dieci giorni**	fra dye-chee jor-nee

WEEK

Sunday	**domenica**	do-me-nee-ka
Monday	**lunedì**	loo-ne-dee
Tuesday	**martedì**	mar-te-dee
Wednesday	**mercoledì**	mair-ko-le-dee
Thursday	**giovedì**	jo-ve-dee
Friday	**venerdì**	ven-air-dee
Saturday	**sabato**	sa-ba-to
on Tuesday	**martedì**	mar-te-dee
on Sundays	**la domenica**	la do-me-nee-ka
fortnight	**quindicina di giorni**	kween-dee-chee-na dee jor-nee

MONTH

January	**gennaio**	jen-na-yo
February	**febbraio**	feb-bra-yo
March	**marzo**	mart-so
April	**aprile**	a-pree-leh
May	**maggio**	mad-jo
June	**giugno**	joon-yo
July	**luglio**	lool-yo
August	**agosto**	a-gos-to
September	**settembre**	set-tem-breh

October	**ottobre**	ot-to-breh
November	**novembre**	no-vem-breh
December	**dicembre**	dee-chem-breh

SEASON

spring	**la primavera**	pree-ma-vair-a
summer	**l'estate** *f*	es-ta-teh
autumn	**l'autunno** *m*	ow-toon-no
winter	**l'inverno** *m*	een-vair-no
in spring	**a primavera**	a pree-ma-vair-a
during the summer	**durante l'estate**	doo-ran-teh les-ta-teh

YEAR

this year	**quest'anno**	kwest-an-no
next year	**l'anno prossimo**	an-no pros-see-mo
last year	**l'anno scorso**	an-no skor-so

PUBLIC HOLIDAYS

1 January	**Capodanno**
Easter Monday	**Lunedì dell'angelo**
25 April (Liberation day)	**Anniversario della Liberazione**

1 May (Labour day)	**Festa del lavoro**
15 August (The Assumption)	**Assunzione**
1 November (All Saints' Day)	**Tutti i Santi**
8 December (Conception of the Virgin)	**Immacolata Concezione**
25 December	**Natale**
26 December	**S Stefano**

Local feast days are held in honour of the patron saints of various towns, such as:

25 April   (St Mark) Venice
24 June   (St John the Baptist) Florence, Genoa and Turin
19 September   (St Gennaro) Naples
4 October   (St Petronio) Bologna
7 December   (St Ambrose) Milan

NUMBERS

CARDINAL

0	zero	dze-ro
1	uno	oon-o
2	due	doo-eh
3	tre	treh
4	quattro	kwat-tro
5	cinque	cheen-kweh
6	sei	say
7	sette	set-teh
8	otto	ot-to
9	nove	no-veh
10	dieci	dye-chee
11	undici	oon-dee-chee

12	**dodici**	do-dee-chee
13	**tredici**	tre-dee-chee
14	**quattordici**	kwat-tor-dee-chee
15	**quindici**	kween-dee-chee
16	**sedici**	se-dee-chee
17	**diciassette**	dee-chas-set-teh
18	**diciotto**	dee-chot-to
19	**diciannove**	dee-chan-no-veh
20	**venti**	ven-tee
21	**ventuno**	ven-toon-o
22	**ventidue**	ven-tee-doo-eh
30	**trenta**	tren-ta
31	**trentuno**	tren-toon-o
40	**quaranta**	kwa-ran-ta
50	**cinquanta**	cheen-kwan-ta
60	**sessanta**	ses-san-ta
70	**settanta**	set-tan-ta
80	**ottanta**	ot-tan-ta
90	**novanta**	no-van-ta
100	**cento**	chen-to
101	**cento uno**	chen-to oon-o
200	**duecento**	doo-eh-chen-to
1,000	**mille**	meel-leh
2,000	**due mila**	doo-eh mee-la
1,000,000	**un milione**	meel-yo-neh

ORDINAL

1st	**primo**	pree-mo
2nd	**secondo**	se-kon-do
3rd	**terzo**	tairt-so
4th	**quarto**	kwar-to
5th	**quinto**	kween-to
6th	**sesto**	ses-to
7th	**settimo**	set-tee-mo
8th	**ottavo**	ot-ta-vo
9th	**nono**	no-no
10th	**decimo**	de-chee-mo
11th	**undicesimo**	oon-dee-**che**-zee-mo
12th	**dodicesimo**	do-dee-**che**-zee-mo
13th	**tredicesimo**	tre-dee-**che**-zee-mo
14th	**quattordicesimo**	kwat-tor-dee-**che**-zee-mo
15th	**quindicesimo**	kween-dee-**che**-zee-mo
16th	**sedicesimo**	se-dee-**che**-zee-mo
17th	**diciassettesimo**	dee-chas-set-te-zee-mo
18th	**diciottesimo**	dee-chot-te-zee-mo
19th	**diciannovesimo**	dee-chan-nov-ve-zee-mo
20th	**ventesimo**	ven-te-zee-mo
30th	**trentesimo**	tren-te-zee-mo
40th	**quarantesimo**	kwa-ran-te-zee-mo
50th	**cinquantesimo**	cheen-kwan-te-zee-mo

60th	**sessantesimo**	ses-san-te-zee-mo
70th	**settantesimo**	set-tan-te-zee-mo
80th	**ottantesimo**	ot-tan-te-zee-mo
90th	**novantesimo**	no-van-te-zee-mo
100th	**centesimo**	chen-te-zee-mo
half	**un mezzo**	med-zo
quarter	**un quarto**	kwar-to
three quarters	**tre quarti**	treh kwar-tee
a third	**un terzo**	tairt-so
two thirds	**due terzi**	doo-eh tairt-see

WEIGHTS & MEASURES

DISTANCE

kilometres – miles

km	*miles or km*	miles	km	*miles or km*	miles
1·6	*1*	0·6	14·5	*9*	5·6
3·2	*2*	1·2	16·1	*10*	6·2
4·8	*3*	1·9	32·2	*20*	12·4
6·4	*4*	2·5	40·2	*25*	15·3
8	*5*	3·1	80·5	*50*	31·1
9·7	*6*	3·7	160·9	*100*	62·1
11·3	*7*	4·4	804·7	*500*	310·7
12·9	*8*	5·0			

A rough way to convert from miles to km: divide by 5 and multiply by 8; from km to miles, divide by 8 and multiply by 5.

LENGTH AND HEIGHT

centimetres – inches

cm	inch or cm	inch	cm	inch or cm	inch
2·5	1	0·4	17·8	7	2·8
5·1	2	0·8	20·3	8	3·2
7·6	3	1·2	22·9	9	3·5
10·2	4	1·6	25·4	10	3·9
12·7	5	2·0	50·8	20	7·9
15·2	6	2·4	127	50	19·7

A rough way to convert from inches to cm: divide by 2 and multiply by 5; from cm to inches, divide by 5 and multiply by 2.

metres – feet

m	ft or m	ft	m	ft or m	ft
0·3	1	3·3	2·4	8	26·2
0·6	2	6·6	2·7	9	29·5
0·9	3	9·8	3	10	32·8
1·2	4	13·1	6·1	20	65·6
1·5	5	16·4	15·2	50	164
1·8	6	19·7	30·5	100	328·1
2·1	7	23			

A rough way to convert from ft to m: divide by 10 and multiply by 3; from m to ft, divide by 3 and multiply by 10.

metres – yards

m	yds or m	yds	m	yds or m	yds
0·9	1	1·1	7·3	8	8·7
1·8	2	2·2	8·2	9	9·8
2·7	3	3·3	9·1	10	10·9
3·7	4	4·4	18·3	20	21·9
4·6	5	5·5	45·7	50	54·7
5·5	6	6·6	91·4	100	109·4
6·4	7	7·7	457·2	500	546·8

A rough way to convert from yds to m: subtract 10 per cent from the number of yds; from m to yds, add 10 per cent to the number of metres.

LIQUID MEASURES

litres – gallons

litres	galls or litres	galls	litres	galls or litres	galls
4·6	1	0·2	36·4	8	1·8
9·1	2	0·4	40·9	9	2·0
13·6	3	0·7	45·5	10	2·2
18·2	4	0·9	90·9	20	4·4
22·7	5	1·1	136·4	30	6·6
27·3	6	1·3	181·8	40	8·8
31·8	7	1·5	227·3	50	11

1 pint = 0·6 litre   1 litre = 1·8 pints

A rough way to convert from galls to litres: divide by 2 and multiply by 9; from litres to galls, divide by 9 and multiply by 2.

WEIGHT

kilogrammes – pounds

kg	lb or kg	lb	kg	lb or kg	lb
0·5	1	2·2	3·2	7	15·4
0·9	2	4·4	3·6	8	17·6
1·4	3	6·6	4·1	9	19·8
1·8	4	8·8	4·5	10	22
2·3	5	11·0	9·1	20	44·1
2·7	6	13·2	22·7	50	110·2

A rough way to convert from lb to kg: divide by 11 and multiply by 5; from kg to lb, divide by 5 and multiply by 11.

grammes – ounces

grammes	oz	oz	grammes
100	3·5	2	56·7
250	8·8	4	114·3
500	17·6	8	228·6
1000 (1 kg)	35	16 (1 lb)	457·2

TEMPERATURE

centigrade (°C) – fahrenheit (°F)

°C	°F
− 10	14
− 5	23
0	32
5	41
10	50
15	59
20	68
25	77
30	86
35	95
37	98·4
38	100·5
39	102
40	104
100	212

To convert °F to °C: deduct 32, divide by 9, multiply by 5; to convert °C to °F: divide by 5, multiply by 9, and add 32.

BASIC GRAMMAR

NOUNS

All Italian nouns are either masculine or feminine. Almost all nouns ending in -o are *masculine* (e.g. ragazzo – boy, biglietto – ticket). Most nouns ending in -a are *feminine* (e.g. ragazza – girl, cartolina – postcard). Those ending in -e are masculine or feminine (e.g. melone – melon *m*, stazione – station *f*).

PLURAL

Nouns ending in -o change to -i in the plural (e.g. ragazzi – boys, biglietti – tickets).

Nouns ending in -a change to -e (e.g. ragazze – girls, cartoline – postcards).

Nouns ending in -e change to -i whether they are masculine or feminine (e.g meloni – melons, stazioni – stations).

N.B. An exception: the plural of uomo is uomini (man, men).

THE ARTICLES

The articles change form to match the gender of the noun, and the definite article has a plural as well as a singular form.

'A' before a *masculine noun* is **un** unless the noun begins with s followed by a consonant, or z, when it is **uno** (e.g. un uomo – a man, un giornale – a newspaper, but uno zio – an uncle, uno specchio – a mirror).

'A' before a *feminine noun* is **una** unless the noun begins with a vowel, when it is shortened to **un'** (e.g. una donna – a woman, but un'avventura – an adventure).

'The' with *masculine singular nouns* is usually **il** (e.g. il ragazzo – the boy). But it is **lo** before a word beginning with s + consonant, or z (e.g. lo specchio – the mirror, lo zio – the uncle). It becomes **l'** before a vowel (e:g. l'anno – the year).

'The' before a *masculine plural noun* is generally **i** (e.g. i giorni – the days). But it is **gli** before a word beginning with s + consonant, z or a vowel (e.g. gli specchi – the mirrors, gli uomini – the men).

'The' before a *feminine singuar noun* is **la**, shortened to **l'** if the noun begins with a vowel (e.g. la madre – the mother, l'opera – the opera). With *feminine nouns in the plural* 'the' is **le** (e.g. le case – the houses).

ADJECTIVES

Adjectives end either in -o or in -e. Those ending in -o form the feminine by changing to -a; those ending in -e are the same in both genders.

All adjectives form their plural in the same way as nouns: -o changes to -i; -a to -e; -e to -i.

	Sing	*Plu*				*Sing*	*Plu*	
m	rosso	rossi	*red*		*m*	verde	verdi	*green*
f	rossa	rosse			*f*	verde	verdi	

Adjectives have the same gender and number as the nouns they qualify, and they sometimes follow the noun (e.g. un ragazzo intelligente – due ragazzi intelligenti).

POSSESSIVE ADJECTIVES

Sing			*Plu*	
m	*f*		*m*	*f*
mio	mia	*my*	miei	mie
tuo	tua	*your*	tuoi	tue
suo	sua	*his, her, its*	suoi	sue
nostro	nostra	*our*	nostri	nostre
vostro	vostra	*your*	vostri	vostre
loro	loro	*their*	loro	loro

Possessive adjectives are usually preceded by the definite article (e.g. la mia macchina – my car, la nostra casa – our house, i suoi fratelli – his/her brothers).

YOU

The polite form of address in Italian is in the third person. 'You' is translated by **lei** if addressing one person; **loro** if addressing more than one. 'Your' is **suo** (sing.) and **Loro** (plu.). **tu** is only used to a close friend or a child.
e.g. Come sta? How are you? Come stanno i suoi figli? How are your children?

VERBS

Personal pronouns (io, tu, etc.) tend to be used only for emphasis.

Essere – *to be*

Present		**Future**	
(io) sono	*I am*	sarò	*I shall be*
(tu) sei	*you are*	sarai	*you will be*
(egli/essa) è	*he/she is*	sarà	*he/she will be*
(lei) è	*you are*	sarà	*you will be*
(noi) siamo	*we are*	saremo	*we shall be*
(voi) siete	*you are*	sarete	*you will be*
(essi/esse) sono	*they are*	saranno	*they will be*
(loro) sono	*you are*	saranno	*you will be*

Past

sono stato	*I was or I have been, etc.*
sei stato	*you were*
è stato/a	*he/she was*
è stato/a	*you were*
siamo stati/e	*we were*
siete stati/e	*you were*
sono stati/e	*they were*
sono stati/e	*you were*

Avere – *to have*

Present		**Future**	
(io) ho	*I have*	avrò	*I shall have*
(tu) hai	*you have*	avrai	*you will have*
(egli/essa) ha	*he/she has*	avrà	*he/she will have*
(lei) ha	*you have*	avrà	*you will have*
(noi) abbiamo	*we have*	avremo	*we shall have*
(voi) avete	*you have*	avrete	*you will have*
(essi/esse) hanno	*they have*	avranno	*they will have*
(loro) hanno	*you have*	avranno	*you will have*

Past

ho avuto	*I had* **or** *I have had, etc.*	abbiamo avuto	*we had*
hai avuto	*you had*	avete avuto	*you had*
ha avuto	*he/she had*	hanno avuto	*they had*
ha avuto	*you had*	hanno avuto	*you had*

REGULAR VERBS

Italian regular verbs fall into three conjugations, determined by the ending of the infinitive.

1st conjugation	infinitives ending in **-are**	e.g.	parlare – to speak
			comprare – to buy
2nd conjugation	infinitives ending in **-ere**	e.g.	vedere – to see
			vendere – to sell
3rd conjugation	infinitives ending in **-ire**	e.g.	sentire – to hear
			capire – to understand

Present tense

	1st conj.	2nd conj.	3rd conj.
io	parl-**o**	vend-**o**	sent-**o**
tu	parl-**i**	vend-**i**	sent-**i**
egli	parl-**a**	vend-**e**	sent-**e**
lei	parl-**a**	vend-**e**	sent-**e**
noi	parl-**iamo**	vend-**iamo**	sent-**iamo**
voi	parl-**ate**	vend-**ete**	sent-**ite**
essi	parl-**ano**	vend-**ono**	sent-**ono**
loro	parl-**ano**	vend-**ono**	sent-**ono**

Some 3rd conjugation verbs add -isc before the normal present tense endings in the singular and in the third person plural, e.g. io capisco, from capire – to understand.

Future tense

The future tense of almost all Italian verbs is formed from the infinitive in the following way:

io	parl-er-**ò**	vend-er-**ò**	sent-ir-**ò**
tu	parl-er-**ai**	vend-er-**ai**	sent-ir-**ai**
egli	parl-er-**à**	vend-er-**à**	sent-ir-**à**
lei	parl-ler-**à**	vend-er-**à**	sent-ir-**à**
noi	parl-er-**emo**	vend-er-**emo**	sent-ir-**emo**
voi	parl-er-**ete**	vend-er-**ete**	sent-ir-**ete**
essi	parl-er-**anno**	vend-er-**anno**	sent-ir-**anno**
loro	parl-er-**anno**	vend-er-**anno**	sent-ir-**anno**

Note that in the 1st conjugation **-are** changes to **-ere** before the future endings are added.

Past tense

The form of the past tense given in this book can be used to translate the English 'I did (something)' as well as 'I have done (something)'. It is formed by using the present tense of avere, or sometimes essere, with the past participle of the verb.

When essere – to be – is used to form the past tense, past participles agree with the subject of the verb in number and gender, using the same endings as adjectives ending in **-o**. E.g. Maria è venuta – Maria has come; I miei amici sono andati a Roma – My friends have gone to Rome.

The past participle of 1st conjugation verbs ends in **-ato**, e.g. parlato.

The past participle of 2nd conjugation verbs usually ends in **-uto**, e.g. venduto.

The past participle of 3rd conjugation verbs usually ends in **-ito**, e.g. sentito.

The past tense is formed as follows:

(io) ho parlato, etc.	ho venduto, etc.	ho sentito, etc.

SOME COMMON IRREGULAR VERBS

Andare – *to go*

Present		**Future**	
(io) vado	*I go, etc.*	andrò	*I shall go, etc.*
(tu) vai		andrai	
(egli) va		andrà	
(lei) va		andrà	
(noi) andiamo		andremo	
(voi) andate		andrete	
(essi) vanno		andranno	
(loro) vanno		andranno	

Past
sono andato   *I went/have been, etc.*

Dire – *to say*

Present		**Future**	
(io) dico	*I say, etc.*	dirò	*I shall say, etc.*
(tu) dici		dirai	
(egli) dice		dirà	
(lei) dice		dirà	
(noi) diciamo		diremo	
(voi) dite		direte	
(essi) dicono		diranno	
(loro) dicono		diranno	

Past
ho detto   *I said/have said, etc.*

Dovere – *to have to, must*

Present		*Future*	
(io) devo	*I have to, etc.*	dovrò	*I shall have to, etc.*
(tu) devi		dovrai	
(egli) deve		dovrà	
(lei) deve		dovrà	
(noi) dobbiamo		dovremo	
(voi) dovete		dovrete	
(essi) devono		dovranno	
(loro) devono		dovranno	

Past
ho dovuto   *I had to/have had to, etc.*

Fare – *to do, to make*

Present		*Future*	
(io) faccio	*I do, etc.*	farò	*I shall do, etc.*
(tu) fai		farai	
(egli) fa		farà	
(lei) fa		farà	
(noi) facciamo		faremo	
(voi) fate		farete	
(essi) fanno		faranno	
(loro) fanno		faranno	

Past
ho fatto   *I did/have done, etc.*

Potere – *to be able to, can*

Present		**Future**	
(io) posso	*I can, etc.*	potrò	*I shall be able to, etc.*
(tu) puoi		potrai	
(egli) può		potrà	
(lei) può		potrà	
(noi) possiamo		potremo	
(voi) potete		potrete	
(essi) possono		potranno	
(loro) possono		potranno	

Past
ho potuto   *I could/was able to, etc.*

Venire – *to come*

Present		**Future**	
(io) vengo	*I come, etc.*	verrò	*I shall come, etc.*
(tu) vieni		verrai	
(egli) viene		verrà	
(lei) viene		verrà	
(noi) veniamo		verremo	
(voi) venite		verrete	
(essi) vengono		verranno	
(loro) vengono		verranno	

Past
sono venuto   *I came/have come, etc.*

Volere – *to want*

Present		**Future**	
(io) voglio	*I want, etc.*	vorrò	*I shall want, etc.*
(tu) vuoi		vorrai	
(egli) vuole		vorrà	
(lei) vuole		vorrà	
(noi) vogliamo		vorremo	
(voi) volete		vorrete	
(essi) vogliono		vorranno	
(loro) vogliono		vorranno	

Past
io ho voluto *I wanted/have wanted, etc.*

PREPOSITIONS

The most common prepositions are:

a, ad	*at, to*	in	*in, to*
di	*of*	su	*on, over*
da	*from*	con	*with*

When they are followed by the definite article they are joined to it as follows:

	il	*lo*	*l'*	*la*	*i*	*gli*	*le*
a	al	allo	all'	alla	ai	agli	alle
di	del	dello	dell'	della	dei	degli	delle
da	dal	dallo	dall'	dalla	dai	dagli	dalle
in	nel	nello	nell'	nella	nei	negli	nelle
su	sul	sullo	sull'	sulla	sui	sugli	sulle
con	col	collo	coll'	colla	coi	cogli	colle

e.g. al mercato – to the market; nel giardino – in the garden; dall'Italia – from Italy; sulla tavola – on the table. Con often remains separate, e.g. con la famiglia – with the family.

VOCABULARY

Various groups of specialized words are given elsewhere in this book and these words are usually not repeated in the Vocabulary:

A

a, an	un, una	oon, oon-a
abbey	l'abbazia *f*	ab-bat-see-a
able (to be)	potere	po-tair-eh
about	circa	cheer-ka
above	sopra	sop-ra
abroad	all'estero	al-les-tair-o
accept (to)	accettare	a-chet-tar-eh
accident	l'incidente *m*	een-chee-den-teh
accommodation	l'alloggio *m*	al-lod-jo
account	il conto	kon-to
ache (to)	dolere	do-lair-eh
acquaintance	il conoscente	ko-no-shen-teh
across	attraverso	at-tra-vair-so
act (to)	agire	a-jeer-eh
add (to)	aggiungere	ad-joon-jair-eh
address	l'indirizzo *m*	een-dee-reet-so
admire (to)	ammirare	am-meer-ar-eh
admission	l'ingresso *m*/ l'entrata *f*	een-gres-so/en-tra-ta
adventure	l'avventura *f*	av-ven-too-ra
advertisement	l'annunzio *m*	an-noont-syo
advice	il consiglio	kon-seel-yo
aeroplane	l'aeroplano *m*	a-air-o-pla-no
afford (to)	permettersi (di)	pair-met-tair-see (dee)

afraid (to be)	(aver) paura	(a-vair) pa-oo-ra
after	dopo	do-po
afternoon	il pomeriggio	po-mair-eed-jo
again	ancora	an-kor-a
against	contro	kon-tro
age	l'età *f*	e-ta
ago	(tempo) fa	(tem-po) fa
agree (to)	essere d'accordo	es-sair-eh da-kor-do
air	l'aria *f*	ar-ee-a
air-conditioning	il condizionatore (d'aria)	kon-deet-syo-na-tor-eh (dar-ee-a)
alarm clock	la sveglia	zvel-ya
alcoholic (drink)	alcolico	al-ko-lee-ko
alive	vivo	vee-vo
all	tutto	toot-to
all right	va bene	va be-neh
allow (to)	permettere	pair-met-tair-eh
almost	quasi	kwa-zee
alone	solo	so-lo
along	lungo	loon-go
already	già	ja
also	anche	an-keh
alter (to)	modificare	mo-dee-fee-kar-eh
alternative	l'alternativa *f*	al-tair-na-tee-va
although	benchè	ben-keh
always	sempre	sem-preh

ambulance	l'ambulanza f	am-boo-lant-sa
America	America f	a-me-ree-ka
American	americano	a-me-ree-ka-no
amuse (to)	divertire	dee-vair-teer-eh
amusing	divertente	dee-vair-ten-teh
amusement park	parco dei divertimenti	par-ko day dee-vair-tee-men-tee
ancient	vecchio	vek-kyo
and	e	eh
angry	arrabbiato	ar-rab-bya-to
animal	l'animale m	a-nee-ma-leh
anniversary	l'anniversario m	an-nee-vair-sar-yo
annoyed	seccato	sek-ka-to
another	un altro	oon al-tro
answer	la risposta	rees-pos-ta
answer (to)	rispondere	rees-pon-dair-eh
antique	antico	an-tee-ko
any	qualche/qualunque	kwal-keh/kwal-oon-kweh
anyone	qualcuno/chiunque	kwal-koo-no/kee-oon-kweh
anything	qualchecosa	kwal-keh-ko-za
anywhere	dovunque	do-voon-kweh
apartment	l'appartamento m	ap-par-ta-men-to
apologize (to)	scusarsi	skoo-zar-see
appetite	l'appetito m	ap-pe-tee-to
appointment	l'appuntamento m	ap-poon-ta-men-to

architect	l'architetto *m*	ar-kee-tet-to
architecture	l'architettura *f*	ar-kee-tet-too-ra
area	la zona/la regione	tso-na/re-jo-neh
area code	il prefisso	pre-fees-so
arm	il braccio	bra-cho
armchair	la poltrona	pol-tro-na
army	l'esercito *m*	e-zair-chee-to
arrange (to)	combinare	kom-bee-nar-eh
arrival	l'arrivo *m*	ar-ree-vo
arrive (to)	arrivare	ar-ree-var-eh
art	l'arte *f*	ar-teh
art gallery	la galleria d'arte	ga-lair-ee-a dar-teh
artificial	sintetico	seen-te-tee-ko
artist	l'artista	ar-tees-ta
as	come	ko-meh
as much as	tanto quanto	tan-to kwan-to
as soon as	appena che	ap-pe-na keh
as well	in più/come pure	een pyoo/ko-meh poo-reh
ashtray	il portacenere	por-ta-che-nair-eh
ask (to)	chiedere	kye-dair-eh
asleep	addormentato	ad-dor-men-ta-to
at	a	a
at last	finalmente	fee-nal-men-teh
at once	subito	soo-bee-to
atmosphere	l'atmosfera *f*	at-mos-fair-a
attention	l'attenzione *f*	at-tent-syo-neh

attractive	attraente	at-tra-en-teh
auction	l'asta	as-ta
audience	il pubblico	eel poob-lee-ko
aunt	la zia	tsee-a
Australia	Australia *f*	ow-stra-lya
Australian	australiano	ow-stra-lya-no
author	l'autore *m*	ow-tor-eh
autumn	l'autunno *m*	ow-toon-no
available	disponibile	dees-po-nee-bee-leh
avalanche	la valanga	va-lan-ga
avenue	il viale	vya-leh
average	la media	med-ya
avoid (to)	evitare	e-vee-tar-eh
awake	sveglio	zvel-yo
away	via	vee-a

B

baby	il bambino	bam-bee-no
baby food	il cibo per bambini	chee-bo pair bam-bee-nee
baby sitter	il/la baby sitter	baby sitter
bachelor	il celibe	che-lee-beh
back *adv*	indietro	een-dye-tro
bad	cattivo	kat-tee-vo
bad *food*	guasto	gwas-to
bag	la borsa	bor-sa
baggage	i bagagli	ba-gal-yee

baggage cart	il carello	ka-rel-lo
bait	lo spuntino	spoon-tee-no
balcony	il balcone	bal-ko-neh
ball *sport*	la palla	pal-la
ballet	il balletto	bal-let-to
balloon	il palloncino	pal-lon-chee-no
band *music*	l'orchestra *f*	or-kes-tra
bank	la banca	ban-ka
bank account	il conto in banca	kon-to een ban-ka
barn	la stalla	stal-la
basket	il cesto	ches-to
bath	il bagno	ban-yo
bath essence	l'estratto per il bagno	es-trat-to pair eel ban-yo
bathe (to)	fare un bagno	fa-reh oon ban-yo
bathing cap	la cuffia da bagno	koof-fya dan ban-yo
bathing costume	il costume da bagno	kos-too-meh da ban-yo
bathing trunks	i calzoncini da bagno	kalt-son-chee-nee da ban-yo
bathroom	la stanza da bagno	stan-za da ban-yo
battery	la batteria	bat-tair-ee-a
bay *sea*	la baia	ba-ya
be (to)	essere	es-sair-eh
beach	la spiaggia	spyad-ja
beard	la barba	bar-ba
beautiful	bello	bel-lo
because	perchè	pair-keh

become (to)	divenire	dee-ve-neer-eh
bed	il letto	let-to
bed and breakfast	l'alloggio e prima collazione	al-lod-jo eh pree-ma kol-lat-syo-neh
bedroom	la camera	ka-mair-a
before *space*	davanti a	da-van-tee a
time	prima di	pree-ma dee
begin (to)	cominciare	ko-meen-char-eh
beginning	il principio	preen-chee-pyo
behind	dietro	dye-tro
believe (to)	credere	kre-dair-eh
bell	il campanello	kam-pa-nel-lo
belong (to)	appartenere	ap-par-te-nair-eh
below	sotto	sot-to
belt	la cintura	cheen-too-ra
bench	la panchina	pan-kee-na
bend	la curva	koor-va
berth	il letto	let-to
best	il migliore	meel-yor-eh
bet	la scommessa	skom-mes-sa
better	meglio/migliore	mel-yo/meel-yor-eh
between	fra	fra
bicycle	la bicicletta	bee-chee-klet-ta
big	grande	gran-deh
bill	il conto	kon-to
binoculars	il binocolo	bee-no-ko-lo

bird	l'uccello *m*	oo-chel-lo
birthday	il compleanno	kom-ple-an-no
bite (to)	mordere	mor-dair-eh
bitter	amaro	a-ma-ro
blanket	la coperta	ko-pair-ta
bleach (to)	ossigenare	os-see-jen-ar-eh
bleed (to)	sanguinare	san-gwee-nar-eh
blind	cieco	chye-ko
blister	la vescica	ve-shee-ka
blood	il sangue	san-gweh
blouse	la blusa	bloo-za
blow *hit*	il colpo	kol-po
blow (to)	soffiare	sof-fyar-eh
(on) board	a bordo	a bor-do
boarding house	la pensione	pen-syo-neh
boat	il battello	bat-tel-lo
body	il corpo	kor-po
bone	l'osso *m*	os-so
bonfire	il falò	fa-lo
book	il libro	leeb-ro
book (to)	riservare	ree-zair-var-eh
boot *for foot*	lo stivale	stee-va-leh
border	la frontiera/il confine	front-yair-a/kon-fee-neh
bored	annoiato	an-no-ya-to
boring	noioso	no-yo-zo

borrow (to)	**prendere in prestito**	pren-dair-eh een pres-tee-to
both	**entrambi**	en-tram-bee
bother (to) *annoy*	**disturbare**	dees-toor-bar-eh
bottle	**la bottiglia**	bot-teel-ya
bottle opener	**il cavatappi**	ka-va-tap-pee
bottom	**il fondo**	fon-do
bow tie	**la cravatta a farfalla**	kra-vat-ta a far-fal-la
bowl	**la tazza**	tat-sa
box *container*	**la scatola**	ska-to-la
theatre	**il palco**	pal-ko
box office	**il botteghino**	bot-te-gee-no
boy	**il ragazzo**	ra-gat-so
bracelet	**il braccialetto**	bra-cha-let-to
braces	**le bretelle**	bre-tel-leh
brain	**il cervello**	chair-vel-lo
brains	**le cervella**	chair-vel-la
branch *tree*	**il ramo**	ra-mo
office	**la filiale/la succursale**	feel-ya-leh/sook-koor-sa-leh
brassière	**il reggiseno**	red-jee-se-no
break (to)	**rompere**	rom-pair-eh
breakfast	**la prima colazione**	pree-ma ko-lat-syo-neh
breathe (to)	**respirare**	res-peer-ar-eh
brick	**il mattone**	mat-to-neh
bridge	**il ponte**	pon-teh

briefs	**le mutandine**	moo-tan-dee-neh
bright *light*	**lucente**	loo-chen-teh
bring (to)	**portare**	por-tar-reh
British	**britannico**	bree-tan-nee-ko
broken	**rotto**	rot-to
brooch	**la spilla**	speel-la
brother	**il fratello**	fra-tel-lo
bruise (to)	**ammaccarsi**	am-mak-kar-see
brush	**la spazzola**	spat-so-la
brush (to)	**spazzolare**	spat-so-lar-eh
bucket	**la secchia**	sek-kya
buckle	**la fibbia**	feeb-bya
build (to)	**costruire**	kos-tru-eer-eh
building	**l'edificio** *m*	e-dee-fee-cho
bunch *flowers, keys*	**il mazzo**	mad-zo
buoy	**la boa**	bo-a
burn (to)	**bruciare**	broo-char-eh
burst (to)	**scoppiare**	skop-pyar-eh
bus	**l'autobus** *m*	ow-to-boos
bus stop	**la fermata d'autobus**	fair-ma-ta dow-to-boos
business	**gli affari**	af-far-ee
busy	**occupato**	ok-koo-pa-to
but	**ma**	ma
butterfly	**la farfalla**	far-fal-la
button	**il bottone**	bot-to-neh
buy (to)	**comprare**	kom-prar-eh

C

cab	**il taxi**	taxi
cabin	**la cabina**	ka-bee-na
calculator	**il calcolatore**	kal-ko-la-tor-eh
calendar	**il calendario**	ka-len-dar-yo
call *telephone*	**la chiamata**	kya-ma-ta
call (to) *summon*	**chiamare**	kya-mar-eh
visit	**visitare**	vee-zee-tar-eh
calm	**calmo**	kal-mo
camp (to)	**accamparsi**	ak-kam-par-see
camp site	**un camping**	camping
can (to be able)	**potere**	po-tair-eh
can *tin*	**il barattolo**	ba-rat-to-lo
can opener	**l'apriscatole** *m*	ap-ree-**ska**-to-leh
Canada	**Canada** *m*	ka-na-da
Canadian	**canadese**	ka-na-de-zeh
cancel (to)	**cancellare**	kan-chel-lar-eh
candle	**la candela**	kan-de-la
canoe	**la canoa**	ka-no-a
cap	**il berretto**	ber-ret-to
capital city	**la capitale**	ka-pee-ta-leh
car	**la macchina**	mak-kee-na
car park	**il parcheggio**	par-ked-jo
carafe	**la caraffa**	ka-raf-fa
caravan	**la roulotte**	roo-lot
care	**la cura**	koo-ra

careful	**attento**	at-ten-to
careless	**disordinato**	dee-zor-dee-na-to
caretaker	**il/la custode**	koos-to-deh
carpet	**il tappeto**	tap-pe-to
carry (to)	**portare**	por-tar-eh
cash	**i contanti**	kon-tan-tee
cash (to)	**incassare**	een-kas-sar-eh
cashier	**il cassiere**	kas-syair-eh
casino	**il casinò**	ka-zee-no
cassette	**la cassetta**	kas-set-ta
cassette recorder	**il registratore a cassetta**	re-jees-tra-tor-eh a kas-set-ta
castle	**il castello**	kas-tel-lo
cat	**il gatto**	gat-to
catalogue	**il catalogo**	ka-ta-lo-go
catch (to)	**prendere**	pren-dair-eh
cathedral	**la cattedrale/il duomo**	kat-te-dra-leh/dwo-mo
catholic	**cattolico**	kat-to-lee-ko
cave	**la grotta**	grot-ta
cement	**il cemento**	che-men-to
centre	**il centro**	chen-tro
central	**centrale**	chen-tra-leh
century	**il secolo**	se-ko-lo
ceremony	**la cerimonia**	che-ree-mo-nya
certain(ly)	**certo**	chair-to

chain *jewellery*	la catena	ka-te-na
chair	la sedia	sed-ya
chambermaid	la cameriera	ka-mair-yair-a
chance	il caso	ka-zo
(small) change	gli spiccioli	spee-cho-lee
change (to)	cambiare	kam-byar-eh
chapel	la cappella	kap-pel-la
charge *money*	il costo	kos-to
charge (to) *money*	far pagare	far pa-gar-eh
cheap	a buon mercato	a bwon mair-ka-to
check (to)	controllare	kon-trol-lar-eh
chef	il capocuoco	ka-po-kwo-ko
cheque	l'assegno *m*	as-sen-yo
chess	il gioco degli scacchi	jo-ko del-yee skak-kee
chess set	gli scacchi	skak-kee
child	il bambino	bam-bee-no
chill (to)	mettere in fresco	met-tair-eh een fres-ko
china	la porcellana	por-chel-la-na
choice	la scelta	shel-ta
choose (to)	scegliere	shel-yair-eh
church	la chiesa	kye-za
cigarette case	il portasigarette	por-ta-see-ga-ret-teh
cinema	il cinema	chee-ne-ma
circle *theatre*	la galleria	gal-lair-ee-a
circus	il circo	cheer-ko
city	la città	cheet-ta

class	la classe	klas-seh
clean	pulito	poo-lee-to
clean (to)	pulire	poo-leer-eh
cleansing cream	la crema detergente	kre-ma de-tair-jen-teh
clear	chiaro	kya-ro
cliff	la scogliera	skol-yair-a
climb (to)	arrampicarsi	ar-ram-pee-kar-see
cloakroom	il guardaroba	gwar-da-ro-ba
clock	l'orologio *m*	or-o-lo-jo
close (to)	chiudere	kyoo-dair-eh
closed	chiuso	kyoo-zo
cloth	la stoffa	stof-fa
clothes	i vestiti	ves-tee-tee
cloud	la nube	noo-beh
coach	il pullman	pool-man
coast	la costa	kos-ta
coat	il soprabito	sop-ra-bee-to
coathanger	l'attaccapanni *m*	at-tak-ka-pan-nee
coin	la moneta	mo-ne-ta
cold	freddo	fred-do
cold (to have a)	essere raffreddato	es-sair-eh raf-fred-da-to
collar	il colletto	kol-let-to
collect (to)	raccogliere	rak-kol-yair-eh
colour	il colore	ko-lor-eh
comb	il pettine	pet-tee-neh
come (to)	venire	ve-neer-eh

come in	entrate	en-tra-teh
comfortable	comodo	ko-mo-do
compact disc	il compact disc	compact disc
company	la compagnia	kom-pan-yee-a
compartment *train*	lo scompartimento	skom-par-tee-men-to
compass	la bussola	boos-so-la
compensation	il risarcimento	ree-zar-chee-men-to
complain (to)	lagnarsi	lan-yar-see
complaint	la lagnanza	lan-yant-sa
complete	completo	kom-ple-to
computer	il computer	computer
concert	il concerto	kon-chair-to
concert hall	la sala dei concerti	sa-la day kon-chair-tee
concrete	il calcestruzzo	kal-che-stroot-so
condition	la condizione	kon-deet-syo-neh
conductor *bus*	il fattorino	fat-tor-ee-no
orchestra	il direttore	dee-ret-tor-teh
congratulations	congratulazioni	kon-gra-too-lat-syo-nee
connect (to)	connettere	kon-net-tair-eh
connection *train, etc.*	la coincidenza	ko-een-chee-dent-sa
consul	il console	kon-so-leh
consulate	il consolato	kon-so-la-to
contact lenses	le lenti a contatto	len-tee a kon-tat-to
contain (to)	contenere	kon-te-nair-eh
contraceptive	l'antifecondativo *m*	an-tee-fe-kon-da-tee-vo
contrast	il contrasto	kon-tras-to

convenient	conveniente	kon-ven-yen-teh
convent	il convento	kon-ven-to
conversation	la conversazione	kon-vair-sat-syo-neh
cook	il cuoco	kwo-ko
cook (to)	cucinare	koo-chee-nar-eh
cool	fresco	fres-ko
copper	il rame	ra-meh
copy	la copia	ko-pya
copy (to)	copiare	ko-pyar-eh
cork	il tappo	tap-po
corkscrew	il cavatappi	ka-va-tap-pee
corner	l'angolo *m*	an-go-lo
correct	corretto	kor-ret-to
corridor	il corridoio	kor-ree-do-yo
cosmetics	i cosmetici	kos-me-tee-chee
cost	il costo	kos-to
cost (to)	costare	kos-tar-eh
costume jewellery	la bigiotteria	bee-jot-tair-ee-a
cottage	la casetta di campagna	ka-zet-ta dee kam-pan-ya
cotton	il cotone	ko-to-neh
cotton wool	l'ovatta *f*	o-vat-ta
couchette	la cuccetta	koo-chet-ta
count (to)	contare	kon-tar-eh
country *nation*	il paese	pa-e-zeh
not town	la campagna	kam-pan-ya

course *dish*	la portata	por-ta-ta
cousin	il cugino	koo-jee-no
cover charge	il coperto	ko-pair-to
crash *collision*	l'urto *m*	oor-to
credit card	la carta di credito	kar-ta dee kre-dee-to
cross	la croce	kro-cheh
cross (to)	attraversare	at-tra-vair-sar-eh
cross country skiing	lo sci di fondo	shee dee fon-do
crossroads	il crocevia	kro-che-vee-a
crystal	il cristallo	krees-tal-lo
cufflinks	i gemelli	je-mel-lee
cup	la tazza	tat-sa
cupboard	l'armadio *m*	ar-ma-dyo
cure (to)	guarire	gwa-reer-eh
curious	curioso	koo-ree-o-zo
curl	il riccio	ree-cho
current	la corrente	kor-ren-teh
curtain	la tenda	ten-da
cushion	il cuscino	koo-shee-no
customs	la dogana	do-ga-na
customs officer	l'ufficiale di dogana *m*	oof-fee-cha-leh dee do-ga-na
cut	il taglio	tal-yo
cut (to)	tagliare	tal-yar-eh
cycling	il ciclismo	chee-kleez-mo
cyclist	il/la ciclista	chee-klees-ta

D

daily	**quotidiano**	kwo-tee-dya-no
damaged	**danneggiato**	dan-ned-ja-to
damp	**umido**	oo-mee-do
dance	**il ballo**	bal-lo
dance (to)	**ballare**	bal-lar-eh
danger	**pericolo**	pe-ree-ko-lo
dangerous	**pericoloso**	pe-ree-ko-lo-zo
dark	**scuro**	skoo-ro
date *appointment*	**l'appuntamento** *m*	ap-poon-ta-men-to
calendar	**la data**	da-ta
daughter	**la figlia**	feel-ya
day	**il giorno**	jor-no
dead	**morto**	mor-to
deaf	**sordo**	sor-do
dealer	**il commerciante**	kom-mair-chan-teh
dear	**caro**	ka-ro
decanter	**la caraffa**	ka-raf-fa
decide (to)	**decidere**	de-chee-dair-eh
deckchair	**la sedia a sdraio**	sed-ya a zdra-yo
declare (to)	**dichiarare**	dee-kyar-ar-eh
deep	**profondo**	pro-fon-do
delay	**il ritardo**	ree-tar-do
deliver (to)	**consegnare**	kon-sen-yar-eh
delivery	**la consegna**	kon-sen-ya
demi-pension	**la mezza pensione**	med-za pen-syo-neh

dentist	**il dentista**	den-tees-ta
dentures	**la dentiera**	dent-yair-a
deodorant	**il deodorante**	de-o-dor-an-teh
depart (to)	**partire**	par-teer-eh
department	**il dipartimento**	dee-par-tee-men-to
department stores	**i grandi magazzini**	gran-dee ma-gad-zee-nee
departure	**la partenza**	par-tent-sa
dessert	**i dolci**	dol-chee
detour	**la deviazione**	de-vyat-syo-neh
dial (to)	**comporre il numero**	kom-por-reh eel noo-mair-o
dialling code	**il prefisso**	pre-fees-so
diamond	**il diamante**	dee-a-man-teh
dice	**i dadi**	da-dee
dictionary	**i dizionario**	deet-syo-nar-yo
diet	**la dieta**	dye-ta
diet (to)	**stare a dieta**	star-eh a dye-ta
different	**differente**	deef-fair-en-teh
difficult	**difficile**	deef-fee-chee-leh
dine (to)	**pranzare**	pran-zar-eh
dining room	**la sala da pranzo**	sa-la da pran-zo
dinner	**il pranzo**	pran-zo
dinner jacket	**il smoking**	smoking
direct	**diretto**	deer-et-to
direction	**la direzione**	deer-et-syo-neh
dirty	**sporco**	spor-ko

disappointed	**deluso**	de-loo-zo
discothèque	**la discoteca**	dees-ko-te-ka
discount	**lo sconto**	skon-to
dish	**il piatto**	pyat-to
disinfectant	**il disinfettante**	dees-een-fet-tan-teh
distance	**la distanza**	dees-tant-sa
disturb (to)	**disturbare**	dees-toor-bar-eh
ditch	**il fosso**	fos-so
dive (to)	**tuffarsi**	toof-far-see
diving board	**il trampolino di lancio**	tram-po-lee-no dee lan-cho
divorced	**divorziato**	dee-vort-sya-to
do (to)	**fare**	far-eh
dock (to)	**attraccare**	at-trak-kar-eh
doctor	**il medico**	me-dee-ko
dog	**il cane**	ka-neh
doll	**la bambola**	bam-bo-la
door	**la porta**	por-ta
double	**doppio**	dop-pyo
double bed	**il letto matrimoniale**	let-to mat-ree-mo-nya-leh
double room	**la camera matrimoniale**	ka-mair-a mat-ree-mo-nya-leh
down (stairs)	**giù**	joo
dozen	**la dozzina**	dod-zee-na
draughty	**pieno di correnti d'aria**	pye-no dee kor-ren-tee dar-ya
draw (to)	**disegnare**	dee-zen-yar-eh

drawer	il cassetto	kas-set-to
drawing	il disegno	dee-zen-yo
dream	il sogno	son-yo
dress	l'abito *m*	a-bee-to
dressing gown	la vestaglia	ves-tal-ya
dressmaker	il sarto	sar-to
drink (to)	bere	ber-eh
drinking water	acqua potabile	ak-wa po-ta-bee-leh
drive (to)	guidare	gwee-dar-eh
driver	il conduttore	kon-doot-tor-eh
driving licence	il patente	pa-ten-teh
drop (to)	cadere	ka-dair-eh
drunk	ubriaco	oo-bree-a-ko
dry	secco, asciutto	sek-ko, a-shoot-to
during	durante	doo-ran-teh
duvet	il duvet	duvet
dye	la tinta	teen-ta

E

each	ciascuno	chas-koo-no
early	di buon'ora	dee bwon or-a
earrings	gli orecchini	or-ek-kee-nee
east	est *m*	est
Easter	pasqua *f*	pas-kwa
easy	facile	fa-chee-leh
eat (to)	mangiare	man-jar-eh

edge	**la sponda**	spon-da
EEC	**Comunità economica europea (CEE)**	Ko-moo-nee-ta e-ko-no-mee-ka e-oo-ro-pe-a
eiderdown	**il piumino**	pyoo-mee-no
elastic	**l'elastico** *m*	e-**las**-tee-ko
electric light bulb	**la lampadina**	lam-pa-dee-na
electric point	**la presa elettrica**	pre-za el-et-tree-ka
electricity	**l'elettricità**	el-et-tree-chee-ta
elevator	**l'ascensore** *m*	a-shen-sor-eh
embarrassed	**imbarazzato**	eem-ba-rad-za-to
embassy	**l'ambasciata** *f*	am-ba-sha-ta
emergency exit	**l'uscita di sicurezza** *f*	oo-shee-ta dee see-koo-ret-sa
empty	**vuoto**	vwo-to
end	**la fine**	fee-neh
engaged *people*	**fidanzato**	fee-dant-sa-to
busy	**occupato**	ok-koo-pa-to
engine	**il motore**	mo-tor-eh
England	**Inghilterra** *f*	een-geel-ter-ra
English	**inglese**	een-gle-zeh
enjoy (to)	**godere**	go-dair-eh
enjoy oneself (to)	**divertirsi**	dee-vair-teer-see
enough	**abbastanza**	ab-bas-tant-sa
enquiries	**gli informazioni**	een-for-mat-syo-nee
enter (to)	**entrare**	en-trar-eh
entrance	**l'ingresso** *m*	een-gres-so

entrance fee	l'entrata *f*	ent-ra-ta
envelope	la busta	boos-ta
equipment	l'attrezzatura *f*	at-tret-sa-too-ra
escalator	la scala mobile	ska-la mo-bee-leh
escape (to)	scappare	skap-par-eh
estate agent	l'agente immobiliare *m*	a-jen-teh eem-mo-beel-yar-eh
Europe	Europa *f*	e-oo-ro-pa
even *not odd*	pari	pa-ree
evening	la sera	se-ra
event	l'evento *m*	e-ven-to
every	ogni	on-yee
everybody	ognuno	on-yoo-no
everything	tutto	toot-to
everywhere	dovunque	do-voon-kweh
example	l'esempio *m*	e-zem-pyo
excellent	eccellente	e-chel-len-teh
except	eccetto	e-chet-to
excess	l'eccesso *m*	e-ches-so
exchange bureau	il cambio	kam-byo
exchange rate	il cambio	kam-byo
excursion	la gita	jee-ta
excuse (to)	scusare	skoo-zar-eh
exhibition	l'esposizione *f*	es-po-zeet-syo-ñeh
exit	l'uscita *f*	oo-shee-ta
expect (to)	aspettare	as-pet-tar-eh

expensive	**costoso**	kos-to-zo
express *letter*	**espresso**	es-pres-so
express train	**il rapido**	ra-pee-do
extra	**extra, in più**	ex-tra/een pyoo
eye shadow	**l'ombretto** *m*	om-bret-to

F

fabric	**il tessuto**	tes-soo-to
face	**la faccia**	fa-cha
face cloth	**pezzuola per lavarsi**	pet-swo-la pair la-var-see
face cream	**la crema per il viso**	kre-ma pair eel vee-zo
fact	**il fatto**	fat-to
factory	**la fabbrica**	fab-bree-ka
fade (to)	**scolorire**	sko-lor-eer-eh
faint (to)	**svenire**	zve-neer-eh
fair *colour*	**chiaro**	kya-ro
fête	**la fiera**	fyair-a
fall (to)	**cadere**	ka-dair-eh
family	**la famiglia**	fa-meel-ya
far	**lontano**	lon-ta-no
fare	**il prezzo (del biglietto)**	pret-so (del beel-yet-to)
farm	**la fattoria**	fat-tor-ee-a
farmer	**l'agricoltore** *m*	ag-ree-kol-tor-eh
farmhouse	**la fattoria**	fat-tor-ee-a
farther	**più lontano**	pyoo lon-ta-no

fashion	la moda	mo-da
fast	veloce	ve-lo-cheh
fat	grasso	gras-so
father	il padre	pa-dreh
fault	lo sbaglio	zbal-yo
fear	la paura	pa-oo-ra
feed (to)	alimentare	a-lee-men-tar-eh
feeding bottle	il poppatoio	pop-pa-to-yo
feel (to)	sentire	sen-teer-eh
felt-tip pen	il pennarello	pen-na-rel-lo
female *adj*	femminile	fem-mee-nee-leh
ferry	il traghetto	tra-get-to
fetch (to)	andare a prendere	an-dar-eh a pren-dair-eh
fever	la febbre	feb-breh
a few	alcuni	al-koo-nee
fiancé(e)	il fidanzato/la fidanzata	fee-dant-sa-to/fee-dant-sa-ta
field	il campo	kam-po
field glasses	il binocolo	bee-no-ko-lo
fight (to)	combattere	kom-bat-tair-eh
fill (to)	riempire	ree-em-peer-eh
fill in (to)	riempire	ryem-peer-eh
film	il film/la pellicola	pel-lee-ko-la
find (to)	trovare	tro-var-eh
fine *money*	la multa	mool-ta
finish (to)	finire	fee-neer-eh

finished	finito	fee-nee-to
fire	il fuoco	fwo-ko
fire escape	l'uscita di sicurezza	oo-shee-ta dee see-koo-ret-sa
fire extinguisher	l'estintore *m*	es-teen-tor-eh
fireworks	i fuochi d'artificio	fwo-kee dar-tee-fee-cho
first	primo	pree-mo
first aid	il pronto soccorso	pron-to sok-kor-so
first class	la prima classe	pree-ma klas-seh
fish	il pesce	pe-sheh
fish (to)	pescare	pes-kar-eh
fisherman	il pescatore	pes-ka-tor-eh
fit (to)	star bene	star be-neh
flag	la bandiera	ban-dyair-a
flavour	il sapore	sa-por-eh
flat *adj*	piatto	pyat-to
noun	l'appartamento *m*	ap-par-ta-men-to
flea market	il mercato delle pulci	mair-ka-to del-leh pool-chee
flight	il volo	vo-lo
flood	l'inondazione *f*	een-on-dat-syo-neh
floor *ground*	il pavimento	pa-vee-men-to
storey	il piano	pya-no
floorshow	il cabaret	ka-ba-reh
flower	il fiore	fyor-eh
fly	la mosca	mos-ka
fly (to)	volare	vo-lar-eh

fog	**la nebbia**	neb-bya
fold (to)	**piegare**	pye-gar-eh
follow (to)	**seguire**	seg-weer-eh
food	**il cibo**	chee-bo
foot	**il piede**	pye-deh
football	**il calcio**	kal-cho
footpath	**il sentiero**	sen-tyair-o
for	**per**	pair
forbid (to)	**vietare**	vye-tar-eh
foreign	**straniero**	stran-yair-o
forest	**la foresta**	for-es-ta
forget (to)	**dimenticare**	dee-men-tee-kar-eh
fork	**la forchetta**	for-ket-ta
forward	**avanti**	a-van-tee
forward (to)	**inoltrare**	een-ol-trar-eh
fountain	**la fontana**	fon-ta-na
fragile	**fragile**	fra-jee-leh
free	**libero**	lee-bair-o
freight	**il nolo**	no-lo
fresh	**fresco**	fres-ko
fresh water	**l'acqua dolce** *f*	ak-wa dol-cheh
friend	**l'amico** *m*/**l'amica** *f*	a-mee-ko/a-mee-ka
friendly	**amichevole**	a-mee-ke-vo-leh
from	**da**	da
front	**il fronte**	fron-teh
frontier	**la frontiera**	fron-tyair-a

frost	la brina	bree-na
frozen	congelato	kon-je-la-to
fruit	il frutto	froot-to
full	pieno	pye-no
full board	la pensione completa	pen-syo-neh kom-ple-ta
fun	il divertimento	dee-vair-tee-men-to
funny	divertente	dee-vair-ten-teh
fur	la pelliccia	pel-lee-cha
furniture	il mobilio	mo-beel-yo

G

gallery	la galleria	gal-lair-ee-a
gamble (to)	giocare d'azzardo	jo-kar-eh dat-sar-do
game	il gioco	jo-ko
garage	il garage	ga-raj
garbage	i rifiuti	reef-yoo-tee
garden	il giardino	jar-dee-no
gas	il gas	gaz
gate	il cancello	kan-chel-lo
gentlemen	signori, uomini	seen-yor-ee, wo-mee-nee
genuine	autentico	ow-ten-tee-ko
get (to)	ottenere	ot-te-nair-eh
get off (to)	scendere	shen-dair-eh
get on (to)	salire	sa-leer-eh
get up (to)	alzarsi	alt-sar-see
gift	il regalo	re-ga-lo

gift wrap (to)	fare una confezione regalo	far-eh oon-a kon-fet-syo-neh re-ga-lo
girdle	il busto	boos-to
girl	la ragazza	ra-gat-sa
give (to)	dare	dar-eh
glad	contento	kon-ten-to
glass	il bicchiere	beek-kyair-eh
glasses	gli occhiali	ok-kya-lee
gloomy	oscuro	os-koo-ro
glove	il guanto	gwan-to
go (to)	andare	an-dar-eh
god	dio *m*	dee-o
gold	l'oro *m*	or-o
gold-plate	il vasellame d'oro	va-sel-la-meh do-ro
golf course	il campo di golf	kam-po dee golf
good	buono	bwo-no
government	il governo	go-vair-no
granddaughter	la nipote	nee-po-teh
grandfather	il nonno	non-no
grandmother	la nonna	non-na
grandson	il nipote	nee-po-teh
grass	l'erba *f*	air-ba
grateful	grato	gra-to
great	grande	gran-deh
ground	il terreno/la terra	ter-re-no/ter-ra
grow (to)	crescere	kre-shair-eh

guarantee	**la garanzia**	gar-ant-see-a
guard	**la guardia**	gwar-dya
guest	**l'ospite** *m/f*	os-pee-teh
guest house	**la pensione**	pen-syo-neh
guide	**la guida**	gwee-da
guide book	**la guida**	gwee-da
guided tour	**il giro organizzato**	jee-ro or-ga-neet-sa-to

H

hair	**i capelli**	ka-pel-lee
hair brush	**la spazzola da capelli**	spat-so-la da ka-pel-lee
hair dryer	**l'asciugacapelli** *m*/il fon	a-shoo-ga-ka-pel-lee/fon
hair spray	**la lacca per capelli**	lak-ka pair ka-pel-lee
hairpin	**la forcina**	for-chee-na
half	**mezzo**	med-zo
half board	**la mezza pensione**	med-za pen-syo-neh
half fare	**metà prezzo** *m*	me-ta pret-so
hammer	**il martello**	mar-tel-lo
hand	**la mano**	ma-no
handbag	**la borsetta**	bor-set-ta
handkerchief	**il fazzoletto**	fat-so-let-to
handmade	**fatto a mano**	fat-to a ma-no
hang (to)	**attaccare/appendere**	at-tak-kar-eh/ap-pen-dair-eh
hanger	**l'attaccapanni** *m*	at-tak-ka-pan-nee

happen (to)	**accadere**	ak-ka-dair-eh
happy	**felice**	fe-lee-cheh
happy birthday	**buon compleanno**	bwon kom-ple-an-no
harbour	**il porto**	por-to
hard	**duro**	doo-ro
harmful	**dannoso**	dan-no-zo
harmless	**innocuo**	een-nok-wo
hat	**il cappello**	kap-pel-lo
have (to)	**avere**	a-vair-eh
haversack	**la bisaccia**	bee-za-cha
he	**egli/lui**	el-yee, loo-ee
head	**la testa**	tes-ta
headphones	**la cuffia**	koof-fya
health	**la salute**	sa-loo-teh
hear (to)	**sentire**	sen-teer-eh
heart	**il cuore**	kwor-eh
heat	**il calore**	ka-lor-eh
heating	**il riscaldamento**	rees-kal-da-men-to
heavy	**pesante**	pe-zan-teh
hedge	**la siepe**	sye-peh
heel *shoe*	**il tacco**	tak-ko
helicopter	**l'elicottero** *m*	e-lee-kot-tair-o
help	**l'aiuto** *m*	a-yoo-to
help (to)	**aiutare**	a-yoo-tar-eh
hem	**l'orlo** *m*	or-lo
her *adj*	**suo**	soo-o

her *pron.*	lei	lay
here	qui	kwee
high	alto	al-to
hike (to)	fare un'escursione a piedi	fa-reh oon-es-koor-syo-neh a pye-dee
hill	la collina	kol-lee-na
him	lui	loo-ee
hire (to)	noleggiare	no-led-jar-eh
his	suo	soo-o
history	la storia	stor-ya
hitchhike (to)	fare l'autostop	fa-reh low-to-stop
hobby	il passatempo	pas-sa-tem-po
hold (to)	tenere	te-nair-eh
hole	il buco	boo-ko
holiday	la vacanza	va-kant-sa
hollow	vuoto/concavo	vwo-to/kon-ka-vo
(at) home	a casa	a ka-za
honeymoon	la luna di miele	loo-na dee mye-leh
hope	la speranza	spe-rant-sa
hope (to)	sperare	spe-rar-eh
horse	il cavallo	ka-val-lo
horse races	le corse di cavalli	kor-seh dee ka-val-lee
horse riding	l'equitazione	ek-wee-tat-syo-neh
hose	il tubo flessibile	too-bo fles-see-bee-leh
hospital	l'ospedale *m*	os-pe-da-leh
host/hostess	l'ospite *m/f*	os-pee-teh

hostel	l'ostello *m*	os-tel-lo
hot	caldo	kal-do
hot water bottle	la borsa d'acqua calda	bor-sa dak-wa kal-da
hotel	l'albergo *m*	al-bair-go
hotel keeper	l'albergatore *m*	al-bair-ga-tor-eh
hour	l'ora *f*	or-a
house	la casa	ka-za
how?	come?	ko-meh
how much/many?	quanto/quanti?	kwan-to/kwan-tee
hungry (to be)	aver fame	a-vair fa-meh
hunt (to)	cacciare	ka-char-eh
hurry (to)	affrettarsi	af-fret-tar-see
hurt (to)	far male	far ma-leh
husband	il marito	ma-ree-to
hydrofoil	l'aliscafo *m*	a-lee-ska-fo

I

I	io	ee-o
ice	il ghiaccio	gya-cho
ice cream	il gelato	je-la-to
ice lolly	il ghiacciolo	gya-cho-lo
identify (to)	identificare	ee-den-tee-fee-kar-eh
if	se	seh
imagine (to)	immaginare	eem-ma-jee-nar-eh
immediately	subito	soo-bee-to

immersion heater	il riscaldatore a immersione	rees-kal-da-tor-eh a eem-mair-syo-neh
important	importante	eem-por-tan-teh
in	in, a	een, a
include (to)	includere	een-kloo-dair-eh
included	compreso	kom-pre-zo
inconvenient	scomodo	sko-mo-do
incorrect	scorretto	skor-ret-to
independent	independente	een-de-pen-den-teh
indoors	in casa	een ka-za
industry	l'industria *f*	een-doos-trya
inexpensive	poco costoso	po-ko kos-to-zo
inflammable	infiammabile	een-fyam-ma-bee-leh
inflatable	pneumatico	pne-oo-ma-tee-ko
inflation	l'inflazione *f*	een-flat-syo-neh
information	l'informazione *f*	een-for-mat-syo-neh
ink	l'inchiostro *m*	een-kyos-tro
inn	l'osteria *f*	os-tair-ee-a
insect	l'insetto *m*	een-set-to
insect bite	la puntura d'insetto	poon-too-ra deen-set-to
insect repellent	la lozione anti-insetti	lot-syo-neh an-tee een-set-tee
inside	dentro	den-tro
instead	invece	een-ve-cheh
instructor	l'istruttore *m*	ees-troot-tor-eh
insurance	l'assicurazione *f*	as-see-koo-rat-syo-neh

insure (to)	**assicurarsi**	as-see-koo-rar-see
interest	**l'interesse** *m*	een-tair-es-seh
interested	**interessato**	een-tair-es-sa-to
interesting	**interessante**	een-tair-es-san-teh
interpreter	**l'interprete** *m*	een-tair-pre-teh
into	**in, dentro**	een, den-tro
introduce (to)	**presentare**	pre-zen-tar-eh
invitation	**l'invito** *m*	een-vee-to
invite (to)	**invitare**	een-vee-tar-eh
Ireland	**Irlanda** *f*	eer-lan-da
Irish	**irlandese** *f*	eer-lan-de-zeh
iron (to)	**stirare**	steer-ar-eh
island	**l'isola** *f*	ee-zo-la
it	**lo**	lo
Italian	**italiano**	ee-tal-ya-no
Italy	**Italia** *f*	ee-tal-ya

J

jacket	**la giacchetta**	jak-ket-ta
jar	**la brocca**	brok-ka
jelly fish	**la medusa**	me-doo-za
Jew	**l'ebreo** *m*	e-bre-o
jewellery	**la gioielleria**	joy-el-lair-ee-a
Jewish	**ebraico**	e-bray-ko
job	**il lavoro**	la-vo-ro
journey	**il viaggio**	vyad-jo

jump (to)	**saltare**	sal-ta-reh
jumper	**il maglione**	mal-yo-neh

K

keep (to)	**tenere**	te-nair-eh
key	**la chiave**	kya-veh
kick (to)	**dare calci a**	da-reh kal-chee a
kind *adj*	**gentile**	jen-tee-leh
king	**il re**	reh
kiss	**il bacio**	ba-cho
kiss (to)	**baciare**	ba-cha-reh
kitchen	**la cucina**	koo-chee-na
knee	**il ginocchio**	jee-nok-kyo
knickers	**le mutandine per donna**	moo-tan-dee-neh pair don-na
knife	**il coltello**	kol-tel-lo
knock (to)	**bussare**	boos-sar-eh
know (to) *fact*	**sapere**	sa-pair-eh
person	**conoscere**	ko-no-shair-eh

L

label	**l'etichetta** *f*	e-tee-ket-ta
lace	**il merletto**	mair-let-to
ladies	**signore/donne**	seen-yor-eh/don-neh
lake	**il lago**	la-go
lamp	**la lampada**	lam-pa-da

land	**la terra**	ter-ra
landing *plane*	**l'atterraggio** *m*	at-ter-rad-jo
stairs	**il pianerottolo**	pya-nair-ot-to-lo
landlady/lord	**la padrona/il padrone di casa**	pa-dro-na/pa-dro-neh dee ka-za
landmark	**il punto di riferimento**	poon-to dee ree-fe-ree-men-to
landscape	**il paesaggio**	pa-e-zad-jo
lane	**il vicolo**	vee-ko-lo
language	**la lingua**	leen-gwa
large	**grande**	gran-deh
last	**ultimo**	ool-tee-mo
late	**tardi**	tar-dee
laugh (to)	**ridere**	ree-dair-eh
launderette	**la lavanderia automatica**	la-van-dair-ee-a ow-to-ma-tee-ka
lavatory	**il gabinetto/la toilette**	ga-bee-net-to/twa-let
lavatory paper	**la carta igienica**	kar-ta ee-jen-ee-ka
law	**la legge**	led-jeh
lawn	**il prato inglese**	pra-to een-gle-zeh
lawyer	**l'avvocato** *m*	av-vo-ka-to
lead (to)	**condurre**	kon-door-reh
leaf	**la foglia**	fol-ya
leak (to)	**perdere**	pair-dair-eh
learn (to)	**imparare**	eem-pa-rar-eh
least *adj*	**minimo**	mee-nee-mo

at least	**almeno**	al-me-no
leather	**la pelle**	pel-leh
leave (to) *abandon*	**lasciare**	la-shar-eh
go away	**partire**	par-teer-eh
left *opp. right*	**sinistro**	see-nees-tro
left luggage	**il deposito bagagli**	de-po-zee-to ba-gal-yee
leg	**la gamba**	gam-ba
lend (to)	**prestare**	pres-tar-eh
length	**la lunghezza**	loon-get-sa
less	**meno**	me-no
lesson	**la lezione**	let-syo-neh
let (to) *allow*	**permettere**	pair-met-tair-eh
rent	**affittare**	af-fee-tar-eh
letter	**la lettera**	let-tair-a
level crossing	**il passaggio a livello**	pas-sad-jo a lee-vel-lo
library	**la biblioteca**	beeb-lee-o-te-ka
licence	**la patente**	pa-ten-teh
life	**la vita**	vee-ta
lifebelt	**la cintura di salvataggio**	cheen-too-ra dee sal-va-tad-jo
lifeboat	**il battello di salvataggio**	bat-tel-lo dee sal-va-tad-jo
lifeguard	**il bagnino**	ban-yee-no
lift	**l'ascensore** *m*	a-shen-sor-eh
light	**la luce**	loo-cheh
colour	**chiaro**	kya-ro

weight	**leggero**	led-jair-o
lighthouse	**il faro**	fa-ro
lightning	**il lampo**	lam-po
like (to) *it pleases me*	**mi piace**	mee pya-cheh
wish	**volere**	vo-lair-eh
like *prep*	**come**	ko-meh
like that	**così**	ko-zee
line	**la linea**	lee-ne-a
linen	**la tela**	te-la
lingerie	**la biancheria per signore**	byan-kair-ee-a pair seen-yor-eh
lipsalve	**la pomata per labbra**	po-ma-ta pair lab-bra
lipstick	**il rossetto**	ros-set-to
liquid *adj*	**liquido**	lee-kwee-do
noun	**il liquido**	lee-kwee-do
listen (to)	**ascoltare**	as-kol-tar-eh
little *amount*	**poco**	po-ko
size	**piccolo**	peek-ko-lo
live (to)	**vivere**	vee-vair-eh
local	**locale**	lo-ka-leh
lock	**la serratura**	ser-ra-too-ra
lock (to)	**chiudere a chiave**	kyoo-dair-eh a kya-veh
long	**lungo**	loon-go
look at (to)	**guardare**	gwar-dar-eh
look for (to)	**cercare**	chair-kar-eh
look like (to)	**sembrare**	sem-brar-eh

lorry	**il camion**	ka-myon
lose (to)	**perdere**	pair-dair-eh
lost property office	**gli oggetti smarriti**	od-jet-tee zmar-ree-tee
(a) lot	**molto**	mol-to
loud	**forte**	for-teh
love (to)	**amare**	a-mar-eh
lovely	**bello**	bel-lo
low	**basso**	bas-so
lucky	**fortunato**	for-too-na-to
luggage	**i bagagli**	ba-gal-yee
lunch	**la colazione/il pranzo**	ko-lat-syo-neh/pran-zo

M

magazine	**la rivista**	ree-vees-ta
maid	**la cameriera**	ka-mair-yair-a
mail	**la posta**	pos-ta
main street	**la strada principale**	stra-da preen-chee-pa-leh
make (to)	**fare**	far-eh
make love (to)	**fare l'amore**	far-eh la-mo-reh
make-up	**il trucco**	trook-ko
male *adj*	**maschile**	mas-kee-leh
man	**l'uomo** *m*	wo-mo
man-made	**artificiale**	ar-tee-fee-cha-leh
manage (to)	**dirigere**	dee-ree-jair-eh
manager	**il direttore**	dee-ret-tor-eh
manicure	**la manicure**	ma-nee-koo-reh

many	**molti**	mol-tee
map *country*	**la carta geografica**	kar-ta je-o-gra-fee-ka
town, small area	**la mappa**	map-pa
market	**il mercato**	mair-ka-to
market place	**la piazza del mercato**	pyat-sa del mair-ka-to
married	**sposato**	spo-za-to
marsh	**il palude**	pa-loo-deh
Mass	**la messa**	mes-sa
massage	**il massaggio**	mas-sad-jo
match *light*	**il fiammifero**	fyam-mee-fair-o
sport	**la partita**	par-tee-ta
material *fabric*	**la stoffa**	stof-fa
mattress	**il materasso**	ma-tair-as-so
me	**mi, me**	mee, meh
meal	**il pasto**	pas-to
mean (to)	**voler dire**	vo-lair deer-eh
measurements	**le misure**	mee-zoo-reh
meet (to)	**incontrare**	een-kon-trar-eh
mend (to)	**riparare**	ree-pa-rar-eh
menstruation	**la mestruazione**	mes-troo-at-syo-neh
mess	**la confusione**	kon-foo-zyo-neh
message	**il messaggio**	mes-sad-jo
messenger	**il messaggero**	mes-sad-je-ro
metal	**il metallo**	me-tal-lo
midday	**mezzogiorno**	med-zo-jor-no
middle	**centro, mezzo**	chen-tro, med-zo

middle-aged	di una certa età	dee oon-a chair-ta e-ta
middle class *adj*	borghese	bor-ge-zeh
noun	il ceto medio	che-to med-yo
midnight	mezzanotte	med-za-not-teh
mild	mite	mee-teh
mill	il mulino	moo-lee-no
mine *pron*	il mio/la mia *sing*	mee-o/mee-a/me-ay/
	i miei/le mie *pl*	mee-eh
minute	il minuto	mee-noo-to
mirror	lo specchio	spek-kyo
Miss	signorina	seen-yor-ee-na
miss (to) *train, etc.*	perdere	pair-dair-eh
mistake	lo sbaglio	zbal-yo
mix (to)	mescolare	mes-ko-lar-eh
mixed	mescolato/misto	mes-ko-la-to/mees-to
modern	moderno	mo-dair-no
moisturizer	la crema idratante	kre-ma eed-ra-tan-teh
moment	il momento	mo-men-to
monastery	il monastero	mo-nas-te-ro
money	il denaro/i soldi	de-na-ro/sol-dee
monk	il monaco	mo-na-ko
month	il mese	me-zeh
monument	il monumento	mo-noo-men-to
moon	la luna	loo-na
moorland	la brughiera	broog-yair-a
moped	il motorino/il ciao	mo-tor-ee-no/cha-o

more	(di) più	(dee) pyoo
morning	la mattina	mat-tee-na
mortgage	l'ipoteca *f*	ee-po-te-ka
mosque	la moschea	mos-ke-a
mosquito	la zanzara	zan-za-ra
most	il più/la più	pyoo
mother	la madre	ma-dreh
motor bike	la moto	mo-to
motor boat	la motobarca	mo-to-bar-ka
motor cycle	la motocicletta	mo-to-chee-klet-ta
motor racing	la corsa automobilistica	kor-sa ow-to-mo-bee-lees-tee-ka
motorway	l'autostrada	ow-to-stra-da
mountain	la montagna	mon-tan-ya
mouse	il topo	to-po
mouth	la bocca	bok-ka
mouthwash	il colluttorio	kol-loot-tor-yo
move (to)	muovere	mwo-vair-eh
Mr	signor	seen-yor
Mrs	signora	seen-yor-a
much	molto	mol-to
museum	il museo	moo-ze-o
music	la musica	moo-zee-ka
must *to have to*	dovere	do-vair-eh
my	mio	mee-o
myself	io stesso	ee-o stes-so

N

nail *carpentry*	il chiodo	kyo-do
finger	l'unghia *f*	oon-gya
nailbrush	lo spazzolino da unghie	spat-so-lee-no da oon-gyeh
nailfile	la limetta da unghie	lee-met-ta da oon-gyeh
nail polish	lo smalto per unghie	smal-to pair oon-gyeh
name	il nome	no-meh
napkin	il tovagliolo	to-val-yo-lo
nappy	il pannolino	pan-no-lee-no
narrow	stretto	stret-to
natural	naturale	na-too-ra-leh
near	vicino	vee-chee-no
nearly	quasi	kwa-zee
necessary	necessario	ne-ches-sar-yo
necklace	la collana	kol-la-na
need (to)	aver bisogno di	a-vair bee-zon-yo dee
needle	l'ago *m*	a-go
nephew	il nipote	nee-po-teh
never	mai	my
new	nuovo	nwo-vo
New Zealand	la Nuova Zelanda	nwo-va ze-lan-da
news	le notizie *f*	no-teet-syeh
newspaper	il giornale	jor-na-leh
next	prossimo	pros-see-mo
nice	carino	ka-ree-no

niece	**la nipote**	nee-po-teh
nightclub	**il locale notturno**	lo-ka-leh not-toor-no
nightdress	**la camicia da notte**	ka-mee-cha da not-teh
nobody	**nessuno**	nes-soo-no
noisy	**rumoroso**	roo-mo-ro-zo
non-alcoholic	**analcolico**	a-nal-ko-lee-ko
none	**nessuno**	nes-soo-no
no one	**nessuno**	nes-soo-no
normal	**normale**	nor-ma-leh
north	**nord** *m*	nord
nosebleed	**l'emorragia nasale** *f*	e-mor-ra-jee-a na-za-leh
not	**non**	non
note	**il biglietto**	beel-yet-to
notebook	**il taccuino**	tak-kwee-no
nothing	**niente**	nyen-teh
notice	**l'avviso** *m*	av-vee-zo
notice (to)	**osservare**	os-sair-var-eh
novel	**il romanzo**	ro-man-zo
now	**ora/adesso**	or-a/a-des-so
number	**il numero**	noo-mair-o
nylon	**il nailon**	nylon

O

obtain (to)	**ottenere**	ot-te-nair-eh
occasion	**l'occasione** *f*	ok-ka-zyo-neh
occupation	**l'occupazione** *f*	ok-koo-pat-syo-neh

occupied	occupato	ok-koo-pa-to
ocean	l'oceano *m*	o-che-a-no
odd *not even*	dispari	dees-pa-ree
strange	strano	stra-no
of	di	dee
of course	naturalmente	na-too-ral-men-teh
offer	l'offerta *f*	of-fair-ta
office	l'ufficio *m*	oof-fee-cho
official *adj*	ufficiale *m*	oof-fee-cha-leh
noun	l'ufficiale *m*	oof-fee-cha-leh
often	spesso	spes-so
ointment	l'unguento *m*	oon-gwen-to
OK	okay/va bene	va be-neh
old	vecchio	vek-kyo
on	su, sopra	soo, sop-ra
on foot	a piedi	a pye-dee
on time	in orario	een or-ar-yo
once	una volta	oon-a vol-ta
only	soltanto	sol-tan-to
open (to)	aprire	a-preer-eh
open *adj*	aperto	a-pair-to
open-air	all'aperto	al-la-pair-to
opening	l'apertura *f*	a-pair-too-ra
opera	l'opera *f*	o-pair-a
opportunity	l'occasione *f*	ok-ka-zyo-neh
opposite	opposto	op-pos-to

optician	l'ottico *m*	ot-tee-ko
or	o	o
orchard	l'orto *m*	or-to
orchestra	l'orchestra *f*	or-kes-tra
order (to)	ordinare	or-dee-nar-eh
ordinary	solito	so-lee-to
other	altro	al-tro
ought	dovere	do-vair-eh
our, ours	nostro	nos-tro
out(side)	fuori	fwo-ree
out of order	guasto	gwas-to
out of stock	esaurito	e-zow-ree-to
over	sopra	sop-ra
over there	là	la
overcoat	il soprabito	sop-ra-bee-to
overnight	per la notte	pair la not-teh
owe (to)	dovere	do-vair-eh
owner	il proprietario	prop-rye-tar-yo

P

pack (to)	impaccare	eem-pak-kar-eh
packet	il pacchetto	pak-ket-to
paddle (to)	sguazzare	sgwat-sar-eh
paddling pool	la piscina per bambini	pee-shee-na pair bam-bee-nee
page	la pagina	pa-jee-na

paid	**pagato**	pa-ga-to
pain	**il dolore**	do-lor-eh
painkiller	**l'antidolorifico** *m*	an-tee-do-lor-ee-fee-ko
paint (to)	**dipingere**	dee-peen-jair-eh
painting	**la pittura/il quadro**	peet-too-ra/kwad-ro
pair	**il paio**	pa-yo
palace	**il palazzo**	pa-lat-so
pale	**pallido**	pal-lee-do
paper	**la carta**	kar-ta
parcel	**il pacco**	pak-ko
park	**il parco**	par-ko
park (to)	**parcheggiare**	par-ked-jar-eh
parking meter	**il parchimetro**	par-kee-met-ro
parking ticket	**la multa per divieto di sosta**	mool-ta pair dee-vye-to dee sos-ta
parliament	**il parlamento**	par-la-men-to
part	**la parte**	par-teh
party *fête*	**la festa**	fes-ta
political	**il partito**	par-tee-to
pass (to)	**passare**	pas-sar-eh
passenger	**il passeggero**	pas-sed-je-ro
passport	**il passaporto**	pas-sa-por-to
past *adj*	**passato**	pas-sa-to
noun	**il passato**	pas-sa-to
path	**il sentiero**	sen-tyair-o
patient	**il paziente**	pat-syen-teh

pavement	**il marciapiede**	mar-cha-pye-deh
pay (to)	**pagare**	pa-gar-eh
payment	**il pagamento**	pa-ga-men-to
peace	**la pace**	pa-cheh
peak	**la cima**	chee-ma
pearl	**la perla**	pair-la
pebble	**il ciottolo**	chot-to-lo
pedal	**il pedale**	pe-da-leh
pedestrian	**il pedone**	pe-do-neh
pedestrian crossing	**l'attraversamento pedonale** *m*	at-tra-vair-sa-men-to pe-do-nal-eh
pedestrian precinct	**la zona pedonale**	dzo-na pe-do-nal-eh
(fountain) pen	**la penna (stilografica)**	pen-na (stee-lo-**gra**-fee-ka)
pencil	**la matita**	ma-tee-ta
penknife	**il temperino**	tem-pe-ree-no
pensioner	**il pensionato**	pen-syo-na-to
people	**la gente**	jen-teh
perfect	**esatto/perfetto**	e-zat-to/pair-fet-to
performance	**lo spettacolo**	spet-**ta**-ko-lo
perfume	**il profumo**	pro-foo-mo
perhaps	**forse**	for-seh
perishable	**deperibile**	de-pair-ee-bee-leh
perm	**la permanente**	pair-ma-nen-teh
permit	**il permesso**	pair-mes-so
permit (to)	**permettere**	pair-met-tair-eh
person	**la persona**	pair-so-na

(per) person	**a persona**	a pair-so-na
personal	**personale**	pair-so-nal-eh
petticoat	**la sottana**	sot-ta-na
photograph	**la fotografia**	fo-to-gra-fee-a
photographer	**il fotografo**	fo-to-gra-fo
piano	**il pianoforte**	pya-no-for-teh
pick (to) *choose*	**scegliere**	shel-yair-eh
gather, pick up	**cogliere**	kol-yair-eh
picnic	**il picnic**	peek-neek
piece	**il pezzo**	pet-zo
pier	**il molo**	mo-lo
pillow	**il guanciale**	gwan-cha-leh
(safety) pin	**lo spillo (di sicurezza)**	speel-lo (dee see-koo-ret-sa)
pipe	**la pipa**	pee-pa
place	**il posto**	pos-to
plain	**semplice**	sem-plee-cheh
plan	**il piano**	pya-no
plant	**la pianta**	pyan-ta
plastic	**plastica**	plas-tee-ka
plate	**il piatto**	pyat-to
play *theatre*	**la commedia**	kom-me-dya
play (to)	**giocare**	jo-kar-eh
player	**il giocatore**	jo-ka-tor-eh
please	**per favore**	pair fa-vor-eh
pleased	**contento**	kon-ten-to

plenty of	molto, molti	mol-to, mol-tee
pliers	le pinze	peent-seh
plimsoll	le scarpe da tela	skar-peh da te-la
plug *bath*	il tappo	tap-po
electric	la spina elettrica	spee-na el-et-tree-ka
pocket	la tasca	tas-ka
point	il punto	poon-to
poisonous	velenoso	ve-le-no-zo
police station	il commissariato di polizia	kom-mees-sar-ya-to dee pol-eet-see-a
policeman	il poliziotto	pol-eet-syot-to
political	politico	po-lee-tee-ko
politician	il politico	po-lee-tee-ko
politics	la politica	po-lee-tee-ka
pollution	l'inquinamento *m*	een-kwee-na-men-to
pond	lo stagno	stan-yo
poor	povero	po-vair-o
pope	il papa	pa-pa
popular	popolare	po-po-lar-eh
porcelain	la porcellana	por-chel-la-na
port	il porto	por-to
possible	possibile	pos-see-bee-leh
post (to)	imbucare	eem-boo-kar-eh
post box	la buca delle lettere	boo-ka del-leh let-tair-eh
post office	l'ufficio postale *m*	oof-fee-cho pos-ta-leh
postcard	la cartolina postale	kar-to-lee-na pos-ta-leh

postman	**il postino**	pos-tee-no
postpone	**rimandare**	ree-man-dar-eh
pound	**la sterlina**	stair-lee-na
(face) powder	**la cipria**	cheep-ree-a
prefer (to)	**preferire**	pre-fe-reer-eh
pregnant	**incinta**	een-cheen-ta
prepare (to)	**preparare**	pre-pa-rar-eh
present *gift*	**il regalo**	re-ga-lo
president	**il presidente**	pre-zee-den-teh
press (to)	**premere**	pre-mair-eh
pretty	**carino**	ka-ree-no
price	**il prezzo**	pret-so
priest	**il prete**	pre-teh
prime minister	**il primo ministro**	pree-mo mee-nees-tro
print	**la stampa**	stam-pa
print (to)	**stampare**	stam-par-eh
private	**privato**	pree-va-to
problem	**il problema**	prob-le-ma
profession	**la professione**	pro-fes-syo-neh
programme	**il programma**	pro-gram-ma
promise	**la promessa**	pro-mes-sa
promise (to)	**promettere**	pro-met-tair-eh
Protestant	**protestante**	pro-tes-tan-teh
provide (to)	**fornire**	for-neer-eh
public	**pubblico**	poob-blee-ko
public holiday	**la festa nazionale**	fes-ta nat-syo-na-leh

pull (to)	**tirare**	tee-rar-eh
pure	**puro**	poo-ro
purse	**il borsellino**	bor-sel-lee-no
push (to)	**spingere**	speen-jair-eh
put (to)	**mettere**	met-tair-eh
pyjamas	**il pigiama**	pee-ja-ma

Q

quality	**la qualità**	kwa-lee-ta
quantity	**la quantità**	kwan-tee-ta
quarter	**il quarto**	kwar-to
queen	**la regina**	re-jee-na
question	**la domanda**	do-man-da
quick	**presto**	pres-to
quiet	**tranquillo**	tran-kweel-lo

R

race	**la corsa**	kor-sa
racecourse	**l'ippodromo** m	eep-po-dro-mo
radiator	**il radiatore**	rad-ya-tor-eh
radio	**la radio**	rad-yo
railway	**la ferrovia**	fer-ro-vee-a
rain	**la pioggia**	pyod-ja
raincoat	**l'impermeabile** m	eem-pair-me-a-bee-leh
(it is) raining	**piove**	pyo-veh
rare	**raro**	ra-ro

rash	l'esantema *m*	e-zan-te-ma
rate	la tariffa	ta-reef-fa
rather	piuttosto	pyoot-tos-to
raw	crudo	kroo-do
razor	il rasoio	ra-zo-yo
razor blade	la lametta per barba	lam-et-ta pair bar-ba
reach (to)	raggiungere	rad-joon-jair-eh
read (to)	leggere	led-jair-eh
ready	pronto	pron-to
real	vero	ve-ro
really	veramente	ver-a-men-teh
reason	la ragione	ra-jo-neh
receipt	la ricevuta	ree-che-voo-ta
receive (to)	ricevere	ree-che-vair-eh
recent	recente	re-chen-teh
recipe	la ricetta	ree-chet-ta
recognize (to)	riconoscere	ree-ko-no-shair-eh
recommend	raccomandare	rak-ko-man-dar-eh
record *music*	il disco	dees-ko
refill	riempire	ryem-peer-eh
refrigerator	il frigorifero	free-go-ree-fe-ro
refund	il rimborso	reem-bor-so
registered letter	la lettera raccomandata	let-tair-a rak-ko-man-da-ta
relatives	i parenti	pa-ren-tee
religion	la religione	re-lee-jo-neh

remember (to)	**ricordare**	ree-kor-dar-eh
rent (to)	**affittare**	af-feet-tar-eh
repair (to)	**riparare**	ree-pa-rar-eh
repeat (to)	**ripetere**	ree-pe-tair-eh
reply (to)	**rispondere**	rees-pon-dair-eh
reservation	**la prenotazione**	pre-no-tat-syo-neh
reserve (to)	**prenotare/riservare**	pre-no-tar-eh ree-zair-var-eh
reserved	**prenotato**	pre-no-ta-to
restaurant	**il ristorante**	rees-tor-an-teh
restaurant car	**il vagone ristorante**	va-go-neh rees-tor-an-teh
return (to)	**ritornare**	ree-tor-nar-eh
reward	**la ricompensa**	ree-kom-pen-sa
ribbon	**il nastro**	nas-tro
rich	**ricco**	reek-ko
right *opp. left*	**destro**	des-tro
opp. wrong	**corretto**	kor-ret-to
right (to be)	**aver ragione**	a-vair ra-jo-neh
ring *finger*	**l'anello** *m*	a-nel-lo
ripe	**maturo**	ma-too-ro
rise (to)	**sorgere**	sor-jair-eh
river	**il fiume**	fyoo-meh
road	**la strada**	stra-da
road map	**la carta stradale**	kar-ta stra-da-leh
road sign	**il cartello stradale**	kar-tel-lo stra-da-leh
road works	**lavori in corso**	la-vor-ee een kor-so

rock	**lo scoglio**	skol-yo
roll *bread*	**il panino**	pa-nee-no
roll (to)	**rotolare**	ro-to-lar-eh
roof	**il tetto**	tet-to
room	**la stanza**	stant-sa
rope	**la fune**	foo-neh
round	**rotondo**	ro-ton-do
rowing boat	**la barca a remi**	bar-ka a re-mee
rubber	**la gomma**	gom-ma
rubbish	**le immondizie**	eem-mon-deet-syeh
rucksack	**il sacco da montagna**	sak-ko da mon-tan-ya
ruins	**le rovine**	ro-vee-neh
run (to)	**correre**	kor-rair-eh
rush hour	**l'ora di punta** *f*	or-a dee poon-ta

S

sad	**triste**	trees-teh
saddle	**la sella**	sel-la
safe *adj*	**sicuro**	see-koo-ro
noun	**la cassaforte**	kas-sa-for-teh
sail (to)	**andare in barca vela**	an-dar-eh een bar-ka ve-la
sailing boat	**la barca vela**	bar-ka ve-la
sailor	**il marinaio**	ma-ree-na-yo
saint	**il santo/la santa**	san-to/san-ta
sale *clearance*	**la svendita**	sven-dee-ta

(for) sale	**in vendita**	een ven-dee-ta
salesman	**il commesso (di negozio)**	kom-mes-so (dee ne-got-syo)
saleswoman	**la commessa (di negozio)**	kom-mes-sa (dee ne-got-syo)
salt	**il sale**	sa-leh
salt water	**l'acqua salata** *f*	ak-wa sa-la-ta
same	**stesso**	stes-so
sand	**la sabbia**	sab-bya
sandals	**i sandali**	san-da-lee
sanitary towel	**l'assorbente igienico** *m*	as-sor-ben-teh ee-jen-ee-ko
satisfactory	**soddisfacente**	sod-dees-fa-chen-teh
saucer	**il piattino**	pyat-tee-no
save (to) *money*	**risparmiare**	rees-par-myar-eh
rescue	**salvare**	sal-var-eh
say (to)	**dire**	deer-eh
scald (to)	**scottare**	skot-tar-eh
scarf	**la sciarpa**	shar-pa
scenery	**il paesaggio**	pa-e-zad-jo
scent	**il profumo**	pro-foo-mo
school	**la scuola**	skwo-la
scissors	**le forbici**	for-bee-chee
Scotland	**Scozia** *f*	skot-sya
Scottish	**scozzese**	skot-se-zeh
scratch (to)	**graffiare**	graf-fyar-eh
screw	**la vite**	vee-teh

sculpture	la scultura	skool-too-ra
sea	il mare	mar-eh
sea food	i frutti di mare	froot-tee dee mar-eh
seashore	la spiaggia	spyad-ja
seasickness	il mal di mare	mal dee mar-eh
season	la stagione	sta-jo-neh
seat	il posto	pos-to
seat belt	la cintura di sicurezza	cheen-too-ra dee see-koo-ret-sa
second	secondo	se-kon-do
second hand	di seconda mano	dee se-kon-da ma-no
see (to)	vedere	ve-dair-eh
seem (to)	parere	pa-rair-eh
self-catering	casa da affitto	ca-za da af-feet-to
self-contained	indipendente	een-dee-pen-den-teh
sell (to)	vendere	ven-dair-eh
send (to)	mandare	man-dar-eh
separate *adj*	a parte	a par-teh
serious	serio	sair-yo
serve (to)	servire	sair-veer-eh
service	il servizio	sair-veet-syo
service *church*	il servizio religioso	sair-veet-syo re-lee-jo-zo
service charge	il servizio	sair-veet-syo
several	parecchi	pa-rek-kee
sew (to)	cucire	koo-cheer-eh
shade *colour*	la tinta	teen-ta

shade/shadow	l'ombra *f*	om-bra
shallow	basso	bas-so
shampoo	lo shampoo	sham-poo
shape	la forma	for-ma
share (to)	dividere	dee-vee-dair-eh
sharp	tagliente	tal-yen-teh
shave (to)	farsi la barba	far-see-la bar-ba
shaving brush	il pennello	pen-nel-lo
shaving cream	la crema da barba	kre-ma da bar-ba
she	essa, lei	es-sa, lay
sheet	il lenzuolo	lent-swo-lo
shelf	lo scaffale	skaf-fa-leh
shell	la conchiglia	kon-keel-ya
shelter	il riparo	ree-pa-ro
shine (to)	splendere	splen-dair-eh
shingle	i ciottoli	chot-to-lee
ship	la nave	na-veh
shipping line	la compagnia di navigazione	kom-pan-yee-a dee na-vee-gat-syo-neh
shirt	la camicia	ka-mee-cha
shock	il colpo	kol-po
shoe	la scarpa	skar-pa
shoelaces	le stringhe da scarpe	streen-geh da skar-peh
shoe polish	la tinta da scarpe	teen-ta da skar-peh
shop	la bottega	bot-te-ga
shopping centre	il centro dei negozi	chen-tro day ne-got-see

shore	la spiaggia	spyad-ja
short	corto	kor-to
shorts	i calzoncini	kalt-son-chee-nee
shoulder	la spalla	spal-la
show	lo spettacolo	spet-ta-ko-lo
show (to)	mostrare	mos-trar-eh
shower	la doccia	do-cha
shut (to)	chiudere	kyoo-dair-eh
shut *adj*	chiuso	kyoo-zo
side	il lato	la-to
sights	le vedute	ve-doo-teh
sightseeing	il giro turistico	jee-ro toor-ees-tee-ko
sign	il segno	sen-yo
sign (to)	firmare	feer-mar-eh
silk	la seta	se-ta
silver	l'argento *m*	ar-jen-to
simple	semplice	sem-plee-cheh
since	da	da
sing (to)	cantare	kan-tar-eh
single *just one*	singolo	seen-go-lo
unmarried	scapolo *of man*	ska-po-lo
	nubile *of woman*	noo-bee-leh
single room	la camera ad un letto	ka-mair-a ad oon let-to
sister	la sorella	so-rel-la
sit (to)	sedere	se-dair-eh
sit down (to)	accomodarsi	ak-ko-mo-dar-see

size	la misura	mee-zoo-ra
skate (to)	pattinare	pat-tee-nar-eh
ski (to)	sciare	shee-ar-eh
skid (to)	slittare	sleet-tar-eh
skirt	la gonna	gon-na
sky	il cielo	che-lo
sleep (to)	dormire	dor-meer-eh
sleeper	il vagone letto	va-go-neh let-to
sleeping bag	il sacco a pelo	sak-ko a pe-lo
sleeve	la manica	ma-nee-ka
slice	la fetta	fet-ta
slip *garment*	la sottoveste	sot-to-ves-teh
slippers	le pantofole/le ciabatte	pan-to-fo-leh/cha-bat-teh
slowly	lentamente	len-ta-men-teh
small	piccolo	peek-ko-lo
smart	elegante	e-le-gan-teh
smell	l'odore *m*	o-dor-eh
smile	sorridere	sor-ree-dair-eh
smoke (to)	fumare	foo-mar-eh
smoking (compartment)	(scompartimento) fumatori	(skom-par-tee-men-to) foo-ma-tor-ee
no smoking	vietato fumare	vye-ta-to foo-mar-eh
snack	lo spuntino	spoon-tee-no
snorkel	il respiratore a tubo	res-pee-ra-tor-eh a too-bo
snow	la neve	ne-veh

(it is) snowing	nevica	ne-vee-ka
so	così	ko-zee
soap	il sapone	sa-po-neh
soap powder	il sapone in polvere	sa-po-neh een pol-vair-eh
sober	sobrio	sob-ryo
socks	i calzini	kalt-see-nee
soft	molle	mol-leh
sold	venduto	ven-doo-to
sold out	esaurito	e-zow-ree-to
sole *shoe*	la suola	swo-la
solid	solido	so-lee-do
some	qualche	kwal-keh
somebody	qualcuno	kwal-koo-no
something	qualcosa	kwal-ko-za
sometimes	qualche volta	kwal-keh vol-ta
somewhere	qualche parte	kwal-keh par-teh
son	il figlio	feel-yo
song	la canzone	kant-so-neh
soon	presto	pres-to
sour	acido	a-chee-do
south	sud *m*	sood
souvenir	il ricordo	ree-kor-do
space	lo spazio	spat-syo
spanner	la chiave	kya-veh
speak (to)	parlare	par-lar-eh
speciality	la specialità	spe-cha-lee-ta

spectacles	gli occhiali	ok-kya-lee
speed	la velocità	ve-lo-chee-ta
speed limit	il limite di velocità	lee-mee-teh dee ve-lo-chee-ta
spend (to)	spendere	spen-dair-eh
spice	la spezia	spet-sya
spoon	il cucchiaio	kook-kya-yo
sport	lo sport	sport
sprain (to)	slogare	zlo-gar-eh
spring *water*	la sorgente	sor-jen-teh
season	la primavera	pree-ma-vair-a
square *adj*	quadrato	kwad-ra-to
noun	la piazza	pyat-sa
stage	il palcoscenico	pal-ko-she-nee-ko
stain	la macchia	mak-kya
stained	macchiato	mak-kya-to
stairs	le scale	ska-leh
stalls	le poltrone	pol-tro-neh
stamp	il francobollo	fran-ko-bol-lo
stand (to)	stare in piedi	star-eh een pye-dee
start (to)	cominciare	ko-meen-char-eh
statue	la statua	stat-wa
stay (to)	stare	star-eh
step *foot*	il passo	pas-so
stick	il bastone	bas-to-neh
stiff	rigido	ree-jee-do

still	**ancora**	an-ko-ra
not moving	**immobile**	eem-mo-bee-leh
sting	**la puntura**	poon-too-ra
stockings	**le calze**	kalt-seh
stolen	**rubato**	roo-ba-to
stone	**la pietra**	pye-tra
stool	**lo sgabello**	zga-bel-lo
stop (to)	**fermare**	fair-mar-eh
store	**il magazzino**	ma-gad-zee-no
straight	**diritto**	dee-reet-to
straight on	**a diritto**	a dee-reet-to
strap	**la cinghia**	cheen-gya
stream	**il ruscello**	roo-shel-lo
street	**la strada**	stra-da
street map	**lo stradario**	stra-dar-yo
string	**lo spago**	spa-go
strong	**forte**	for-teh
student	**lo studente**	stoo-den-teh
style	**lo stile**	stee-leh
suburb	**la periferia**	pair-ee-fair-ee-a
subway	**il sottopassaggio**	sot-to-pas-sad-jo
suddenly	**improvvisamente**	eem-prov-vee-za-men-teh
suede	**il camoscio**	ka-mo-sho
suit	**l'abito** *m*	a-bee-to
suitcase	**la valigia**	va-lee-ja
summer	**l'estate** *f*	es-ta-teh

sun	**il sole**	so-leh
sunbathing	**il bagno di sole**	ban-yo dee so-leh
sunburn	**la scottatura di sole**	skot-ta-too-ra dee so-leh
sunglasses	**gli occhiali da sole**	ok-kya-lee da so-leh
sunhat	**il cappello da sole**	kap-pel-lo da so-leh
sunny	**soleggiato**	so-led-ja-to
sunshade	**il parasole**	pa-ra-so-leh
suntan cream	**la pomata solare**	po-ma-ta so-lar-eh
supper	**la cena**	che-na
sure	**sicuro**	see-koo-ro
surfboard	**il sandolino**	san-do-lee-no
surgery	**l'ambulatorio** *m*	am-boo-la-tor-yo
surprise	**la sorpresa**	sor-pre-za
surprise (to)	**sorprendere**	sor-pren-dair-eh
surroundings	**i dintorni**	deen-tor-nee
suspender belt	**le giarrettiere**	jar-ret-tyair-eh
sweater	**il maglione**	mal-yo-neh
sweet	**dolce**	dol-cheh
sweets	**le caramelle**	ka-ra-mel-leh
swell (to)	**gonfiare**	gon-fyar-eh
swim (to)	**nuotare**	nwo-tar-eh
swimming pool (open)	**la piscina (all'aperto)**	pee-shee-na (al-la-pair-to)
swings	**l'altalena** *f*	al-ta-le-na
switch *light*	**l'interruttore** *m*	een-tair-root-tor-eh

T

table	**la tavola**	ta-vo-la
tablecloth	**la tovaglia**	to-val-ya
tablet	**la pastiglia**	pas-teel-ya
tailor	**il sarto**	sar-to
take (to)	**prendere**	pren-dair-eh
talk (to)	**parlare**	par-lar-eh
tall	**alto**	al-to
tampon	**il tampone**	tam-po-neh
tank	**il serbatoio**	ser-ba-to-yo
tap	**il rubinetto**	roo-bee-net-to
tapestry	**l'arazzo** *m*	a-rat-so
taste	**il gusto**	goos-to
taste (to)	**gustare**	goos-tar-eh
tax	**la tassa**	tas-sa
taxi	**il taxi**	taxi
teach (to)	**insegnare**	een-sen-yar-eh
tear *eye*	**la lacrima**	lak-ree-ma
tear (to)	**strappare**	strap-par-eh
telegram	**il telegramma**	te-le-gram-ma
telephone	**il telefono**	te-le-fo-no
telephone (to)	**telefonare**	te-le-fo-nar-eh
telephone box	**la cabina telefonica**	ka-bee-na te-le-fo-nee-ka
telephone call	**la telefonata**	te-le-fo-na-ta
telephone directory	**l'elenco telefonico** *m*	e-len-ko te-le-fo-nee-ko

telephone number	**il numero di telefono**	noo-mair-o dee te-le-fo-no
telephone operator	**il centralino**	chen-tra-lee-no
television	**la televisione**	te-le-vee-zyo-neh
telex	**il telex**	telex
tell (to)	**raccontare**	rak-kon-tar-eh
temperature	**la temperatura**	tem-pe-ra-too-ra
temporary	**provvisorio**	prov-vee-zor-yo
tennis	**il tennis**	tennis
tent	**la tenda**	ten-da
tent peg	**il cavicchio per tenda**	ka-veek-kyo pair ten-da
tent pole	**il palo per tenda**	pa-lo pair ten-da
terrace	**la terrazza**	ter-rat-sa
than	**che, di**	keh, dee
that	**quello**	kwel-lo
the	**il/lo/la/i/gli/le**	eel/lo/la/ee/lyee/leh
theatre	**il teatro**	te-at-ro
their, theirs	**loro**	lo-ro
them	**li, loro**	lee, lo-ro
then	**poi, allora**	poy, al-lor-a
there	**lì, là**	lee, la
there is	**c'è**	cheh
there are	**ci sono**	chee so-no
thermometer	**il termometro**	tair-mo-met-ro
these	**questi**	kwes-tee
they	**essi**	es-see

thick	**grosso**	gros-so
thief	**il ladro**	lad-ro
thin	**sottile**	sot-tee-leh
thing	**la cosa**	ko-za
think (to)	**pensare**	pen-sar-eh
thirsty (to be)	**aver sete**	a-vair se-teh
this	**questo**	kwes-to
those	**quelli**	kwel-lee
thread	**il filo**	fee-lo
throat	**la gola**	go-la
through	**attraverso**	at-tra-vair-so
throw (to)	**gettare**	jet-tar-eh
thunder	**il tuono**	two-no
thunderstorm	**la tempesta**	tem-pes-ta
ticket	**il biglietto**	beel-yet-to
ticket office	**la biglietteria**	beel-yet-tair-ee-a
tide	**la marea**	ma-re-a
tie	**la cravatta**	kra-vat-ta
tight	**stretto**	stret-to
tights	**la calzamaglia**	kalt-sa-mal-ya
time	**il tempo**	tem-po
timetable	**l'orario** *m*	o-rar-yo
tin	**il barattolo**	ba-rat-to-lo
tin opener	**l'apriscatole** *m*	a-pree-skat-to-leh
tip *money*	**la mancia**	man-cha
tip (to) *money*	**dare una mancia**	dar-eh oon-a man-cha

tired	stanco	stan-ko
to	a/in	a/een
tobacco (brown)	il tabacco (scuro)	ta-bak-ko (skoo-ro)
tobacco pouch	la borsa da tabacco	bor-sa da ta-bak-ko
together	insieme	een-sye-meh
toilet	il gabinetto	ga-bee-net-to
toilet paper	la carta igienica	kar-ta ee-jen-ee-ka
toll	il pedaggio	pe-dad-jo
tomorrow	domani	do-ma-nee
tongue	la lingua	leen-gwa
too *also*	anche	an-keh
excessive	troppo	trop-po
too much/many	troppo/troppi	trop-po/trop-pee
toothbrush	lo spazzolino da denti	spat-so-lee-no da den-tee
toothpaste	il dentifricio	den-tee-free-cho
toothpick	lo stuzzicadenti	stoot-see-ka-den-tee
top	la cima	chee-ma
torch *electric*	la lampadina tascabile	lam-pa-dee-na tas-ka-bee-leh
torn	strappato	strap-pa-to
touch (to)	toccare	tok-kar-eh
tough	duro	doo-ro
tourist	il turista	too-rees-ta
tourist office	l'agenzia turistica	a-jent-see-a too-rees-tee-ka
towards	verso	vair-so

towel	l'asciugamano *m*	a-shoo-ga-ma-no
tower	la torre	tor-reh
town	la città	cheet-ta
town hall	il municipio	moo-nee-cheep-yo
toy	il giocattolo	jo-kat-to-lo
traffic	il traffico	traf-fee-ko
traffic jam	l'ingorgo di traffico *m*	een-gor-go dee traf-fee-ko
traffic lights	il semaforo	se-ma-for-o
train	il treno	tre-no
transfer	trasferire	tras-fair-eer-eh
translate (to)	tradurre	tra-door-reh
travel (to)	viaggiare	vyad-jar-eh
travel agent	l'agenzia di viaggi *f*	agent-see-a dee vyad-jee
traveller	il viaggiatore	vyad-ja-tor-eh
treat (to)	trattare	trat-tar-eh
medical	curare	koo-rar-eh
treatment	la cura	koo-ra
tree	l'albero *m*	al-bair-o
trip	il viaggio	vyad-jo
trouble	il guaio	gwa-yo
trousers	i pantaloni	pan-ta-lo-nee
true	vero	vair-o
trunk *luggage*	il baule	ba-oo-leh
trunks	i calzoncini	kalt-son-chee-nee
truth	la verità	ve-ree-ta

try, try on (to)	provare	pro-var-eh
tunnel	la galleria	gal-lair-ee-a
turn (to)	voltare	vol-tar-eh
turning	la svolta	svol-ta
tweezers	le pinzette	peent-set-teh
twisted	slogato	zlo-ga-to
typewriter	la macchina da scrivere	mak-kee-na da skree-vair-eh

U

ugly	brutto	broot-to
umbrella	l'ombrello *m*	om-brel-lo
uncle	lo zio	tsee-o
uncomfortable	scomodo	sko-mo-do
unconscious	svenuto	zve-noo-to
under	sotto	sot-to
underground	la metropolitana	met-ro-po-lee-ta-na
underneath	sotto	sot-to
understand	capire	ka-peer-eh
underwear	la biancheria intima	byan-kair-ee-a een-tee-ma
university	l'università *f*	oo-nee-vair-see-ta
unpack (to)	disfare le valigie	dees-far-eh leh va-lee-jeh
until	fino a	fee-no a
unusual	insolito	een-so-lee-to
up	sopra	sop-ra

upstairs	**di sopra**	dee sop-ra
urgent	**urgente**	oor-jen-teh
us	**noi/ci**	noy/chee
use (to)	**usare**	oo-zar-eh
useful	**utile**	oo-tee-leh
useless	**inutile**	een-oo-tee-leh
usual	**solito**	so-lee-to

V

vacant	**libero**	lee-bair-o
vacation	**la vacanze**	va-kant-seh
valid	**valido**	va-lee-do
valley	**la valle**	val-leh
valuable	**di valore**	dee va-lor-eh
value	**il valore**	va-lor-eh
vase	**il vaso**	va-zo
VAT	**IVA**	ee-va
vegetables	**la verdura**	vair-doo-ra
vegetarian	**vegetariano**	ve-je-tar-ya-no
vein	**la vena**	ve-na
velvet	**il velluto**	vel-loo-to
ventilation	**la ventilazione**	ven-tee-lat-syo-neh
very	**molto**	mol-to
very little	**pochissimo**	po-kees-see-mo
very much	**moltissimo**	mol-tees-see-mo
vest	**la maglietta**	mal-yet-ta

viaduct	**il viadotto**	vee-a-dot-to
video cassette	**la video-cassetta**	veed-yo-kas-set-ta
video recorder	**il videoregistratore**	veed-yo-re-jees-tra-tor-eh
view	**la vista**	vees-ta
village	**il villaggio**	veel-lad-jo
vineyard	**il vigneto**	veen-ye-to
violin	**il violino**	vyo-lee-no
visa	**il visto**	vees-to
visit	**la visita**	vee-zee-ta
visit (to)	**visitare**	vee-zee-tar-eh
voice	**la voce**	vo-cheh
voltage	**il voltaggio**	vol-tad-jo
voucher	**il buono**	bwo-no
voyage	**il viaggio**	vyad-jo

W

wait (to)	**aspettare**	as-pet-tar-eh
waiter	**il cameriere**	ka-mair-yair-eh
waiting room	**la sala d'aspetto**	sa-la das-pet-to
waitress	**la cameriera**	ka-mair-yair-a
wake (to) *someone*	**svegliare**	zvel-yar-eh
wake up (to)	**svegliarsi**	zvel-yar-see
Wales	**Galles** *m*	gal-lez
walk (to)	**passeggiare**	pas-sed-jar-eh
wallet	**il portafoglio**	por-ta-fol-yo
want (to)	**volere**	vo-lair-eh

wardrobe	il guardaroba	gwar-da-ro-ba
warm	caldo	kal-do
wash (to)	lavare	la-var-eh
washbasin	il lavandino	la-van-dee-no
waste	il rifiuto	ree-fyoo-to
waste (to)	sprecare	spre-kar-eh
watch	l'orologio *m*	o-ro-lo-jo
water	l'acqua *f*	ak-wa
waterfall	la cascata	kas-ka-ta
waterproof	impermeabile	eem-pair-me-a-bee-leh
water ski-ing	lo sci nautico	shee naw-tee-ko
wave	l'onda *f*	on-da
way	la via	vee-a
we	noi	noy
wear (to)	indossare	een-dos-sar-eh
weather	il tempo	tem-po
weather forecast	le previsioni del tempo	pre-vee-syo-nee del tem-po
wedding ring	la fede	fe-deh
week	la settimana	set-tee-ma-na
weigh (to)	pesare	pe-zar-eh
weight	il peso	pe-zo
well *adv*	bene	be-neh
well *water*	il pozzo	pot-so
Welsh	gallese	gal-le-zeh
west	ovest *m*	o-vest

wet	bagnato	ban-ya-to
what?	che cosa?	keh ko-za
wheel	la ruota	rwo-ta
wheelchair	la sedia a rotelle	se-dya a ro-tel-leh
when?	quando?	kwan-do
where?	dove?	do-veh
which?	quale?	kwa-leh
while	mentre	men-treh
who?	chi?	kee
whole	intero	een-tair-o
whose?	di chi?	dee kee
why?	perchè?	pair-keh
wide	largo	lar-go
widow	la vedova	ve-do-va
widower	il vedovo	ve-do-vo
wife	la moglie	mol-yeh
wild	selvaggio	sel-vad-jo
win (to)	vincere	veen-chair-eh
wind	il vento	ven-to
window	la finestra	fee-nes-tra
wine merchant	la rivendita di vino	ree-ven-dee-ta dee vee-no
wing	l'ala *f*	a-la
winter	l'inverno *m*	een-vair-no
winter sports	gli sport invernali	sport een-vair-na-lee
wish (to)	desiderare	de-zee-dair-ar-eh

with	**con**	kon
without	**senza**	sen-za
woman	**la donna**	don-na
wonderful	**meraviglioso**	me-ra-veel-yo-zo
wood *forest*	**il bosco**	bos-ko
timber	**il legno**	len-yo
wool	**la lana**	la-na
word	**la parola**	pa-ro-la
work	**il lavoro**	la-vo-ro
work (to)	**lavorare**	la-vo-rar-eh
worried	**preoccupato**	pre-ok-koo-pa-to
worse	**peggiore**	ped-jor-eh
worth (to be)	**valore**	va-lor-eh
wrap	**avvolgere**	av-vol-jair-eh
write (to)	**scrivere**	scree-vair-eh
writing paper	**la carta da scrivere**	kar-ta da scree-vair-eh
wrong	**sbagliato**	zbal-ya-to
wrong (to be)	**aver torto**	a-vair tor-to

X

| xerox | **la fotocopia** | fo-to-kop-ya |
| X-ray | **la radiografia** | rad-yo-gra-fee-a |

Y

| yacht | **lo yacht** | yacht |
| year | **l'anno** *m* | an-no |

yesterday	ieri	yair-ee
you	voi/lei	voy/lay
young	giovane	jo-van-eh
your	vostro/suo	vos-tro/soo-o
youth hostel	l'ostello della gioventù *m*	os-tel-lo del-la jo-ven-too

Z

| zip | la chiusura lampo | kyoo-zoo-ra lam-po |
| zoo | lo zoo | zoo |

INDEX

NOTES